D1535389

PEREGRINE BOOKS
Y22
SELECTED PROSE
T. S. ELIOT

T. S. ELIOT

SELECTED PROSE

EDITED BY
JOHN HAYWARD

PENGUIN BOOKS
IN ASSOCIATION WITH
FABER AND FABER

Penguin Books Ltd, Harmondsworth, Middlesex
AUSTRALIA: Penguin Books Pty Ltd, 762 Whitehorse Road,
Mitcham, Victoria

—

This selection first published in Penguin Books 1953
Reprinted 1953, 1958
Reprinted in Peregrine Books 1963

—

Made and printed in Great Britain
by Hazell Watson & Viney Ltd
Aylesbury and Slough
Set in Linotype Plantin

96784

CONTENTS

[*The titles marked with an asterisk have been supplied by the editor. The dates are those of first publication.*]

5

CONTENTS

2. SOCIAL CRITICISM

INTRODUCTION

In the essay on Matthew Arnold, from which the first extract in this book is taken, there is an important statement about the purpose of literary criticism, which throws light on T. S. Eliot's own critical method and achievement. 'From time to time,' it runs, 'it is desirable that some critic shall appear to review the past of our literature, and set the poets and the poems in a new order.' Such critics are rare, for they must possess, in addition to an unusual capacity for judgement, an independence of mind powerful enough to recognize and to interpret for their generation its own values and categories of appreciation. Matthew Arnold was such a critic, as were Coleridge and Johnson and Dryden before him; and such, in our own day, is Mr Eliot himself.

The influence of a critic capable of undertaking this periodical task of revaluation may not be impressive at first, for canons of literary taste are not altered suddenly by revolutionary methods. Their alteration can only be effected gradually and in accordance with that evolutionary process by which habits of mind of educated men and women are changed from time to time. The initiative will come from the exceptional critic, but it may be a long while before he succeeds in imposing his standards on cultivated society as a whole. After thirty years it is now clear that Mr Eliot's critical writings have made a deep impression on literary opinions and taste. Without his perspicuous and stimulating direction, we should be the poorer for much that we now take for granted in our knowledge and enjoyment of the literature which satisfies our particular needs. I am thinking especially of his reassessment of our early poetic drama, and the poetry of Donne and his school; his judgements on Milton and Dryden; and his appraisal of Baudelaire and the French symbolists. Evidence of his imposing influence as a critic is perhaps most apparent in our appreciation of his own work as a poet and dramatist; for much of the satisfaction we derive from it is due to those very elements in the literature of the past which he has re-valued, for his own profit as well as ours. It is indeed through knowledge of his criticism that we may often arrive at a clearer and deeper understanding of his poems and plays.

When Mr Eliot settled in London and began his work as a critic during the First World War, society was ready for change in its habits of thoughts and its attitude to life in general. This is not the place to discuss how much the ensuing reorientation of ideas and emotions was the cause or the effect of one of those profound disturbances in history which reform the spirit of the times. In the arts and in the literature of those days, the signs of change were isolated but ominous. The theory and the technique of atonalism and of cubism were already established on the Continent, where the first surrealists had staked their claims in the Freudian unconscious and were consciously exploiting them. In this country, Schoenberg and Picasso, though already recognized as masters abroad, were then just beginning to be accepted as innovators; but few people had yet heard of T. S. Eliot or of his mentor, Ezra Pound, the subject of the former's first, anonymous, book of criticism, published in New York exactly a year before the Armistice.*

Mr Eliot's first volume of poems, *Prufrock and Other Observations*, published in June 1917, had made little, if any, mark; and his first signed criticism (apart from undergraduate contributions to the *Harvard Advocate*), printed eighteen months earlier in the *International Journal of Ethics*, was of academic interest only. Even when he began soon after to review for the *New Statesman* the total number of readers he could command was not much more than six thousand; and in March 1917 only a very few of them would have recognized the import of his 'Reflections on *Vers Libre*' (the earliest specimen of his criticism in this selection). When, during the same year, he was appointed assistant editor of the *Egoist* and became a regular contributor to its pages, his potential public was considerably smaller, though it was at least an interested one. Apart from two reviews, his first contribution to the *Egoist* was the series

* A most interesting account of their early association as literary rebels will be found in *The Letters of Ezra Pound*, 1951.

of three articles, entitled 'Reflections on Contemporary Poetry', which were published in three consecutive monthly issues between September and November 1917. It is, of course, impossible to measure the impact they made at that time on enlightened opinion; nor, indeed, can one distinguish their effectiveness from that of similar articles in similar periodicals, such as *Others* and *Blast*, or the *Little Review* and *Poetry* (Chicago), in which the poems in *Prufrock* had originally appeared in print. But they were, as we can now see, among the earliest intimations of a movement out of the dead-end into which the so-called Georgian Poets had been driven by the last impulse of nineteenth-century romanticism. The literary historian, looking for signs and portents of that movement, would find a significant one in a review by 'Apteryx' in the *Egoist* for March 1918, of *Georgian Poetry 1916–17* and *Wheels, A Second Cycle*. The title of the review was 'Verse Pleasant and Unpleasant' and the pseudonymous Mr Eliot left no doubt which in his judgement was which. It was not until the following year, however, that his influence as a critic began to command respect outside the select circle into which he had been drawn soon after his arrival in London in 1915. In the spring of 1919 he began to write regular reviews for the *Athenaeum*, under Middleton Murry's editorship, and it was principally from those reviews that his first collection of essays, *The Sacred Wood*, was made and published in 1920. There are three notable exceptions from this common source – the now famous statement of poetic faith printed in the *Egoist* for October 1919, as 'Tradition and the Individual Talent'; and the essays on Ben Jonson and Massinger, commissioned as front-page articles by Bruce Richmond, the editor of *The Times Literary Supplement*. These essays were to be the first two in a series of critical re-estimations of the dramatists and poets of the seventeenth century, which remain unrivalled in the criticism of the first half of the twentieth; and it is proper, in passing, to acknowledge the perception of the editor who originally gave them a far wider currency than any of Mr Eliot's work had previously obtained.

There is no need to recall in detail Mr Eliot's work as a critic after the year 1920. With the publication, two years later, of *The*

Waste Land, in the first number of the *Criterion,** his poetic reputation was securely established and his authority as a critic correspondingly enhanced. For the past thirty years that authority has steadily increased; and has gradually extended beyond the limits of formal literary criticism until it is now at least acknowledged wherever the critical faculty is operative. I cannot indeed think of a critic who has ever been more widely read and discussed in his own lifetime; and not only in English, but in almost every language, except Russian, throughout the civilized world.

Although Mr Eliot contributed a quarterly 'Commentary', as well as occasional reviews, to the *Criterion* for nearly twenty years, his critical work was never directed, either by necessity or choice, into a regular channel, after he had accepted in 1925 a full-time directorship in a publishing firm. From that time forward his criticism tended more and more to be given, in the first place, in the form of lectures and addresses, which were later to be selected and revised for publication. For example, *The Use of Poetry and the Use of Criticism* incorporated the lectures he gave at Harvard in 1932-3 as Charles Eliot Norton Professor of Poetry; and *The Idea of a Christian Society* those given on the Boutwell foundation at Corpus Christi College, Cambridge, in the spring of 1939. But, in addition to such collections as these, a number of important single addresses were afterwards published separately, among them the W. P. Ker Lecture at Glasgow in 1942 on *The Music of Poetry*; the presidential address to the Classical Association in the same year; the British Academy Lecture on *Milton* in 1947; and the lecture on *Poetry and Drama* delivered at Harvard in 1950, all of which are printed together in full, for the first time, in this selection.

It was in Mr Eliot's second collection of essays, published in 1928 under the title *For Lancelot Andrewes,*† that the scope of his criti-

---

* For some account of the policy and history of this literary quarterly, which was edited by Mr Eliot during the seventeen years of its existence, see pp. 228-30 of this selection.

† The essays he chose to preserve from this discarded collection and from *The Sacred Wood* are included in *Selected Essays* (1932; revised edition, 1951).

cism was first noticeably enlarged. This development was un-doubtedly connected with two crucial steps he took about that time: his reception into the Anglican Church, and his adoption of British nationality. An allusive personal statement, which he made at this turning-point in his life and which was printed in the preface to that book, has often since been quoted and misquoted, as well as mis-understood, and, like all dogmatic assertions, assumed to be valid for all times and all occasions. And yet that peremptory statement, defining his critical standpoint at that juncture as 'classicist in litera-ture, royalist in politics, and anglo-catholic in religion', does, not-withstanding its vagueness, summarize the nature of the beliefs to which Mr Eliot has adhered, and which, in his writings, he has expounded, ever since. I do not see that we need to define its terms or to analyse their context. It is sufficient, surely, if we understand it to be a triple affirmation of a single belief – belief in the value of Tradition. This implies, of course, respect for established order, in the sense both of authority and of form. Mr Eliot's sense of the past is intensely expressed or intimated throughout his writings, in prose as well as verse, and with consummate effect in his *Four Quartets*; but the past evoked by him is not something dead and done with, an object merely of nostalgic retrospect. It is rather a continuing tradition, as much involved in the present, and indeed *present* in it, as the present is involved in the future, and to which we are all bound, as it were, to conform; and it is only when we regard it in this way that we can realize not merely our indebtedness to the past but also what the past, paradoxically, owes to us. It is in this respect that Mr Eliot's aesthetic revaluation of certain parts of our literary inheritance is such an important and illuminating contribution to the history of criticism.

In his social criticism, beginning in 1934 with his 'primer of modern heresy', *After Strange Gods*,* his constant awareness of the past, transmitting its vitality to the living and imposing its order on the present, is equally apparent. His observations on contemporary

* The Page-Barbour Lectures given at the University of Virginia in 1933. The author was dissatisfied with them and has chosen to allow them to go out of print.

society and, even more, his speculations about the future of society, especially those relating to religion and culture – I refer in particular to *The Idea of a Christian Society* and *Notes towards the Definition of Culture* – are deeply informed with this belief in tradition, in hierarchical order, and in the need for conformity. There is, perhaps inevitably, an element of didacticism in these later essays and addresses, which is not wholly disguised, though it is mitigated, by Mr Eliot's characteristic method of exposition, by cautious stages of definition, doubt, reservation, and qualification to the final affirmation. In this dialectical teasing of his subject he shows a kind of feline skill worthy of his progeny of 'practical' cats. Often, indeed, when he seems to invite controversy he disarms us with an unexpected stroke of diffidence, or retires momentarily into a cloud of unknowing, from which he will emerge to enlist our cooperation and finally to command our assent. Thus, if he is occasionally pontifical, or seemingly condescending, it is not from arrogance or complacency; for he is without intellectual pride or vanity, and, in print at least, more tolerant than most moralists of human folly and frailty. Moreover, he has what is, in a critic, the saving grace of irony, an unfailing specific for dogmatism. His prose style reflects his detachment and calm, and is, in its lack of metaphor or other ornament, the mirror of an inquiring, dispassionate, yet incisive mind. Although his critical faculties have been increasingly exercised in recent years on social problems, his latest published essay, *Poetry and Drama* (the most revealing, incidentally, of his own poetic and dramatic practice), is, we may hope, an earnest of his inclination, if not intention, to continue to write literary criticism, even if he feels, as he may well do, that he has accomplished as much as he can in this field. For it is in his reconsideration and consequent revitalization of literature, and above all, of English poetry of the past, that his influence, as a critic, has been most fruitful and inspiring. No critic, indeed, since Coleridge, has shown more clearly the *use* of poetry and of criticism.

The present selection from his prose works has, therefore, been designed primarily to emphasize this aspect of his critical activity and contains a larger proportion of literary criticism, both general and particular, than of any other kind. It has been made with the author's approval (though he is not, of course, responsible for it), and is, I hope, fairly representative of his considerable output during the past thirty years and more. Even those who need no such introduction as this to Mr Eliot's critical writings, probably do not know how numerous they are. We tend to think of him as unprolific, but in fact he has had published, to date, between four and five hundred separate pieces of prose criticism, in the form of essays, reviews, lectures, addresses, and broadcasts. Many of them, having served their purpose on the occasion for which they were composed, have been forgotten and have little claim, beyond that of curiosity, to be preserved. But in their totality, they are evidence of the constancy and zeal with which his critical intelligence has been applied to understanding and demonstrating the relationship of life and letters in our time. The essays reprinted here, in whole or in part, sufficiently exemplify the genius with which he has fulfilled this task.

JOHN HAYWARD

· I ·

LITERARY CRITICISM

Literary Criticism: General

THE FUNCTION OF CRITICISM

FROM time to time, every hundred years or so, it is desirable that some critic shall appear to review the past of our literature, and set the poets and the poems in a new order. This task is not one of revolution but of readjustment. What we observe is partly the same scene, but in a different and more distant perspective; there are new and strange objects in the foreground, to be drawn accurately in proportion to the more familiar ones which now approach the horizon, where all but the most eminent become invisible to the naked eye. The exhaustive critic, armed with a powerful glass, will be able to sweep the distance and gain an acquaintance with minute objects in the landscape with which to compare minute objects close at hand; he will be able to gauge nicely the position and proportion of the objects surrounding us, in the whole of the vast panorama. This metaphorical fancy only represents the ideal; but Dryden, Johnson, and Arnold have each performed the task as well as human frailty will allow. The majority of critics can be expected only to parrot the opinions of the last master of criticism; among more independent minds a period of destruction, of preposterous over-estimation, and of successive fashions takes place, until a new authority comes to introduce some order. And it is not merely the passage of time and accumulation of new artistic experience, nor the ineradicable tendency of the great majority of men to repeat the opinions of those few who have taken the trouble to think, nor the tendency of a nimble but myopic minority to progenerate heterodoxies, that makes new assessments necessary. It is that no generation is interested in Art in quite the same way as any other; each generation, like each individual, brings to the contemplation of art its own categories of appreciation, makes its own demands upon art, and has its own uses for art. 'Pure' artistic appreciation is to my thinking only an ideal, when not merely a figment, and must be, so long as the appreciation of art is an affair of limited and transient human beings existing in space and time. Both artist and audience are limited. There is for each time, for each artist, a kind of alloy required to make the metal workable into art; and each generation prefers its own alloy to any other. Hence each new master of criticism performs a useful service merely by the fact that his errors are of a different kind from the last; and the longer the sequence of critics we have, the greater amount of correction is possible.

[From *The Use of Poetry and the Use of Criticism*, 1933]

CRITICISM

CRITICISM must always profess an end in view, which, roughly speaking, appears to be the elucidation of works of art and the correction of taste. The critic's task, therefore, appears to be quite clearly cut out for him; and it ought to be comparatively easy to decide whether he performs it satisfactorily, and, in general, what kinds of criticism are useful and what are otiose. But on giving the matter a little attention, we perceive that criticism, far from being a simple and orderly field of beneficent activity, from which imposters can be readily ejected, is no better than a Sunday park of contending and contentious orators, who have not even arrived at the articulation of their differences. Here, one would suppose, was a place for quiet cooperative labour. The critic, one would suppose, if he is to justify his existence, should endeavour to discipline his personal prejudices and cranks – tares to which we are all subject – and compose his differences with as many of his fellows as possible, in the common pursuit of true judgement. When we find that quite the contrary prevails, we begin to suspect that the critic owes his livelihood to the violence and extremity of his opposition to other critics, or else to some trifling oddities of his own with which he contrives to season the opinions which men already hold, and which out of vanity or sloth they prefer to maintain. We are tempted to expel the lot.

Immediately after such an eviction, or as soon as relief has abated our rage, we are compelled to admit that there remain certain books, certain essays, certain sentences, certain men, who have been 'useful' to us. And our next step is to attempt to classify these, and find out whether we establish any principles for deciding what kinds of books should be preserved, and what aims and methods of criticism should be followed.

We must ourselves decide what is useful to us and what is not; and it is quite likely that we are not competent to decide. But it is fairly certain that 'interpretation' (I am not touching upon the acrostic element in literature) is only legitimate when it is not interpretation at all, but merely putting the reader in possession of facts which he would otherwise have missed. I have had some experience of Extension lecturing, and I have found only two ways of leading any pupils to like anything with the right liking: to present them with a selection of the simple kind of facts about a work – its conditions, its setting, its genesis – or else to spring the work on them in such a way that they were not prepared to be prejudiced against it.

Comparison and analysis are the chief tools of the critic. It is obvious indeed that they *are* tools, to be handled with care, and not employed in an inquiry into the number of times giraffes are mentioned in the English novel. They are not used with conspicuous success by many contemporary writers. You must know what to compare and what to analyse. The late Professor Ker had skill in the use of these tools. Comparison and analysis need only the cadavers on the table; but interpretation is always producing parts of the body from its pockets, and fixing them in place. And any book, any essay, any note in *Notes and Queries*, which produces a fact even of the lowest order about a work of art is a better piece of work than nine-tenths of the most pretentious critical journalism, in journals or in books. We assume, of course, that we are masters and not servants of facts, and that we know that the discovery of Shakespeare's laundry bills would not be of much use to us; but we must always reserve final judgement as to the futility of the research which has discovered them, in the possibility that some genius will appear who will know of a use to which to put them. Scholarship, even in its humblest forms, has its rights; we assume that we know how to use it, and how to neglect it. Of course the multiplication of critical books and essays may create, and I have seen it create, a vicious taste for reading about works of art instead of reading the works themselves, it may supply opinion instead of educating taste. But *fact* cannot corrupt taste; it can at worst gratify one taste – a taste for history, let us say, or antiquities, or biography – under the illusion that it is assisting another. The real corrupters are those who supply opinion or fancy; and Goethe and Coleridge are not guiltless – for what is Coleridge's *Hamlet*: is it an honest inquiry as far as the data permit, or is it an attempt to present Coleridge in an attractive costume?

[From 'The Function of Criticism', 1923]

TRADITION

TRADITION is not solely, or even primarily, the maintenance of certain dogmatic beliefs; these beliefs have come to take their living form in the course of the formation of a tradition. What I mean by tradition involves all those habitual actions, habits, and customs, from the most significant religious rite to our conventional way of greeting a stranger, which represent the blood kinship of 'the same people living in the same place'. It involves a good deal which can be called *taboo*: that this word is used in our time in an exclusively derogatory sense is to me a curiosity of some significance. We become conscious of these items, or conscious of their importance, usually only after they have begun to fall into desuetude, as we are aware of the leaves of a tree when the autumn wind begins to blow them off – when they have separately ceased to be vital. Energy may be wasted at that point in a frantic endeavour to collect the leaves as they fall and gum them on to the branches: but the sound tree will put forth new leaves, and the dry tree should be put to the axe. We are always in danger, in clinging to an old tradition, or attempting to re-establish one, of confusing the vital and the unessential, the real and the sentimental. Our second danger is to associate tradition with the immovable; to think of it as something hostile to all change; to aim to return to some previous condition which we imagine as having been capable of preservation in perpetuity, instead of aiming to stimulate the life which produced that condition in its time.

It is not of advantage to us to indulge a sentimental attitude towards the past. For one thing, in even the very best living tradition there is always a mixture of good and bad, and much that deserves criticism; and for another, tradition is not a matter of feeling alone. Nor can we safely, without very critical examination, dig ourselves in stubbornly to a few dogmatic notions, for what is a healthy belief at one time may, unless it is one of the few fundamental things, be a pernicious prejudice at another. Nor should we cling to traditions as a way of asserting our superiority over less favoured peoples. What we can do is to use our minds, remembering that a tradition without intelligence is not worth having, to discover what is the best life for us not as a political abstraction, but as a particular people in a particular place; what in the past is worth preserving and what should be rejected; and what conditions, within our power to bring about, would foster the society that we desire.

[From *After Strange Gods*, 1934]

TRADITION AND THE INDIVIDUAL TALENT

I

IN English writing we seldom speak of tradition, though we occasionally apply its name in deploring its absence. We cannot refer to 'the tradition' or to 'a tradition'; at most, we employ the adjective in saying that the poetry of So-and-so is 'traditional' or even 'too traditional'. Seldom, perhaps, does the word appear except in a phrase of censure. If otherwise, it is vaguely approbative, with the implication, as to the work approved, of some pleasing archaeological reconstruction. You can hardly make the word agreeable to English ears without this comfortable reference to the reassuring science of archaeology.

Certainly the word is not likely to appear in our appreciations of living or dead writers. Every nation, every race, has not only its own creative, but its own critical turn of mind; and is even more oblivious of the shortcomings and limitations of its critical habits than of those of its creative genius. We know, or think we know, from the enormous mass of critical writing that has appeared in the French language the critical method or habit of the French; we only conclude (we are such unconscious people) that the French are 'more critical' than we, and sometimes even plume ourselves a little with the fact, as if the French were the less spontaneous. Perhaps they are; but we might remind ourselves that criticism is as inevitable as breathing, and that we should be none the worse for articulating what passes in our minds when we read a book and feel an emotion about it, for criticizing our own minds in their work of criticism. One of the facts that might come to light in this process is our tendency to insist, when we praise a poet, upon those aspects of his work in which he least resembles anyone else. In these aspects or parts of his work we pretend to find what is individual, what is the peculiar essence of the man. We dwell with satisfaction upon the poet's difference from his predecessors, especially his immediate predecessors; we endeavour to find something that can be isolated in order to be enjoyed. Whereas if we approach a poet without this prejudice we shall often find that not only the best, but the most individual parts of his work may be those in which the dead poets, his ancestors, assert their immortality most vigorously. And I do not mean the impressionable period of adolescence, but the period of full maturity.

Yet if the only form of tradition, of handing down, consisted in following the ways of the immediate generation before us in a blind or timid adherence to its successes, 'tradition' should positively be discouraged. We have seen many such simple currents soon lost in the sand; and novelty is better than repetition. Tradition is a matter of much wider significance. It cannot be inherited, and if you want it you must obtain it by great labour. It involves, in the first place, the historical sense, which we may call nearly indispensable to anyone who would continue to be a poet beyond his twenty-fifth year; and the historical sense involves a perception, not only of the

22

pastness of the past, but of its presence; the historical sense compels
a man to write not merely with his own generation in his bones, but
with a feeling that the whole of the literature of Europe from Homer
and within it the whole of the literature of his own country has a
simultaneous existence and composes a simultaneous order. This
historical sense, which is a sense of the timeless as well as of the
temporal and of the timeless and of the temporal together, is what
makes a writer traditional. And it is at the same time what makes a
writer most acutely conscious of his place in time, of his own con-
temporaneity.

No poet, no artist of any art, has his complete meaning alone. His
significance, his appreciation is the appreciation of his relation to
the dead poets and artists. You cannot value him alone; you must
set him, for contrast and comparison, among the dead. I mean this as
a principle of aesthetic, not merely historical, criticism. The necessity that he shall conform, that he shall cohere, is not one-sided;
what happens when a new work of art is created is something that
happens simultaneously to all the works of art which preceded it. The
existing monuments form an ideal order among themselves, which
is modified by the introduction of the new (the really new) work of
art among them. The existing order is complete before the new
work arrives; for order to persist after the supervention of novelty,
the *whole* existing order must be, if ever so slightly, altered; and so
the relations, proportions, values of each work of art toward the whole
are readjusted; and this is conformity between the old and the new.
Whoever has approved this idea of order, of the form of European,
of English literature will not find it preposterous that the past should
be altered by the present as much as the present is directed by the
past. And the poet who is aware of this will be aware of great difficulties and responsibilities.*

* Cf. In poetry there is no such thing as complete originality owing
nothing to the past. Whenever a Virgil, a Dante, a Shakespeare, a Goethe
is born, the whole future of European poetry is altered. When a great poet
has lived, certain things have been done once and for all, and cannot be
achieved again; but on the other hand, every great poet adds something to
the complex material out of which future poetry will be written. *Notes
towards the Definition of Culture.* [Editor's note]

In a peculiar sense he will be aware also that he must inevitably be judged by the standards of the past. I say judged, not amputated, by them; not judged to be as good as, or worse or better than, the dead; and certainly not judged by the canons of dead critics. It is a judgement, a comparison, in which two things are measured by each other. To conform merely would be for the new work not really to conform at all; it would not be new, and would therefore not be a work of art. And we do not quite say that the new is more valuable because it fits in; but its fitting in is a test of its value — a test, it is true, which can only be slowly and cautiously applied, for we are none of us infallible judges of conformity. We say: it appears to conform, and is perhaps individual, or it appears individual, and may conform; but we are hardly likely to find that it is one and not the other.

To proceed to a more intelligible exposition of the relation of the poet to the past: he can neither take the past as a lump, an indiscriminate bolus, nor can he form himself wholly on one or two private admirations, nor can he form himself wholly upon one preferred period. The first course is inadmissible, the second is an important experience of youth, and the third is a pleasant and highly desirable supplement. The poet must be very conscious of the main current, which does not at all flow invariably through the most distinguished reputations. He must be quite aware of the obvious fact that art never improves, but that the material of art is never quite the same. He must be aware that the mind of Europe — the mind of his own country — a mind which he learns in time to be much more important than his own private mind — is a mind which changes, and that this change is a development which abandons nothing *en route*, which does not superannuate either Shakespeare, or Homer, or the rock drawing of the Magdalenian draughtsmen. That this development, refinement perhaps, complication certainly, is not, from the point of view of the artist, any improvement. Perhaps not even an improvement from the point of view of the psychologist or not to the extent which we imagine; perhaps only in the end based upon a complication in economics and machinery. But the difference between the present and the past is that the conscious present is an

24

awareness of the past in a way and to an extent which the past's awareness of itself cannot show.

Someone said: 'The dead writers are remote from us because we *know* so much more than they did.' Precisely, and they are that which we know.

I am alive to a usual objection to what is clearly part of my programme for the *métier* of poetry. The objection is that the doctrine requires a ridiculous amount of erudition (pendantry), a claim which can be rejected by appeal to the lives of poets in any pantheon. It will even be affirmed that much learning deadens or perverts poetic sensibility. While, however, we persist in believing that a poet ought to know as much as will not encroach upon his necessary receptivity and necessary laziness, it is not desirable to confine knowledge to whatever can be put into a useful shape for examinations, drawing-rooms, or the still more pretentious modes of publicity. Some can absorb knowledge, the more tardy must sweat for it. Shakespeare acquired more essential history from Plutarch than most men could from the whole British Museum. What is to be insisted upon is that the poet must develop or procure the consciousness of the past and that he should continue to develop this consciousness throughout his career.

What happens is a continual surrender of himself as he is at the moment to something which is more valuable. The progress of an artist is a continual self-sacrifice, a continual extinction of personality.

There remains to define this process of depersonalization and its relation to the sense of tradition. It is in this depersonalization that art may be said to approach the condition of science. I therefore invite you to consider, as a suggestive analogy, the action which takes place when a bit of finely filiated platinum is introduced into a chamber containing oxygen and sulphur dioxide.

I I

Honest criticism and sensitive appreciation is directed not upon the poet but upon the poetry. If we attend to the confused cries of the newspaper critics and the susurrus of popular repetition that follows, we shall hear the names of poets in great numbers; if we seek not

Blue-book knowledge but the enjoyment of poetry, and ask for a poem, we shall seldom find it. I have tried to point out the importance of the relation of the poem to other poems by other authors, and suggested the conception of poetry as a living whole of all the poetry that has ever been written. The other aspect of this Impersonal theory of poetry is the relation of the poem to its author. And I hinted, by an analogy, that the mind of the mature poet differs from that of the immature one not precisely in any valuation of 'personality', not being necessarily more interesting, or having 'more to say', but rather by being a more finely perfected medium in which special, or very varied, feelings are at liberty to enter into new combinations.

The analogy was that of the catalyst. When the two gases previously mentioned are mixed in the presence of a filament of platinum, they form sulphurous acid. This combination takes place only if the platinum is present; nevertheless the newly formed acid contains no trace of platinum, and the platinum itself is apparently unaffected: has remained inert, neutral, and unchanged. The mind of the poet is the shred of platinum. It may partly or exclusively operate upon the experience of the man himself; but, the more perfect the artist, the more completely separate in him will be the man who suffers and the mind which creates; the more perfectly will the mind digest and transmute the passions which are its material.

The experience, you will notice, the elements which enter the presence of the transforming catalyst, are of two kinds: emotions and feelings. The effect of a work of art upon the person who enjoys it is an experience different in kind from any experience not of art. It may be formed out of one emotion, or may be a combination of several; and various feelings, inhering for the writer in particular words or phrases or images, may be added to compose the final result. Or great poetry may be made without the direct use of any emotion whatever: composed out of feelings solely. Canto xv of the *Inferno* (Brunetto Latini) is a working up of the emotion evident in the situation; but the effect, though single as that of any work of art, is obtained by considerable complexity of detail. The last quatrain gives an image, a feeling attaching to an image, which 'came', which did not develop simply out of what precedes, but which was probably in suspension in the poet's mind until the proper combination arrived for it to add itself to. The poet's mind is in fact a receptacle for seizing and storing up numberless feelings, phrases, images, which remain there until all the particles which can unite to form a new compound are present together.

If you compare several representative passages of the greatest poetry you see how great is the variety of types of combination, and also how completely any semi-ethical criterion of 'sublimity' misses the mark. For it is not the 'greatness', the intensity, of the emotions, the components, but the intensity of the artistic process, the pressure, so to speak, under which the fusion takes place, that counts. The episode of Paolo and Francesca employs a definite emotion, but the intensity of the poetry is something quite different from whatever intensity in the supposed experience it may give the impression of. It is no more intense, furthermore, than Canto XXVI, the voyage of Ulysses, which has not the direct dependence upon an emotion. Great variety is possible in the process of transmutation of emotion: the murder of Agamemnon, or the agony of Othello, gives an artistic effect apparently closer to a possible original than the scenes from Dante. In the *Agamemnon*, the artistic emotion approximates to the emotion of an actual spectator; in *Othello* to the emotion of the protagonist himself. But the difference between art and the event is always absolute; the combination which is the murder of Agamemnon is probably as complex as that which is the voyage of Ulysses. In either case there has been a fusion of elements. The ode of Keats contains a number of feelings which have nothing particular to do with the nightingale, but which the nightingale, partly perhaps because of its attractive name, and partly because of its reputation, served to bring together.

The point of view which I am struggling to attack is perhaps related to the metaphysical theory of the substantial unity of the soul: for my meaning is, that the poet has, not a 'personality' to express, but a particular medium, which is only a medium and not a personality, in which impressions and experiences combine in

27

peculiar and unexpected ways. Impressions and experiences which are important for the man may take no place in the poetry, and those which become important in the poetry may play quite a negligible part in the man, the personality.

I will quote a passage which is unfamiliar enough to be regarded with fresh attention in the light – or darkness – of these observations:

> And now methinks I could e'en chide myself
> For doating on her beauty, though her death
> Shall be revenged after no common action.
> Does the silkworm expend her yellow labours
> For thee? For thee does she undo herself?
> Are lordships sold to maintain ladyships
> For the poor benefit of a bewildering minute?
> Why does yon fellow falsify highways,
> And put his life between the judge's lips,
> To refine such a thing – keeps horse and men
> To beat their valours for her? ...

In this passage (as is evident if it is taken in its context) there is a combination of positive and negative emotions: an intensely strong attraction toward beauty and an equally intense fascination by the ugliness which is contrasted with it and which destroys it. This balance of contrasted emotion is in the dramatic situation to which the speech is pertinent, but that situation alone is inadequate to it. This is, so to speak, the structural emotion, provided by the drama. But the whole effect, the dominant tone, is due to the fact that a number of floating feelings, having an affinity to this emotion by no means superficially evident, have combined with it to give us a new art emotion.

It is not in his personal emotions, the emotions provoked by particular events in his life, that the poet is in any way remarkable or interesting. His particular emotions may be simple, or crude, or flat. The emotion in his poetry will be a very complex thing, but not with the complexity of the emotions of people who have very complex or unusual emotions in life. One error, in fact, of eccentricity in poetry is to seek for new human emotions to express; and in this search for novelty in the wrong place it discovers the perverse. The business of the poet is not to find new emotions, but to use the ordinary ones and, in working them up into poetry, to express feelings which are not in actual emotions at all. And emotions which he has never experienced will serve his turn as well as those familiar to him. Consequently, we must believe that 'emotion recollected in tranquillity' is an inexact formula. For it is neither emotion, nor recollection, nor, without distortion of meaning, tranquillity. It is a concentration, and a new thing resulting from the concentration, of a very great number of experiences which to the practical and active person would not seem to be experiences at all; it is a concentration which does not happen consciously or of deliberation. These experiences are not 'recollected', and they finally unite in an atmosphere which is 'tranquil' only in that it is a passive attending upon the event. Of course this is not quite the whole story. There is a great deal, in the writing of poetry, which must be conscious and deliberate. In fact, the bad poet is usually unconscious where he ought to be conscious, and conscious where he ought to be unconscious. Both errors tend to make him 'personal'. Poetry is not a turning loose of emotion, but an escape from emotion; it is not the expression of personality, but an escape from personality. But, of course, only those who have personality and emotions know what it means to want to escape from these things.

III

ὁ δὲ νοῦς ἴσως θειότερόν τι καὶ ἀπαθές ἐστιν.

This essay proposes to halt at the frontier of metaphysics or mysticism, and confine itself to such practical conclusions as can be applied by the responsible person interested in poetry. To divert interest from the poet to the poetry is a laudable aim: for it would conduce to a juster estimation of actual poetry, good and bad. There are many people who appreciate the expression of sincere emotion in verse, and there is a smaller number of people who can appreciate technical excellence. But very few know when there is an expression of *significant* emotion, emotion which has its life in the poem and

29

not in the history of the poet. The emotion of art is impersonal. And the poet cannot reach this impersonality without surrendering himself wholly to the work to be done. And he is not likely to know what is to be done unless he lives in what is not merely the present, but the present moment of the past, unless he is conscious, not of what is dead, but of what is already living.

[1919]

'ROMANTIC' AND 'CLASSIC'

ROMANTICISM and classicism are not matters with which creative writers can afford to bother overmuch, or with which they do, as a rule, in practice greatly concern themselves. It is true that from time to time writers have labelled themselves 'romanticists' or 'classicists', just as they have from time to time banded themselves together under other names. These names which groups of writers and artists give themselves are the delight of professors and historians of literature, but should not be taken very seriously; their chief value is temporary and political – that, simply, of helping to make the authors known to a contemporary public; and I doubt whether any poet has ever done himself anything but harm by attempting to write as a 'romantic' or as a 'classicist'. No sensible author, in the midst of something that he is trying to write, can stop to consider whether it is going to be romantic or the opposite. At the moment when one writes, one is what one is, and the damage of a lifetime, and of having been born into an unsettled society, cannot be repaired at the moment of composition.

The danger of using terms like 'romantic' and 'classic' – this does not, however, give us permission to avoid them altogether – does not spring so much from the confusion caused by those who use these terms about their own work, as from inevitable shifts of meaning in context. We do not mean quite the same thing when we speak of a writer as romantic, as we do when we speak of a literary period as romantic. Furthermore, we may have in mind, on any particular occasion, certain virtues or vices more or less justly associated with one term or the other, and it is doubtful whether there is any total sum of virtues or of vices which may be arrogated to either class. The opportunities for systematic misunderstanding, and for futile controversy, are accordingly almost ideal; and discussion of the subject is generally conducted by excitement of passion and prejudice, rather than by reason. Finally – and this is the most important point – the differences represented by these two terms are not such as can be confined to a purely literary context. In using them, you are ultimately bringing in all human values, and according to your own schemes of valuation.

[From *After Strange Gods*, 1934]

RELIGION AND LITERATURE

WHAT I have to say is largely in support of the following propositions : Literary criticism should be completed by criticism from a definite ethical and theological standpoint. In so far as in any age there is common agreement on ethical and theological matters, so far can literary criticism be substantive. In ages like our own, in which there is no such common agreement, it is the more necessary for Christian readers to scrutinize their reading, especially of works of imagination, with explicit ethical and theological standards. The 'greatness' of literature cannot be determined solely by literary standards; though we must remember that whether it is literature or not can be determined only by literary standards.

We have tacitly assumed, for some centuries past, that there is *no* relation between literature and theology. This is not to deny that literature – I mean, again, primarily works of imagination – has been, is, and probably always will be judged by some moral standards. But moral judgements of literary works are made only according to the moral code accepted by each generation, whether it lives according to that code or not. In an age which accepts some precise Christian theology, the common code may be fairly orthodox: though even in such periods the common code may exalt such concepts as 'honour', 'glory', or 'revenge' to a position quite intolerable to Christianity. The dramatic ethics of the Elizabethan Age offer an interesting study. But when the common code is detached from its theological background, and is consequently more and more merely a matter of habit, it is exposed both to prejudice and to change. At such times morals are open to being altered *by* literature; so that we find in practice that what is 'objectionable' in literature is merely what the present generation is not used to. It is a commonplace that what shocks one generation is accepted quite calmly by the next. This adaptability to change of moral standards is sometimes greeted with satisfaction as an evidence of human perfectibility: whereas it is only evidence of what unsubstantial foundations people's moral judgements have.

I am not concerned here with religious literature but with the application of our religion to the criticism of any literature. It may be as well, however, to distinguish first what I consider to be the three senses in which we can speak of 'religious literature'. The first is that of which we say that it is 'religious literature' in the same way that we speak of 'historical literature' or or 'scientific literature'. I mean that we can treat the Authorized translation of the Bible, or the works of Jeremy Taylor, as literature, in the same way that we treat the historical writing of Clarendon or of Gibbon – our two great English historians – as literature; or Bradley's *Logic*, or Buffon's *Natural History*. All of these writers were men who, incidentally to their religious, or historical, or philosophic purpose, had a gift of language which makes them delightful to read to all those who can enjoy language well written, even if they are unconcerned with the objects which the writers had in view. And I would add that though a scientific, or historical, or theological, or philosophic work which is also 'literature', may become superannuated as anything but literature, yet it is not likely to be 'literature' unless it had its scientific or other value for its own time. While I acknowledge the legitimacy of this enjoyment, I am more acutely aware of its abuse. The persons who enjoy these writings *solely* because of their literary merit are essentially parasites; and we know that parasites, when they become too numerous, are pests. I could fulminate against the men of letters who have gone into ecstasies over 'the Bible as litera-

32

ture', the Bible as 'the noblest monument of English prose'. Those who talk of the Bible as a 'monument of English prose' are merely admiring it as a monument over the grave of Christianity. I must try to avoid the by-paths of my discouse: it is enough to suggest that just as the work of Clarendon, or Gibbon, or Buffon, or Bradley would be of inferior literary value if it were insignificant as history, science, and philosophy respectively, so the Bible has had a *literary* influence upon English literature *not* because it has been considered as literature, but because it has been considered as the report of the Word of God. And the fact that men of letters now discuss it as 'literature' probably indicates the *end* of its 'literary' influence.

The second kind of relation of religion to literature is that which is found in what is called 'religious' or 'devotional' poetry. Now what is the usual attitude of the lover of poetry – and I mean the person who is a genuine and first-hand enjoyer and appreciator of poetry, not the person who follows the admirations of others – towards this department of poetry? I believe, all that may be implied in his calling it a *department*. He believes, not always explicitly, that when you qualify poetry as 'religious' you are indicating very clear limitations. For the great majority of people who love poetry, *'religious* poetry' is a variety of *minor* poetry: the religious poet is not a poet who is treating the whole subject-matter of poetry in a religious spirit, but a poet who is dealing with a confined part of this subject-matter: who is leaving out what men consider their major passions, and thereby confessing his ignorance of them. I think that this is the real attitude of most poetry lovers towards such poets as Vaughan, or Southwell, or Crashaw, or George Herbert, or Gerard Hopkins.

But what is more, I am ready to admit that up to a point these critics are right. For there is a kind of poetry, such as most of the work of the authors I have mentioned, which is the product of a special religious awareness, which may exist without the general awareness which we expect of the major poet. In some poets, or in some of their works, this general awareness may have existed; but the preliminary steps which represent it may have been suppressed, and only the end-product presented. Between these, and those in which the religious or devotional genius represents the *special* and limited awareness, it may be very difficult to discriminate. I do not pretend to offer Vaughan, or Southwell, or George Herbert, or Hopkins as major poets :* I feel sure that the first three, at least, are poets of this limited awareness. They are not great religious poets in the sense in which Dante, or Corneille, or Racine, even in those of their plays which do not touch upon Christian themes, are great Christian religious poets. Or even in the sense in which Villon and Baudelaire, with all their imperfections and delinquencies, are Christian poets. Since the time of Chaucer, Christian poetry (in the sense in which I shall mean it) has been limited in England almost exclusively to minor poetry.

I repeat that when I am considering Religion and Literature, I speak of these things only to make clear that I am not concerned primarily with Religious Literature. I am concerned with what should be the relation between Religion and all Literature. Therefore the third type of 'religious literature' may be more quickly passed over. I mean the literary works of men who are sincerely desirous of forwarding the cause of religion : that which may come under the heading of Propaganda. I am thinking, of course, of such delightful fiction as Chesterton's *Man Who Was Thursday*, or his *Father Brown*. No one admires and enjoys these things more than I do; I would only remark that when the same effect is aimed at by zealous persons of less talent than Chesterton the effect is negative. But my point is that such writings do not enter into any serious consideration of the relation of Religion and Literature : because they are conscious operations in a world in which it is assumed that Religion and Literature are not related. It is a conscious and limited relating. What I want is a literature which should be *un*consciously, rather than deliberately and defiantly, Christian : because the work of Chesterton has its point from appearing in a world which is definitely not Christian.

---

* I note that in an address delivered in Swansea some years later (subsequently published in *The Welsh Review* under the title of 'What Is Minor Poetry?') I stated with some emphasis my opinion that Herbert is a major, not a minor poet. I agree with my later opinion. [*Author's note*, 1949]

I am convinced that we fail to realize how completely, and yet how irrationally, we separate our literary from our religious judgements. If there could be a complete separation, perhaps it might not matter: but the separation is not, and never can be, complete. If we exemplify literature by the novel – for the novel is the form in which literature affects the greatest number – we may remark this gradual secularization of literature during at least the last three hundred years. Bunyan, and to some extent Defoe, had moral purposes: the former is beyond suspicion, the latter may be suspect. But since Defoe the secularization of the novel has been continuous. There have been three chief phases. In the first, the novel took the Faith, in its contemporary version, for granted, and omitted it from its picture of life. Fielding, Dickens, and Thackeray belong to this phase. In the second, it doubted, worried about, or contested the Faith. To this phase belong George Eliot, George Meredith, and Thomas Hardy. To the third phase, in which we are living, belong nearly all contemporary novelists except James Joyce. It is the phase of those who have never heard the Christian Faith spoken of as anything but an anachronism.

Now, do people in general hold a definite opinion, that is to say religious or anti-religious; and do they read novels, or poetry for that matter, with a separate compartment of their minds? The common ground between religion and fiction is behaviour. Our religion imposes our ethics, our judgement and criticism of ourselves, and our behaviour toward our fellow men. The fiction that we read affects our behaviour towards our fellow men, affects our patterns of ourselves. When we read of human beings behaving in certain ways, with the approval of the author, who gives his benediction to this behaviour by his attitude towards the result of the behaviour arranged by himself, we can be influenced towards behaving in the same way. When the contemporary novelist is an individual thinking for himself in isolation, he may have something important to offer to those who are able to receive it. He who is alone may speak to the individual. But the majority of novelists are persons drifting in the stream, only a little faster. They have some sensitiveness, but little intellect.

We are expected to be broadminded about literature, to put aside prejudice or conviction, and to look at fiction as fiction and at drama as drama. With what is inaccurately called 'censorship' in this country – with what is much more difficult to cope with than an official censorship, because it represents the opinions of individuals in an irresponsible democracy, I have very little sympathy; partly because it so often suppresses the wrong books, and partly because it is little more effective than Prohibition of Liquor; partly because it is one manifestation of the desire that state control should take the place of decent domestic influence; and wholly because it acts only from custom and habit, not from decided theological and moral principles. Incidentally, it gives people a false sense of security in leading them to believe that books which are *not* suppressed are harmless. Whether there *is* such a thing as a harmless book I am not sure : but there very likely are books so utterly unreadable as to be incapable of injuring anybody. But it is certain that a book is not harmless merely because no one is consciously offended by it. And if we, as readers, keep our religious and moral convictions in one compartment, and take our reading merely for entertainment, or on a higher plane, for aesthetic pleasure, I would point out that the author, whatever his conscious intentions in writing, in practice recognizes no such distinctions. The author of a work of imagination is trying to affect us wholly, as human beings, whether he knows it or not; and we are affected by it, as human beings, whether we intend to be or not. I suppose that everything we eat has some other effect upon us than merely the pleasure of taste and mastication; it affects us during the process of assimilation and digestion; and I believe that exactly the same is true of anything we read.

The fact that what we read does not concern merely something called our *literary taste*, but that it affects directly, though only amongst many other influences, the whole of what we are, is best elicited, I think, by a conscientious examination of the history of our individual literary education. Consider the adolescent reading of any person with some literary sensibility. Everyone, I believe, who is at all sensible to the seductions of poetry, can remember some moment in youth when he or she was completely carried away by the work of one poet. Very likely he was carried away by several poets, one after the other. The reason for this passing infatuation is not merely that our sensibility to poetry is keener in adolescence than in maturity. What happens is a kind of inundation, of invasion of the undeveloped personality by the stronger personality of the poet. The same thing may happen at a later age to persons who have not done much reading. One author takes complete possession of us for a time; then another; and finally they begin to affect each other in our mind. We weigh one against another; we see that each has qualities absent from others, and qualities incompatible with the qualities of others: we begin to be, in fact, critical; and it is our growing critical power which protects us from excessive possession by any one literary personality. The good critic – and we should all try to be critics, and not leave criticism to the fellows who write reviews in the papers – is the man who, to a keen and abiding sensibility, joins wide and increasingly discriminating reading. Wide reading is not valuable as a kind of hoarding, an accumulation of knowledge, or what sometimes is meant by the term 'a well-stocked mind'. It is valuable because in the process of being affected by one powerful personality after another, we cease to be dominated by any one, or by any small number. The very different views of life, cohabiting in our minds, affect each other, and our own personality asserts itself and gives each a place in some arrangement peculiar to ourself.

It is simply not true that works of fiction, prose or verse, that is to say works depicting the actions, thoughts, and words and passions of imaginary human beings, *directly* extend our knowledge of life. Direct knowledge of life is knowledge directly in relation to ourselves, it is our knowledge of *how* people behave in general, of *what* they are like in general, in so far as that part of life in which we ourselves have participated gives us material for generalization. Knowledge of life obtained through fiction is only possible by another stage of self-consciousness. That is to say, it can only be a knowledge of other people's knowledge of life, not of life itself. So far as we are taken up with the happenings in any novel in the same way in which we are taken up with what happens under our eyes, we are acquiring at least as much falsehood as truth. But when we are developed enough to say: 'This is the view of life of a person who was a good observer within his limits, Dickens, or Thackeray, or George Eliot, or Balzac; but he looked at it in a different way from me, because he was a different man; he even selected rather different things to look at, or the same things in a different order of importance, because he was a different man; so what I am looking at is the world as seen by a particular mind' – then we are in a position to gain something from reading fiction. We are learning *something* about life from these authors direct, just as we learn something from the reading of history direct; but these authors are only really helping us when we can see, and allow for, their differences from ourselves.

Now what we get, as we gradually grow up and read more and more, and read a greater diversity of authors, is a variety of views of life. But what people commonly assume, I suspect, is that we gain this experience of other men's views of life only by 'improving reading'. This, it is supposed, is a reward we get by applying ourselves to Shakespeare, and Dante, and Goethe, and Emerson, and Carlyle, and dozens of other respectable writers. The rest of our reading for amusement is merely killing time. But I incline to come to the alarming conclusion that it is just the literature that we read for 'amusement' or 'purely for pleasure' that may have the greatest and least suspected influence upon us. It is the literature which we read with the least effort that can have the easiest and most insidious influence upon us. Hence it is that the influence of popular novelists, and of popular plays of contemporary life, requires to be scrutinized most closely. And it is chiefly *contemporary* literature that the majority of people ever read in this attitude of 'purely for pleasure', of pure passivity.

The relation to my subject of what I have been saying should now be a little more apparent. Though we may read literature merely for pleasure, of 'entertainment' or of 'aesthetic enjoyment', this reading never affects simply a sort of special sense: it affects us as entire human beings; it affects our moral and religious existence. And I say that while individual modern writers of eminence can be improving, contemporary literature as a whole tends to be degrading. And that even the effect of the better writers, in an age like ours, may be degrading to some readers; for we must remember that what a writer does to people is not necessarily what he intends to do. It may be only what people are capable of having done to them. People exercise an unconscious selection in being influenced. A writer like D. H. Lawrence may be in his effect either beneficial or pernicious. I am not sure that I have not had some pernicious influence myself.

At this point I anticipate a rejoinder from the liberal-minded, from all those who are convinced that if everybody says what he thinks, and does what he likes, things will somehow, by some automatic compensation and adjustment, come right in the end. 'Let everything be tried,' they say, 'and if it is a mistake, then we shall learn by experience.' This argument might have some value, if we were always the same generation upon earth; or if, as we know to be not the case, people ever learned much from the experience of their elders. These liberals are convinced that only by what is called unrestrained individualism will truth ever emerge. Ideas, views of life, they think, issue distinct from independent heads, and in consequence of their knocking violently against each other, the fittest survive, and truth rises triumphant. Anyone who dissents from this view must be either a medievalist, wishful only to set back the clock, or else a fascist, and probably both.

If the mass of contemporary authors were really individualists, every one of them an inspired Blake, each with his separate vision, and if the mass of the contemporary public were really a mass of *individuals* there might be something to be said for this attitude. But this is not, and never has been, and never will be. It is not only that the reading individual today (or at any day) is not enough an individual to be able to absorb all the 'views of life' of all the authors pressed upon us by the publishers' advertisements and the reviewers, and to be able to arrive at wisdom by considering one against another. It is that the contemporary authors are not individuals enough either. It is not that the world of separate individuals of the liberal democrat is undesirable; it is simply that this world does not exist. For the reader of contemporary literature is not, like the reader of the established great literature of all time, exposing himself to the influence of divers and contradictory personalities; he is exposing himself to a mass movement of writers who, each of them, think that they have something individually to offer, but are really all working together in the same direction. And there never was a time, I believe, when the reading public was so large, or so helplessly exposed to the influences of its own time. There never was a time, I believe, when those who read at all, read so many more books by living authors than books by dead authors; there never was a time so completely parochial, so shut off from the past. There may be too many publishers; there are certainly too many books published; and the journals ever incite the reader to 'keep up' with what is being published. Individualistic democracy has come to high tide: and it is more difficult today to be an individual than it ever was before.

Within itself, modern literature has perfectly valid distinctions of good and bad, better and worse: and I do not wish to suggest that I confound Bernard Shaw with Noel Coward, Virginia Woolf with Miss Mannin. On the other hand, I should like it to be clear that I am not defending a 'high'-brow against a 'low'-brow literature. What I do wish to affirm is that the whole of modern literature is corrupted by what I call Secularism, that it is simply unaware of, simply cannot understand the meaning of, the primacy of the supernatural over the natural life: of something which I assume to be our primary concern.

I do not want to give the impression that I have delivered a mere fretful jeremiad against contemporary literature. Assuming a common attitude between my readers, or some of my readers, and myself, the question is not so much, what is to be done about it? as, how should we behave towards it?

I have suggested that the liberal attitude towards literature will not work. Even if the writers who make their attempt to impose their 'view of life' upon us were really distinct individuals, even if we as readers were distinct individuals, what would be the result? It would be, surely, that each reader would be impressed, in his reading, merely by what he was previously prepared to be impressed by; he would follow the 'line of least resistance', and there would be no assurance that he would be made a better man. For literary judgement we need to be acutely aware of two things at once: of 'what we like', and of 'what we *ought* to like'. Few people are honest enough to know either. The first means knowing what we really feel: very few know that. The second involves understanding our shortcomings; for we do not really know what we ought to like unless we also know why we ought to like it, which involves knowing why we don't yet like it. It is not enough to understand what we ought to be, unless we know what we are; and we do not understand what we are, unless we know what we ought to be. The two forms of self-consciousness, knowing what we are and what we ought to be, must go together.

It is our business, as readers of literature, to know what we like. It is our business, as Christians, *as well as* readers of literature, to know what we ought to like. It is our business as honest men not to assume that whatever we like is what we ought to like; and it is our business as honest Christians not to assume that we do like what we ought to like. And the last thing I would wish for would be the existence of two literatures, one for Christian consumption and the other for the pagan world. What I believe to be incumbent upon all Christians is the duty of maintaining consciously certain standards and criteria of criticism over and above those applied by the rest of the world; and that by these criteria and standards everything that we read must be tested. We must remember that the greater part of our current reading matter is written for us by people who have no real belief in a supernatural order, though some of it may be written by people with individual notions of a supernatural order which are not ours. And the greater part of our reading matter is coming to be written by people who not only have no such belief, but are even ignorant of the fact that there are still people in the world so 'backward' or so 'eccentric' as to continue to believe. So long as we are conscious of the gulf fixed between ourselves and the greater part of contemporary literature, we are more or less protected from being harmed by it, and are in a position to extract from it what good it has to offer us.

There are a very large number of people in the world today who believe that all ills are fundamentally economic. Some believe that various specific economic changes alone would be enough to set the world right; others demand more or less drastic changes in the social as well, changes chiefly of two opposed types. These changes demanded and in some places carried out, are alike in one respect, that they hold the assumptions of what I call Secularism: they concern themselves only with changes of a temporal, material, and external nature; they concern themselves with morals only of a collective nature. In an exposition of one such new faith I read the following words:

'In our morality the one single test of any moral question is whether it impedes or destroys in any way the power of the individual to serve the State. [The individual] must answer the questions: "Does this action injure the nation? Does it injure other members of the nation? Does it injure my ability to serve the nation?" And if the answer is clear on all those questions, the individual has absolute liberty to do as he will.'

Now I do not deny that this is a kind of morality, and that it is capable of great good within limits; but I think that we should all repudiate a morality which had no higher ideal to set before us than that. It represents, of course, one of the violent reactions we are witnessing, against the view that the community is solely for the benefit of the individual; but it is equally a gospel of this world, and of this world alone. My complaint against modern literature is of the same kind. It is not that modern literature is in the ordinary sense 'immoral' or even 'amoral'; and in any case to prefer that charge would not be enough. It is simply that it repudiates, or is wholly ignorant of, our most fundamental and important beliefs; and that in consequence its tendency is to encourage its readers to get what they can out of life while it lasts, to miss no 'experience' that presents itself, and to sacrifice themselves, if they make any sacrifice at all, only for the sake of tangible benefits to others in this world either now or in the future. We shall certainly continue to read the best of its kind, of what our time provides; but we must tirelessly criticize it according to our own principles, and not merely according to the principles admitted by the writers and by the critics who discuss it in the public press.

[Contributed to the symposium, *Faith that Illuminates*, 1935]

THE distinction between 'journalism' and 'literature' is quite futile, unless we are drawing such violent contrast as that between Gibbon's *History* and tonight's evening paper; and such a contrast itself is too violent to have meaning. You cannot, that is, draw any useful distinction between journalism and literature merely in a scale of literary values, as a difference between the well written and the supremely well written: a second-rate novel is not journalism, but it certainly is not literature. The term 'journalism' has deteriorated in the last thirty years; and it is particularly fitting, in the present essay, to try to recall it to its more permanent sense. To my thinking, the most accurate as well as most comprehensive definition of the term is to be obtained through considering the state of mind, and the type of mind, concerned in writing what all would concede to be the *best* journalism. There is a type of mind, and I have a very close sympathy with it, which can only turn to writing, or only produce its best writing, under the pressure of an immediate occasion; and it is this type of mind which I propose to treat as the journalist's. The underlying causes may differ: the cause may be an ardent preoccupation with affairs of the day, or it may be (as with myself) inertia or laziness requiring an immediate stimulus, or a habit formed by early necessity of earning small sums quickly. It is not so much that the journalist works on different material from that of other writers, as that he works from a different, no less and often more honourable, motive.

The indignity commonly thrown at the journalists is this, that his work is said to be of only passing interest, intended to make an immediate strong impression, and destined to eternal oblivion after that instant effect has been produced. To say merely this, however, is to overlook the reasons for which writing may be 'ephemeral', and the loose application of that adjective itself, as well as the curious accidents which protect a piece of writing from oblivion. Those persons who are drawn by the powerful attraction of Jonathan Swift read and re-read with enchanted delight *The Drapier's Letters*; and these letters are journalism acccording to my hint of a definition, if anything is. But *The Drapier's Letters* are such an important item now in English letters, so essential to anyone who would be well read in the literature of England, that we ignore the accident by which we still read them. If Swift had never written *Gulliver's Travels*, and if he had not played a striking and dramatic part in political life, and if this amazing madman had not supplemented these claims to permanence by a most interesting private life, what would be the place of *The Drapier's Letters* now? They would be praised now and then by some student of Anglo-Irish history of the epoch who happened by some odd coincidence to have also an exceptional degree of literary acumen; and they would be read by nobody else. The same fate would have overcome the pamphleteering of Defoe, were he not the author of *Robinson Crusoe* and *Moll Flanders*; or the pamphleteering of Samuel Johnson, were he not the hero of Boswell. To turn to another great English writer of quite a different kind, let us suppose that John Henry Newman had not been also the great leader of the English Church whose defection Gladstone described as a 'catastrophe'; that he had not played the prominent role in the nineteenth century that he did play; supposing also that the material of his *Apologia* was as defunct as the subject of Wood's halfpence in Ireland, who but a few discerning connoisseurs of style would ever read that book now or a century hence? And the *Apologia* of Newman is as surely journalism as is the journalism of Swift, Defoe, or Johnson.

To quote an example on the opposite side: the *Martin Marprelate* tracts are not, certainly, as fine prose as the best of Swift, Defoe, Johnson, or Newman. They belong to a cruder period. But still they contain some very fine passages indeed, and the whole controversy is on a high literary level. Who reads them now? except a very small number of people, those who interest themselves in the religious squabbles of that epoch, and those who interest themselves in the prose styles of that epoch. They are not considered a part of the necessary education of the cultivated English-speaking person. Literary style is sometimes assigned almost magical properties, or is credited with being a mysterious preservative for subject-matter which no longer interests. This is far from being absolutely true.

Style alone cannot preserve; only good style in conjunction with permanently interesting content can preserve. All other preservation, such as that of Swift's or Defoe's journalism, is due to a happy accident. Even poetry is not immune, though poetry usually concerns itself with simpler and more eternal matters than anything else; for who, except scholars, and except the eccentric few who are born with a sympathy for such work, or others who have deliberately studied themselves into the right appreciation, can now read through the whole of *The Faerie Queene* with delight?

[From *Charles Whibley*, 1931]

Literary Criticism: Poetry

THE EXPERIENCE OF POETRY

THE experience of a poem is the experience both of a moment and of a lifetime. It is very much like our intenser experiences of other human beings. There is a first, or an early moment which is unique, of shock and surprise, even of terror (*Ego dominus tuus*); a moment which can never be forgotten, but which is never repeated integrally; and yet which would become destitute of significance if it did not survive in a larger whole of experience; which survives inside a deeper and a calmer feeling. The majority of poems one outgrows and outlives, as one outgrows and outlives the majority of human passions: Dante's is one of those which one can only just hope to grow up to at the end of life.

[From *Dante*, 1929]

THE DEVELOPMENT OF TASTE

THE majority of children, up to say twelve or fourteen, are capable of a certain enjoyment of poetry; at or about puberty the majority of these find little further use for it, but a small minority then find themselves possessed of a craving for poetry which is wholly different from any enjoyment experienced before. I do not know whether little girls have a different taste in poetry from little boys, but the responses of the latter I believe to be fairly uniform. 'Horatius', 'The Burial of Sir John Moore', 'Bannockburn', Tennyson's 'Revenge', some of the border ballads: a liking for martial and sanguinary poetry is no more to be discouraged than engagements with lead soldiers and pea-shooters. The only pleasure that I got from Shakespeare was the pleasure of being commended for reading him; had I been a child of more independent mind I should have refused to read

46

him at all. Recognizing the frequent deceptions of memory, I seem to remember that my early liking for the sort of verse that small boys do like vanished at about the age of twelve, leaving me for a couple of years with no sort of interest in poetry at all. I can recall clearly enough the moment when, at the age of fourteen or so, I happened to pick up a copy of Fitzgerald's *Omar* which was lying about, and the almost overwhelming introduction to a new world of feeling which this poem was the occasion of giving me. It was like a sudden conversion; the world appeared anew, painted with bright, delicious, and painful colours. Thereupon I took the usual adolescent course with Byron, Shelley, Keats, Rossetti, Swinburne.

I take this period to have persisted until about my twenty-second year. Being a period of rapid assimilation the end may not know the beginning, so different may the taste become. Like the first period of childhood, it is one beyond which I dare say many people never advance; so that such taste for poetry as they retain in later life is only a sentimental memory of the pleasures of youth, and is probably entwined with all our other sentimental retrospective feelings. It is, no doubt, a period of keen enjoyment; but we must not confuse the intensity of the poetic experience in adolescence with the intense experience of poetry. At this period, the poem, or the poetry of a single poet, invades the youthful consciousness and assumes complete possession for a time. We do not really see it as something with an existence outside ourselves; much as in our youthful experiences of love, we do not so much see the person as infer the existence of some outside object which sets in motion these new and delightful feelings in which we are absorbed. The frequent result is an outburst of scribbling which we may call imitation, so long as we are aware of the meaning of the word 'imitation' which we employ. It is not deliberate choice of a poet to mimic, but writing under a kind of daemonic possession by one poet.

The third, or mature stage of enjoyment of poetry, comes when we cease to identify ourselves with the poet we happen to be reading; when our critical faculties remain awake; when we are aware of what one poet can be expected to give and what he cannot. The poem has its own existence, apart from us; it was there before us and will endure after us. It is only at this stage that the reader is prepared to distinguish between degrees of greatness in poetry; before that stage he can only be expected to distinguish between the genuine and the sham – the capacity to make this latter distinction must always be practised first. The poets we frequent in adolescence will not be arranged in any objective order of eminence, but by the personal accidents which put them into relation with us; and this is right. I doubt whether it is possible to explain to school children or even undergraduates the differences of degree among poets, and I doubt whether it is wise to try; they have not yet had enough experience of life for these matters to have much meaning. The perception of *why* Shakespeare, or Dante, or Sophocles holds the place he has is something which comes only very slowly in the course of living. And the deliberate attempt to grapple with poetry which is not naturally congenial, and some of which never will be, should be a very mature activity indeed; an activity which well repays the effort, but which cannot be recommended to young people without grave danger of deadening their sensibility to poetry and confounding the genuine *development* of taste with the sham acquisition of it.

[From *The Use of Poetry and the Use of Criticism*, 1933]

THE APPRECIATION OF POETRY

THE rudiment of criticism is the ability to select a good poem and reject a bad poem; and the most severe test of its ability to select a good *new* poem, to respond properly to a new situation. The experience of poetry, as it develops in the conscious and mature person, is not merely the sum of the experiences of good poems. Education in poetry requires an organization of these experiences. There is not one of us who is born with or who suddenly acquires at puberty or later, an infallible discrimination and taste. The person whose experience is limited is always liable to be taken in by the sham or the adulterate article; and we see generation after generation of untrained readers being taken in by the sham and the adulterate in its own time – indeed preferring them, for they are more easily assimilable than the genuine article. Yet a very large number of people, I believe, have the native capacity for enjoying *some* good poetry: how much, or how many degrees of capacity may profitably be distinguished, is not part of my present purpose to inquire. It is only the exceptional reader, certainly, who in the course of time comes to classify and compare his experiences, to see one in the light of others; and who, as his poetic experiences multiply, will be able to understand each more accurately. The element of enjoyment is enlarged into appreciation, which brings a more intellectual addition to the original intensity of feeling. It is a second stage in our understanding of poetry, when we no longer merely select and reject, but organize. We may even speak of a third stage, one of reorganization; a stage at which a person already educated in poetry meets with something new in his own time, and finds a new pattern of poetry arranging itself in consequence.

[From *The Use of Poetry and the Use of Criticism*, 1933]

THE CRITIC OF POETRY

SUCH writing as Johnson's *Lives of the Poets* and his essay on Shakespeare loses none of its permanence from the consideration that every generation must make its own appraisal of the poetry of the past, in the light of the performance of its contemporaries and immediate predecessors. Criticism of poetry moves between two extremes. On the one hand the critic may busy himself so much with the implications of a poem, or of one poet's work – implications moral, social, religious, or other – that the poetry becomes hardly more than a text for a discourse. Such is the tendency of the moralizing critics of the nineteenth century, to which Landor makes a notable exception. Or if you stick too closely to the 'poetry' and adopt no attitude towards what the poet has to say, you will tend to evacuate it of all significance. And furthermore there is a philosophic borderline, which you must not transgress too far or too often, if you wish to preserve your standing as a critic, and are not prepared to present yourself as a philosopher, metaphysician, sociologist, or psychologist instead. Johnson, in these respects, is a type of critical integrity. Within his limitations, he is one of the great critics; and he is a great critic partly because he keeps within his limitations. When you know what they are, you know where you are. Considering all the temptations to which one is exposed in judging contemporary writing, all the prejudices which one is tempted to indulge in judging writers of the immediately preceding generation, I view Johnson's *Lives of the Poets* as a masterpiece of the judicial bench. His style is not so formally perfect as that of some other prose writers of his time. It reads often like the writing of a man who is more habituated to talking than to writing; he seems to think aloud, and in short breaths, rather than in the long periods of the historian or the orator. His criticism is as salutary against the dogmatic excesses of the eighteenth century – more indulged in France than in England – as it is against excessive adulation of individual poets with their faults as well as virtues. For Johnson poetry was still poetry, and not another thing. Had he lived a generation later, he would have been obliged to look more deeply into the foundations, and so would have been unable to leave us an example of what criticism ought to be for a civilization which, being settled, has no need, while it lasts, to inquire into the functions of its parts.

[From *The Use of Poetry and the Use of Criticism*, 1933]

POETRY AND PHILOSOPHY

WE say, in a vague way, that Shakespeare, or Dante, or Lucretius, is a poet who thinks, and that Swinburne is a poet who does not think, even that Tennyson is a poet who does not think. But what we really mean is not a difference in quality of thought, but a difference in quality of emotion. The poet who 'thinks' is merely the poet who can express the emotional equivalent of thought. But he is not necessarily interested in the thought itself. We talk as if thought was precise and emotion was vague. In reality there is precise emotion and there is vague emotion. To express precise emotion requires as great intellectual power as to express precise thought. But by 'thinking' I mean something very different from anything that I find in Shakespeare. Champions of Shakespeare as a great philosopher, have a great deal to say about Shakespeare's power of thought, but they fail to show that he thought to any purpose; that he had any coherent view of life, or that he recommended any procedure to follow. 'We possess a great deal of evidence', says Wyndham Lewis, 'as to what Shakespeare thought of military glory and martial events.' Do we? Or rather, did Shakespeare think anything at all? He was occupied with turning human actions into poetry.

I would suggest that none of the plays of Shakespeare has a 'meaning', although it would be equally false to say that a play of Shakespeare is meaningless. All great poetry gives the illusion of a view of life. When we enter into the world of Homer or Sophocles, or Virgil or Dante, or Shakespeare, we incline to believe that we are apprehending something that can be expressed intellectually; for every precise emotion tends towards intellectual formulation.

We are apt to be deluded by the example of Dante. Here, we think, is a poem which represents an exact intellectual system; Dante has a 'philosophy', therefore every poet as great as Dante has a philosophy too. Dante had behind him the system of Saint Thomas, to which his poem corresponds point to point. Therefore Shakespeare had behind him Seneca, or Montaigne, or Machiavelli; and if his work does not correspond point to point with any or a composition of these, then it must be that he did a little quiet thinking on his own, and was better than any of these people at their own job. I can see no reason for believing that either Dante or Shakespeare did any thinking on his own. The people who think that Shakespeare thought, are always people who are not engaged in writing poetry, but who are engaged in thinking, and we all like to think that great men were like ourselves. The difference between Shakespeare and Dante is that Dante had one coherent system of thought behind him; but that was just his luck, and from the point of view of poetry is an irrelevant accident. It happened that at Dante's time thought was orderly and strong and beautiful, and that it was concentrated in one man of the greatest genius; Dante's poetry receives a boost which in a sense it does not merit, from the fact that the thought behind it is the thought of a man as great and lovely as Dante himself: Saint Thomas. The thought behind Shakespeare is of men far inferior to Shakespeare himself: hence the alternative errors, first, that as Shakespeare was as great a poet as Dante, he must have supplied, out of his own thinking, the difference in quality between a Saint Thomas and a Montaigne or a Machiavelli or a Seneca, or second, that Shakespeare is inferior to Dante. In truth neither Shakespeare nor Dante did any real thinking – that was not their job; and the relative value of the thought current of their time, the material enforced upon each to use as the vehicle of his feeling, is of no importance. It does not make Dante a greater poet, or mean that we can learn more from Dante than from Shakespeare. We can certainly learn more from Aquinas than from Seneca, but that is quite a different matter. When Dante says

la sua voluntade è nostra pace,

it is great poetry, and there is a great philosophy behind it. When Shakespeare says

As flies to wanton boys, are we to the gods;
They kill us for their sport,

it is *equally* great poetry, though the philosophy behind it is not great. But the essential is that each expresses, in perfect language, some permanent human impulse. Emotionally, the latter is just as strong, just as true, and just as informative – just as useful and beneficial in the sense in which poetry is useful and beneficial, as the former.

What every poet starts from is his own emotions. And when we get down to these, there is not much to choose between Shakespeare and Dante. Dante's railings, his personal spleen – sometimes thinly disguised under Old Testament prophetic denunciations – his nostalgia, his bitter regrets for past happiness – or for what seems happiness when it is past – and his brave attempts to fabricate something permanent and holy out of his personal animal feelings – as in the *Vita Nuova* – can all be matched out of Shakespeare. Shakespeare, too, was occupied with the struggle – which alone constitutes life for a poet – to transmute his personal and private agonies into something rich and strange, something universal and impersonal. The rage of Dante against Florence, or Pistoia, or what not, the deep surge of Shakespeare's general cynicism and disillusionment, are merely gigantic attempts to metamorphose private failures and disappointments. The great poet, in writing himself, writes his time. Thus Dante, hardly knowing it, became the voice of the thirteenth century; Shakespeare, hardly knowing it, became the representative of the end of the sixteenth century, of a turning point in history. But you can hardly say that Dante believed, or did not believe, the Thomist philosophy; you can hardly say that Shakespeare believed, or did not believe, the mixed and muddled scepticism of the Renaissance. If Shakespeare had written according to a better philosophy, he would have written worse poetry; it was his business to express the greatest emotional intensity of his time, based on whatever his time happened to think. Poetry is not a substitute for philosophy or theology or religion; it has its own function. But as this function is not intellectual but emotional, it cannot be defined adequately in intellectual terms. We can say that it provides 'consolation': strange consolation, which is provided equally by writers so different as Dante and Shakespeare.

[From *Shakespeare and the Stoicism of Seneca*, 1927]

THE MUSIC OF POETRY*

IT may appear strange, that when I profess to be talking about the 'music' of poetry, I put such emphasis upon conversation. But I would remind you, first, that the music of poetry is not something which exists apart from the meaning. Otherwise, we could have poetry of great musical beauty which made no sense, and I have never come across such poetry. The apparent exceptions only show a difference of degree: there are poems in which we are moved by

* The third W. P. Ker Memorial Lecture delivered at Glasgow University, 24 February 1942. [*Editor's note*]

53

the music and take the sense for granted, just as there are poems in which we attend to the sense and are moved by the music without noticing it. Take an apparently extreme example – the nonsense verse of Edward Lear. His non-sense is not vacuity of sense: it is a parody of sense, and that is the sense of it. 'The Jumblies' is a poem of adventure, and of nostalgia for the romance of foreign voyage and exploration; 'The Yongy-Bongy-Bo' and 'The Dong with a Luminous Nose' are poems of unrequited passion – 'blues' in fact. We enjoy the music, which is of a high order, and we enjoy the feeling of irresponsibility towards the sense. Or take a poem of another type, the 'Blue Closet' of William Morris. It is a delightful poem, though I cannot explain what it means and I doubt whether the author could have explained it. It has an effect somewhat like that of a rune or charm, but runes and charms are very practical formulae designed to produce definite results, such as getting a cow out of a bog. But its obvious intention (and I think the author succeeds) is to produce the effect of a dream. It is not necessary, in order to enjoy the poem, to know what the dream means; but human beings have an unshakeable belief that dreams mean something: they used to believe – and many still believe – that dreams disclose the secrets of the future; the orthodox modern faith is that they reveal the secrets – or at least the more horrid ones – of the past. It is a commonplace to observe that the meaning of a poem may wholly escape paraphrase. It is not quite so commonplace to observe that the meaning of a poem may be something larger than its author's conscious purpose, and something remote from its origins. One of the most obscure of modern poets was the French writer Stéphane Mallarmé, of whom the French sometimes say that his language is so peculiar that it can be understood only by foreigners. The late Roger Fry, and his friend Charles Mauron, published an English translation with notes to unriddle the meanings: when I learn that a difficult sonnet was inspired by seeing a painting on the ceiling reflected on the polished top of a table, or by seeing the light reflected from the foam on a glass of beer, I can only say that this may be a correct embryology, but it is not the meaning. If we are not moved, then it is, as poetry, meaningless. We can be deeply stirred by hearing the recitation of a poem in a language of which we understand no word; but if we are then told that the poem is gibberish and has no meaning, we shall consider that we have been deluded – this was no poem, it was merely an imitation of instrumental music. If, as we are aware, only a part of the meaning can be conveyed by paraphrase, that is because the poet is occupied with frontiers of consciousness beyond which words fail, though meanings still exist. A poem may appear to mean very different things to different readers, and all of these meanings may be different from what the author thought he meant. For instance, the author may have been writing some peculiar personal experience, which he saw quite unrelated to anything outside; yet for the reader the poem may become the expression of a general situation, as well as of some private experience of his own. The reader's interpretation may differ from the author's and be equally valid – it may even be better. There may be much more in a poem than the author was aware of. The different interpretations may all be partial formulations of one thing; the ambiguities may be due to the fact that the poem means more, not less, than ordinary speech can communicate.

So, while poetry attempts to convey something beyond what can be conveyed in prose rhythms, it remains, all the same, one person talking to another; and this is just as true if you sing it, for singing is another way of talking. The immediacy of poetry to conversation is not a matter on which we can lay down exact laws. Every revolution in poetry is apt to be, and sometimes to announce itself as, a return to common speech. That is the revolution which Wordsworth announced in his Prefaces, and he was right; but the same revolution had been carried out a century before by Oldham, Waller, Denham, and Dryden; and the same revolution was due again something over a century later. The followers of a revolution develop the new poetic idiom in one direction or another; they polish or perfect it; meanwhile the spoken language goes on changing, and the poetic idiom goes out of date. Perhaps we do not realize how natural the speech of Dryden must have sounded to the most sensitive of his contemporaries. No poetry, of course, is ever exactly the same speech that the poet talks and hears : but it has to be in such a relation to the speech of his time that the listener or reader can say 'that is how I should

55

talk if I could talk poetry'. This is the reason why the best contemporary poetry can give us a feeling of excitement and a sense of fulfilment different from any sentiment aroused by even very much greater poetry of a past age.

The music of poetry, then, must be a music latent in the common speech of its time. And that means also that it must be latent in the common speech of the poet's *place*. It would not be to my present purpose to inveigh against the ubiquity of standardized, or 'B.B.C.' English. If we all came to talk alike there would no longer be any point in our not writing alike: but until that time comes – and I hope it may be long postponed – it is the poet's business to use the speech which he finds about him, that with which he is most familiar. I shall always remember the impression of W. B. Yeats reading poetry aloud. To hear him read his own works was to be made to recognize how much the Irish way of speech is needed to bring out the beauties of Irish poetry: to hear Yeats reading William Blake was an experience of a different kind, more astonishing than satisfying. Of course, we do not want the poet merely to reproduce exactly the conventional idiom of himself, his family, his friends, and his particular district: but what he finds there is the material out of which he must make his poetry. He must, like the sculptor, be faithful to the medium in which he works; it is out of sounds that he has heard that he must make his melody and harmony.

It would be a mistake, however, to assume that all poetry ought to be melodious, or that melody is more than one of the components of the music of words. Some poetry is meant to be sung; most poetry, in modern times, is meant to be spoken – and there are many other things to be spoken of besides the murmur of innumerable bees or the moan of doves in immemorial elms. Dissonance, even cacophony, has its place: just as, in a poem of any length, there must be transitions between passages of greater and less intensity, to give a rhythm of fluctuating emotion essential to the musical structure of the whole; and the passages of less intensity will be, in relation to the level on which the total poem operates, prosaic – so that, in the sense implied by that context, it may be said that no poet can write a poem of amplitude unless he is a master of the prosaic.

What matters, in short, is the whole poem: and if the whole poem need not be, and often should not be, wholly melodious, it follows that a poem is not made only out of 'beautiful words'. I doubt whether from the point of view of *sound* alone, any word is more or less beautiful than another – within its own language, for the question whether some languages are not more beautiful than others is quite another question. The ugly words are the words not fitted for the company in which they find themselves; there are words which are ugly because of rawness or because of antiquation; there are words which are ugly because of foreignness or ill-breeding (e.g. *television*): but I do not believe that any word well-established in its own language is either beautiful or ugly. The music of a word is, so to speak, at a point of intersection: it arises from its relation first to the words immediately preceding and following it, and indefinitely to the rest of its context; and from another relation, that of its immediate meaning in that context to all the other meanings which it has had in other contexts, to its greater or less wealth of association. Not all words, obviously, are equally rich and well-connected: it is part of the business of the poet to dispose the richer among the poorer, at the right points, and we cannot afford to load a poem too heavily with the former – for it is only at certain moments that a word can be made to insinuate the whole history of a language and a civilization. This is an 'allusiveness' which is not the fashion or eccentricity of a peculiar type of poetry, but an allusiveness which is in the nature of words, and which is equally the concern of every kind of poet. My purpose here is to insist that a 'musical poem' is a poem which has a musical pattern of sound and a musical pattern of the secondary meanings of the words which compose it, and that these two patterns are indissoluble and one. And if you object that it is only the pure sound, apart from the sense, to which the adjective 'musical' can be rightly applied, I can only reaffirm my previous assertion that the sound of a poem is as much an abstraction from the poem as is the sense.

The history of blank verse illustrates two interesting and related points: the dependence upon speech and the striking difference, in what is prosodically the same form, between dramatic blank verse and blank verse employed for epical, philosophical, meditative, and idyllic purposes. The dependence of verse upon speech is much more direct in dramatic poetry than in any other. In most kinds of poetry, the necessity for its reminding us of contemporary speech is reduced by the latitude allowed for personal idiosyncrasy: a poem by Gerard Hopkins, for instance, may sound pretty remote from the way in which you and I express ourselves – or rather, from the way in which our fathers and grandfathers expressed themselves: but Hopkins does give the impression that his poetry has the necessary fidelity to *his* way of thinking and talking to himself. But in dramatic verse the poet is speaking in one character after another, through the medium of a company of actors trained by a producer, and of different actors and different producers at different times: his idiom must be comprehensive of all the voices, but present at a deeper level than is necessary when the poet speaks only for himself. Some of Shakespeare's later verse is very elaborate and peculiar: but it remains the language, not of one person, but of a world of persons. It is based upon the speech of three hundred years ago, yet when we hear it well rendered we can forget the distance of time – as is brought home to us most patently in one of those plays, of which *Hamlet* is the chief, which can fittingly be produced in modern dress. By the time of Otway dramatic blank verse has become artificial and at best reminiscent; and when we get to the verse plays by nineteenth-century poets, of which the greatest is probably *The Cenci*, it is difficult to preserve any illusion of reality. Nearly all the greater poets of the last century tried their hands at verse plays. These plays, which few people read more than once, are treated with respect as fine poetry; and their insipidity is usually attributed to the fact that the authors, though great poets, were amateurs in the theatre. But even if the poets had had greater natural gifts for the theatre, or had toiled to acquire the craft, their plays would have been just as ineffective, unless their theatrical talent and experience had shown them the necessity for a different kind of versification. It is not primarily lack of plot, or lack of action and suspense, or imperfect realization of character, or lack of anything of what is called 'theatre', that makes these plays so lifeless: it is primarily that their rhythm of speech is something that we cannot associate with any human being except a poetry reciter.

Even under the powerful manipulation of Dryden dramatic blank verse shows a grave deterioration. There are splendid passages in *All for Love:* yet Dryden's characters talk more naturally at times in the heroic plays which he wrote in rhymed couplets, than they do in what would seem the more natural form of blank verse – though less naturally in English than the characters of Corneille and Racine in French. The causes for the rise and decline of any form of art are always complex, and we can always trace a number of contributory causes, while there seems to remain some deeper cause incapable of formulation: I should not care to advance any one reason why prose came to supersede verse in the theatre. But I feel sure that one reason why blank verse cannot be employed now in the drama is that so much non-dramatic poetry, and great non-dramatic poetry, has been written in it in the last three hundred years. Our minds are saturated in these non-dramatic works in what is formally the same kind of verse. If we can imagine, as a flight of fancy, Milton coming before Shakespeare, Shakespeare would have had to discover quite a different medium from that which he used and perfected. Milton handled blank verse in a way which no one has ever approached or ever will approach: and in so doing did more than anyone or anything else to make it impossible for the drama: though we may also believe that dramatic blank verse had exhausted its resources, and had no future in any event. Indeed, Milton almost made blank verse impossible for any purpose for a couple of generations. It was the precursors of Wordsworth – Thomson, Young, Cowper – who made the first efforts to rescue it from the degradation to which the eighteenth-century imitators of Milton had reduced it. There is much, and varied, fine blank verse in the nineteenth century: the nearest to colloquial speech is that of Browning – but, significantly, in his monologues rather than in his plays.

To make a generalization like this is not to imply any judgement of the relative stature of poets. It merely calls attention to the profound difference between dramatic and all other kinds of verse: a difference in the music, which is a difference in the relation to the current spoken language. It leads to my next point: which is that the task of the poet will differ, not only according to his personal constitution, but according to the period in which he finds himself. At some periods, the task is to explore the musical possibilities of an established convention of the relation of the idiom of verse to that of speech; at other periods, the task is to catch up with the changes in colloquial speech, which are fundamentally changes in thought and sensibility. This cyclical movement also has a very great influence upon our critical judgement. At a time like ours, when a refreshment of poetic diction similar to that brought about by Wordsworth has been called for (whether it has been satisfactorily accomplished or not), we are inclined, in our judgements upon the past, to exaggerate the importance of the innovators at the expense of the reputation of the developers: which might account for what will seem, surely, to a later age, our undue adulation of Donne and depreciation of Milton.

I have said enough, I think, to make clear that I do not believe that the task of the poet is primarily and always to effect a revolution in language. It would not be desirable, even if it were possible, to live in a state of perpetual revolution: the craving for continual novelty of diction and metric is as unwholesome as the obstinate adherence to the idiom of our grandfathers. There are times for exploration and times for the development of the territory acquired. The poet who did most for the English language is Shakespeare: and he carried out, in one short lifetime, the task of two poets. I have attempted to indicate his dual achievement elsewhere: I can only say here, briefly, that the development of Shakespeare's verse can be roughly divided into two periods. During the first, he was slowly adapting his form to colloquial speech: so that by the time he wrote *Antony and Cleopatra* he had devised a medium in which everything that any dramatic character might have to say, whether high or low, 'poetical' or 'prosaic', could be said with naturalness and beauty. Having got to this point, he began to elaborate. The first period – of the poet who began with *Venus and Adonis*, but who had already, in *Love's Labour's Lost*, begun to see what he had to do – is from artificiality to simplicity, from stiffness to suppleness. The later plays move from simplicity towards elaboration. He is occupied with the other task of the poet – doing the work of two poets in one lifetime – that of experimenting to see how elaborate, how complicated, the music could be made without losing touch with colloquial speech altogether, and without his characters ceasing to be human beings. This is the poet of *Cymbeline*, *The Winter's Tale*, *Pericles*, and *The Tempest*. Of those whose exploration took them in this one direction only, Milton is the greatest master. We may think that Milton, in exploring the orchestral music of language, sometimes ceases to talk a social idiom at all; we may think that Wordsworth, in attempting to recover the social idiom, sometimes oversteps the mark and becomes pedestrian: but it is often true that only by going too far can we find out how far we can go; though one has to be a very great poet to justify such perilous adventures.

So far, I have spoken only of versification and not of poetic structure; and it is time for a reminder that the mystic of verse is not a line by line matter, but a question of the whole poem. Only with this in mind can we approach the vexed question of formal pattern and free verse. In the plays of Shakespeare a musical design can be discovered in particular scenes, and in his more perfect plays as wholes. It is a music of imagery as well as sound: Mr Wilson Knight has shown in his examination of several of the plays, how much the use of recurrent imagery, and dominant imagery, throughout one play, has to do with the total effect. A play of Shakespeare is a very complex musical structure; the more easily grasped structure is that of forms such as the sonnet, the formal ode, the ballade, the villanelle, rondeau, or sestina. It is sometimes assumed that modern poetry has done away with forms like these. I have seen signs of a return to them; and indeed I believe that the tendency to return to set, and even elaborate, patterns is permanent, as permanent as the need for a refrain or a chorus to a popular song. Some forms are more appropriate to some languages than to others, and all are more appropriate to some periods than to others. At one stage the stanza is a right and natural formalization of speech into pattern. But the stanza – and the more elaborate it is, the more rules to be observed in its proper execution, the more surely this happens – tends to become fixed to the idiom of the moment of its perfection. It quickly loses contact with the changing colloquial speech, being possessed by the mental outlook of a past generation; it becomes discredited when employed solely by those writers who, having no impulse to form within them, have recourse to pouring their liquid sentiment into a ready-made mould in which they vainly hope that it will set. In a perfect sonnet, what you admire is not so much the author's skill in adapting himself to the pattern as the skill and power with which he makes the pattern comply with what he has to say. Without this fitness, which is contingent upon period as well as individual genius, the rest is at best virtuosity: and where the musical element is the only element, that also vanishes. Elaborate forms return: but there have to be periods during which they are laid aside.

As for 'free verse', I expressed my view twenty-five years ago by saying that no verse is free for the man who wants to do a good job.* No one has better cause to know than I, that a great deal of bad prose has been written under the name of free verse: though whether its authors wrote bad prose or bad verse, or bad verse in one style or in another, seems to me a matter of indifference. But only a bad poet could welcome free verse as a liberation from form. It was a revolt against dead form, and a preparation for new form or for the renewal of the old; it has an insistence upon the inner unity which is unique to every poem, against the outer unity which is typical. The poem comes before the form, in the sense that a form grows out of the attempt of somebody to say something; just as a system of prosody is only a formulation of the identities in the rhythms of a succession of poets influenced by each other.

Forms have to be broken and remade: but I believe that any language, so long as it remains the same language, imposes its laws and restrictions and permits its own licence, dictates its own speech rhythms and sound patterns. And a language is always changing; its developments in vocabulary, in syntax, pronunciation, and intonation – even, in the long run, its deterioration – must be accepted by the poet and made the best of. He in turn has the privilege of contri-

* 'Reflections on *Vers Libre*' in the *New Statesman*, 3 March 1917. See p. 82. [*Editor's note*]

buting to the development and maintaining the quality, the capacity of the language to express a wide range, and subtle gradation, of feeling and emotion; his task is both to respond to change and make it conscious, and to battle against degradation below the standards which he has learnt from the past. The liberties that he may take are for the sake of order.

At what stage contemporary verse now finds itself, I must leave you to judge for yourselves. I suppose that it will be agreed that if the work of the last twenty years is worthy of being classified at all, it is as belonging to a period of search for a proper modern colloquial idiom. We have still a good way to go in the invention of a verse medium for the theatre; a medium in which we shall be able to hear the speech of contemporary human beings, in which dramatic characters can express the purest poetry without highfalutin and in which they can convey the most commonplace message without absurdity. But when we reach a point at which the poetic idiom can be stabilized, then a period of musical elaboration can follow. I think that a poet may gain much from the study of music: how much technical knowledge of musical form is desirable I do not know, for I have not that technical knowledge myself. But I believe that the properties in which music concerns the poet most nearly, are the sense of rhythm and the sense of structure. I think that it might be possible for a poet to work too closely to musical analogies: the result might be an effect of artificiality; but I know that a poem, or a passage of a poem, may tend to realize itself first as a particular rhythm before it reaches expression in words, and that this rhythm may bring to birth the idea and the image; and I do not believe that this is an experience peculiar to myself. The use of recurrent themes is as natural to poetry as to music. There are possibilities for verse which bear some analogy to the development of a theme by different groups of instruments; there are possibilities of transitions in a poem comparable to the different movements of a symphony or a quartet; there are possibilities of contrapuntal arrangement of subject-matter. It is in the concert room, rather than in the opera house, that the germ of a poem may be quickened. More than this I cannot say, but must leave the matter here to those who have

63

had a musical education. But I would remind you again of the two tasks of poetry, the two directions in which language must at different times be worked: so that however far it may go in musical elaboration, we must expect a time to come when poetry will have again to be recalled to speech. The same problems arise, and always in new forms; and poetry has always before it, as F. S. Oliver said of politics, an 'endless adventure'.

[From *The Music of Poetry*, 1942]

POETRY AND DRAMA*

I

REVIEWING my critical output for the last thirty-odd years, I am surprised to find how constantly I have returned to the drama, whether by examining the work of the contemporaries of Shakespeare, or by reflecting on the possibilities of the future. It may even be that people are weary of hearing me on this subject. But, while I find that I have been composing variations on this theme all my life, my views have been continually modified and renewed by increasing experience; so that I am impelled to take stock of the situation afresh at every stage of my own experimentation.

As I have gradually learned more about the problems of poetic drama, and the conditions which it must fulfil if it is to justify itself, I have made a little clearer to myself, not only my own reasons for wanting to write in this form, but the more general reasons for wanting to see it restored to its place. And I think that if I say something about these problems and conditions, it should make clearer to other people whether and if so why poetic drama has anything potentially to offer the play-goer, that prose drama cannot. For I start with the assumption that if poetry is merely a decoration, an added embellishment, if it merely gives people of literary tastes the pleasure of listening to poetry at the same time that they are witness-

* The first Theodore Spencer Memorial Lecture, delivered at Harvard University, 21 November 1950. The introductory personal tribute is omitted. [*Editor's note*]

ing a play, then it is superfluous. It must justify itself dramatically, and not merely be fine poetry shaped into a dramatic form. From this it follows that no play should be written in verse for which prose is *dramatically* adequate. And from this it follows, again, that the audience, its attention held by the dramatic action, its emotions stirred by the situation between the characters, should be too intent upon the play to be wholly conscious of the medium.

Whether we use prose or verse on the stage, they are both but means to an end. The difference, from one point of view, is not so great as we might think. In those prose plays which survive, which are read and produced on the stage by later generations, the prose in which the characters speak is as remote, for the best part, from the vocabulary, syntax, and rhythm of our ordinary speech – with its fumbling for words, its constant recourse to approximation, its disorder, and its unfinished sentences – as verse is. Like verse, it has been written, and rewritten. Our two greatest prose stylists in the drama – apart from Shakespeare and the other Elizabethans who mixed prose and verse in the same play – are, I believe, Congreve and Bernard Shaw. A speech by a character of Congreve or of Shaw has – however clearly the characters may be differentiated – that unmistakable personal rhythm which is the mark of a prose style, and of which only the most accomplished conversationalists – who are for that matter usually monologuists – show any trace in their talk. We have all heard (too often!) of Molière's character who expressed surprise when told that he spoke prose. But it was M. Jourdain who was right, and not his mentor or his creator: he did not speak prose – he only talked. For I mean to draw a triple distinction: between prose, and verse, and our ordinary speech which is mostly below the level of either verse or prose. So if you look at it in this way, it will appear that prose, on the stage, is as artificial as verse: or alternatively, that verse can be as natural as prose.

But while the sensitive member of the audience will appreciate, when he hears fine prose spoken in a play, that this is something better than ordinary conversation, he does not regard it as a wholly different language from that which he himself speaks, for that would interpose a barrier between himself and the imaginary characters on the stage. Too many people, on the other hand, approach a play which they know to be in verse, with the consciousness of the difference. It is unfortunate when they are repelled by verse, but can also be deplorable when they are attracted by it – if that means that they are prepared to enjoy the play and the language of the play as two separate things. The chief effect of style and rhythm in dramatic speech, whether in prose or verse, should be unconscious.

From this it follows that a mixture of prose and verse in the same play is generally to be avoided: each transition makes the auditor aware, with a jolt, of the medium. It is, we may say, justifiable when the author wishes to produce this jolt: when, that is, he wishes to transport the audience violently from one plane of reality to another. I suspect that this kind of transition was easily acceptable to an Elizabethan audience, to whose ears both prose and verse came naturally; who liked highfalutin and low comedy in the same play; and to whom it seemed perhaps proper that the more humble and rustic characters should speak in a homely language, and that those of more exalted rank should rant in verse. But even in the plays of Shakespeare some of the prose passages seem to be designed for an effect of contrast which, when achieved, is something that can never become old-fashioned. The knocking at the gate in *Macbeth* is an example that comes to everyone's mind; but it has long seemed to me that the alternation of scenes in prose with scenes in verse in *Henry IV* points an ironic contrast between the world of high politics and the world of common life. The audience probably thought they were getting their accustomed chronicle play garnished with amusing scenes of low life; yet the prose scenes of both Part I and Part II provide a sardonic comment upon the bustling ambitions of the chiefs of the parties in the insurrection of the Percys.

Today, however, because of the handicap under which verse drama suffers, I believe that prose should be used very sparingly indeed; that we should aim at a form of verse in which everything can be said that has to be said; and that when we find some situation which is intractable in verse, it is merely that our form of verse is inelastic. And if there prove to be scenes which we cannot put in verse, we must either develop our verse, or avoid having to introduce such scenes. For we have to accustom our audiences to verse to the point at which they will cease to be conscious of it; and to introduce prose dialogue, would only be to distract their attention from the play itself to the medium of its expression. But if our verse is to have so wide a range that it can say anything that has to be said, it follows that it will not be 'poetry' all the time. It will only be 'poetry' when the dramatic situation has reached such a point of intensity that poetry becomes the natural utterance, because then it is the only language in which the emotions can be expressed at all.

It is indeed necessary for any long poem, if it is to escape monotony, to be able to say homely things without bathos, as well as to take the highest flights without sounding exaggerated. And it is still more important in a play, especially if it is concerned with contemporary life. The reason for writing even the more pedestrian parts of a verse play in verse instead of prose is, however, not only to avoid calling the audience's attention to the fact that it is at other moments listening to poetry. It is also that the verse rhythm should have its effect upon the hearers, without their being conscious of it. A brief analysis of one scene of Shakespeare's may illustrate this point. The opening scene of *Hamlet* – as well constructed an opening scene as that of any play ever written – has the advantage of being one that everybody knows.

What we do not notice, when we witness this scene in the theatre, is the great variation of style. Nothing is superfluous, and there is no line of poetry which is not justified by its dramatic value. The first twenty-two lines are built of the simplest words in the most homely idiom. Shakespeare had worked for a long time in the theatre, and written a good many plays, before reaching the point at which he could write those twenty-two lines. There is nothing quite so simplified and sure in his previous work. He first developed conversational, colloquial verse in the monologue of the character part – Faulconbridge in *King John*, and later the Nurse in *Romeo and Juliet*. It was a much further step to carry it unobtrusively into the dialogue of brief replies. No poet has begun to master dramatic verse until he can write lines which, like these in *Hamlet*, are *transparent*. You are consciously attending, not to the poetry, but to the meaning of the poetry. If you were hearing *Hamlet* for the first time, without knowing anything about the play, I do not think that it would occur to you to ask whether the speakers were speaking in verse or prose. The verse is having a different effect upon us from prose; but at the moment, what we are aware of is the frosty night, the officers keeping watch on the battlements, and the foreboding of an ominous action. I do not say that there is no place for the situation in which part of one's pleasure will be the enjoyment of hearing beautiful poetry – providing that the author gives it, in that place, dramatic inevitability. And of course, when we have both seen a play several times and read it between performances, we begin to analyse the means by which the author has produced his effects. But in the immediate impact of this scene we are unconscious of the medium of its expression.

From the short, brusque ejaculations at the beginning, suitable to the situation and to the character of the guards – but not expressing more character than is required for their function in the play – the verse glides into a slower movement with the appearance of the courtiers Horatio and Marcellus.

> *Horatio says 'tis but our fantasy,* . . .

and the movement changes again on the appearance of Royalty, the ghost of the King, into the solemn and sonorous

> *What art thou, that usurp'st this time of night,* . . .

(and note, by the way, this anticipation of the plot conveyed by the use of the verb *usurp*); and majesty is suggested in a reference reminding us whose ghost this is:

> *So frown'd he once, when, in an angry parle,*
> *He smote the sledded Polacks on the ice.*

There is an abrupt change to staccato in Horatio's words to the Ghost on its second appearance; this rhythm changes again with the words

We do it wrong, being so majestical,
To offer it the show of violence;
For it is, as the air, invulnerable,
And our vain blows malicious mockery.

The scene reaches a resolution with the words of Marcellus:

It faded on the crowing of the cock.
Some say that ever 'gainst that season comes
Wherein our Saviour's birth is celebrated,
The bird of dawning singeth all night long;...

and Horatio's answer:

So have I heard and do in part believe it.
But, look, the morn, in russet mantle clad,
Walks o'er the dew of yon high eastern hill.
Break we our watch up.

This is great poetry, and it is dramatic; but besides being poetic and dramatic, it is something more. There emerges, when we analyse it, a kind of musical design also which reinforces and is one with the dramatic movement. It has checked and accelerated the pulse of our emotion without our knowing it. Note that in these last words of Marcellus there is a deliberate brief emergence of the poetic into consciousness. When we hear the lines

But, look, the morn, in russet mantle clad,
Walks o'er the dew of yon high eastern hill,

we are lifted for a moment beyond character, but with no sense of unfitness of the words coming, and at this moment, from the lips of Horatio. The transitions in the scene obey laws of the music of dramatic poetry. Note that the two lines of Horatio which I have quoted twice are preceded by a line of the simplest speech which might be either verse or prose:

So have I heard and do in part believe it,

and that he follows them abruptly with a half line which is hardly more than a stage direction:

> *Break we our watch up.*

It would be interesting to pursue, by a similar analysis, this problem of the double pattern in great poetic drama – the pattern which may be examined from the point of view of stagecraft or from that of the music. But I think that the examination of this one scene is enough to show us that verse is not merely a formalization, or an added decoration, but that it intensifies the drama. It should indicate also the importance of the unconscious effect of the verse upon us. And lastly, I do not think that this effect is felt only by those members of an audience who 'like poetry' but also by those who go for the play alone. By the people who do not like poetry, I mean those who cannot sit down with a book of poetry and enjoy reading it: these people also, when they go to a play in verse, should be affected by the poetry. And these are the audiences whom the writer of such a play ought to keep in mind.

At this point I might say a word about those plays which we call *poetic*, though they are written in prose. The plays of John Millington Synge form rather a special case, because they are based upon the idiom of a rural people whose speech is naturally poetic, both in imagery and in rhythm. I believe that he even incorporated phrases which he had heard from these country people of Ireland. The language of Synge is not available except for plays set among that same people. We can draw more general conclusions from the plays in prose, so much admired in my youth, and now hardly even read, by Maeterlinck. These plays are in a different way restricted in their subject-matter; and to say that the characterization in them is dim is an understatement. I do not deny that they have some poetic quality. But in order to be poetic in prose a dramatist has to be so consistently poetic that his scope is very limited. Synge wrote plays about characters whose originals in life talked poetically, so he could make them talk poetry and remain real people. The poetic prose dramatist who has not this advantage, has to be too poetic. The poetic drama in prose is more limited by poetic convention or by our conventions as to what subject-matter is poetic, than is the poetic drama in verse. A really dramatic verse can be employed, as Shakespeare employed it, to say the most matter-of-fact things.

Yeats is a very different case from Maeterlinck or Synge. A study of his development as a dramatist would show, I think, the great distance he went, and the triumph of his last plays. In his first period, he wrote plays in verse about subjects conventionally accepted as suitable for verse, in a metric which – though even at that early stage having the personal Yeats rhythm – is not really a form of speech quite suitable for anybody except mythical kings and queens. His middle-period *Plays for Dancers* are very beautiful, but they do not solve any problem for the dramatist in verse: they are poetic prose plays with important interludes in verse. It was only in his last play *Purgatory* that he solved his problem of speech in verse, and laid all his successors under obligation to him.

II

Now, I am going to venture to make some observations based on my own experience, which will lead me to comment on my intentions, failures, and partial successes, in my own plays. I do this in the belief that any explorer or experimenter in new territory may, by putting on record a kind of journal of his explorations, say something of use to those who follow him into the same regions and who will perhaps go farther.

The first thing of any importance that I discovered, was that a writer who has worked for years, and achieved some success, in writing other kinds of verse, has to approach the writing of a verse play in a different frame of mind from that to which he has been accustomed in his previous work. In writing other verse, I think that one is writing, so to speak, in terms of one's own voice: the way it sounds when you read it to yourself is the test. For it is yourself speaking. The question of communication, of what the reader will get from it, is not paramount: if your poem is right to you, you can only hope that the readers will eventually come to accept it. The poem can wait a little while; the approval of a few sympathetic and judicious critics is enough to begin with; and it is for future readers to meet the poet more than half way. But in the theatre, the problem of communication presents itself immediately. You are deliberately writing verse for other voices, not for your own, and you do not know whose voices they will be. You are aiming to write lines which will have an immediate effect upon an unknown and unprepared audience, to be interpreted to that audience by unknown actors rehearsed by an unknown producer. And the unknown audience cannot be expected to show any indulgence towards the poet. The poet cannot afford to write his play merely for his admirers, those who know his non-dramatic work and are prepared to receive favourably anything he puts his name to. He must write with an audience in view which knows nothing and cares nothing, about any previous success he may have had before he ventured into the theatre. Hence one finds out that many of the things one likes to do, and knows how to do, are out of place; and that every line must be judged by a new law, that of dramatic relevance.

When I wrote *Murder in the Cathedral* I had the advantage, for a beginner, of an occasion which called for a subject generally admitted to be suitable for verse. Verse plays, it has been generally held, should either take their subject-matter from some mythology, or else should be about some remote historical period, far enough away from the present for the characters not to need to be recognizable as human beings, and therefore for them to be licensed to talk in verse. Picturesque period costume renders verse much more acceptable. Furthermore, my play was to be produced for a rather special kind of audience – an audience of those serious people who go to 'festivals' and expect to have to put up with poetry – though perhaps on this occasion some of them were not quite prepared for what they got. And finally it was a religious play, and people who go deliberately to a religious play at a religious festival expect to be patiently bored and to satisfy themselves with the feeling that they have done something meritorious. So the path was made easy.

It was only when I put my mind to thinking what sort of play I wanted to do next, that I realized that in *Murder in the Cathedral* I had not solved any general problem; but that from my point of view the play was a dead end. For one thing, the problem of language which that play had presented to me was a special problem. Fortunately, I did not have to write in the idiom of the twelfth century, because that idiom, even if I knew Norman French and Anglo-Saxon, would have been unintelligible. But the vocabulary and style could not be exactly those of modern conversation – as in some modern French plays using the plot and personages of Greek drama – because I had to take my audience back to an historical event; and they could not afford to be archaic, first because archaism would only have suggested the wrong period, and second because I wanted to bring home to the audience the contemporary relevance of the situation. The style therefore had to be *neutral*, committed neither to the present nor to the past. As for the versification, I was only aware at this stage that the essential was to avoid any echo of Shakespeare, for I was persuaded that the primary failure of nineteenth-century poets when they wrote for the theatre (and most of the greatest English poets had tried their hand at drama) was not in their theatrical technique, but in their dramatic language; and that this was due largely to their limitation to a strict blank verse which, after extensive use for non-dramatic poetry, had lost the flexibility which blank verse must have if it is to give the effect of conversation. The rhythm of regular blank verse had become too remote from the movement of modern speech. Therefore what I kept in mind was the versification of *Everyman*, hoping that anything unusual in the sound of it would be, on the whole, advantageous. An avoidance of too much iambic, some use of alliteration, and occasional unexpected rhyme, helped to distinguish the versification from that of the nineteenth century.

The versification of the dialogue in *Murder in the Cathedral* has therefore, in my opinion, only a *negative* merit: it succeeded in avoiding what had to be avoided, but it arrived at no positive novelty: in short, in so far as it solved the problem of speech in verse for writing today, it solved if for this play only, and provided me with no clue to the verse I should use in another kind of play. Here, then, were two problems left unsolved: that of the idiom and that of the metric (it is really one and the same problem), for general use in any play I might want to write in future. I next became aware of my reasons for depending, in that play, so heavily upon the assistance of the chorus. There were two reasons for this, which in the circumstances justified it. The first was that the essential action of the play – both the historical facts and the matter which I invented – was somewhat limited. A man comes home, foreseeing that he will be killed, and he is killed. I did not want to increase the number of characters, I did not want to write a chronicle of twelfth-century politics, nor did I want to tamper unscrupulously with the meagre records as Tennyson did (in introducing Fair Rosamund, and in suggesting that Becket had been crossed in love in early youth). I wanted to concentrate on death and martyrdom. The introduction of a chorus of excited and sometimes hysterical women, reflecting in their emotion the significance of the action, helped wonderfully. The second reason was this: that a poet writing for the first time for the stage, is much more at home in choral verse than in dramatic dialogue. This, I felt sure, was something I could do, and perhaps the dramatic weaknesses would be somewhat covered up by the cries of the women. The use of a chorus strengthened the power, and concealed the defects of my theatrical technique. For this reason I decided that next time I would try to integrate the chorus more closely into the play.

I wanted to find out also, whether I could learn to dispense altogether with the use of prose. The two prose passages in *Murder in the Cathedral* could not have been written in verse. Certainly, with the kind of dialogue verse which I used in that play, the audience would have been uncomfortably aware that it was verse they were hearing. A sermon cast in verse is too unusual an experience for even the most regular churchgoer: nobody could have responded to it as a sermon at all. And in the speeches of the knights, who are quite aware that they are addressing an audience of people living eight hundred years after they themselves are dead, the use of platform prose is intended of course to have a special effect: to shock the audience out of their complacency. But this is a kind of trick: that is, a device tolerable only in one play and of no use for any other. I may, for aught I know, have been slightly under the influence of *St Joan*.

I do not wish to give you the impression that I would rule out of dramatic poetry these three things: historical or mythological subject-matter, the chorus, and traditional blank verse. I do not wish to lay down any law that the only suitable characters and situations are those of modern life, or that a verse play should consist of dialogue only, or that a wholly new versification is necessary. I am only tracing out the route of exploration of one writer, and that one myself. If the poetic drama is to reconquer its place, it must, in my opinion, enter into overt competition with prose drama. As I have said, people are prepared to put up with verse from the lips of personages dressed in the fashion of some distant age; they should be made to hear it from people dressed like ourselves, living in houses and apartments like ours, and using telephones and motor cars and radio sets. Audiences are prepared to accept poetry recited by a chorus, for that is a kind of poetry recital, which it does them credit to enjoy. And audiences (those who go to a verse play because it is in verse) expect poetry to be in rhythms which have lost touch with colloquial speech. What we have to do is to bring poetry into the world in which the audience lives and to which it returns when it leaves the theatre; not to transport the audience into some imaginary world totally unlike its own, an unreal world in which poetry is tolerated. What I should hope might be achieved, by a generation of dramatists having the benefit of our experience, is that the audience should find, at the moment of awareness that it is hearing poetry, that it is saying to itself: '*I* could talk in poetry too!' Then we should not be transported into an artificial world; on the contrary, own own sordid, dreary daily world would be suddenly illuminated and transfigured.

I was determined, therefore, in my next play to take a theme of contemporary life, with characters of our own time living in our own world. *The Family Reunion* was the result. Here my first concern was the problem of the versification, to find a rhythm close to contemporary speech, in which the stresses could be made to come wherever we should naturally put them, in uttering the particular phrase on the particular occasion. What I worked out is substantially what I have continued to employ: a line of varying length and varying number of syllables, with a caesura and three stresses. The caesura and the stresses may come at different places, almost anywhere in the line; the stresses may be close together or well separated by light syllables; the only rule being that there must be one stress on one side of the caesura and two on the other. In retrospect, I soon saw that I had given my attention to versification, at the expense of plot and character. I had, indeed, made some progress in dispensing with the chorus; but the device of using four of the minor personages, representing the Family, sometimes as individual character parts and sometimes collectively as chorus, does not seem to me very satisfactory. For one thing, the immediate transition from individual, characterized part to membership of a chorus is asking too much of the actors: it is a very difficult transition to accomplish. For another thing, it seemed to me another trick, one which, even if successful, could not have been applicable in another play. Furthermore, I had in two passages used the device of a lyrical duet further isolated from the rest of the dialogue by being written in shorter lines with only two stresses. These passages are in a sense 'beyond character', the speakers have to be presented as falling into a kind of trance-like state in order to speak them. But they are so remote from the necessity of the action that they are hardly more than passages of poetry which might be spoken by anybody; they are too much like operatic arias. The member of the audience, if he enjoys this sort of thing, is putting up with a suspension of the action in order to enjoy a poetic fantasia: these passages are really less related to the action than are the choruses in *Murder in the Cathedral*.

I observed that when Shakespeare, in one of his mature plays, introduces what might seem a purely poetic line or passage, it never interrupts the action, or is out of character, but on the contrary, in some mysterious way supports both action and character. When Macbeth speaks his so often quoted words beginning

Tomorrow and tomorrow and tomorrow,

or when Othello, confronted at night with his angry father-in-law and friends, utters the beautiful line

Keep up your bright swords, for the dew will rust them,

76

we do not feel that Shakespeare has thought of lines which are beautiful poetry and wishes to fit them in somehow, or that he has for the moment come to the end of his dramatic inspiration and has turned to poetry to fill up with. The lines are surprising, and yet they fit in with the character; or else we are compelled to adjust our conception of the character in such a way that the lines will be appropriate to it. The lines spoken by Macbeth reveal the weariness of the weak man who had been forced by his wife to realize his own half-hearted desires and her ambitions, and who, with her death, is left without the motive to continue. The line of Othello expresses irony, dignity, and fearlessness; and incidentally reminds us of the time of night in which the scene takes place. Only poetry could do this; but it is *dramatic* poetry: that is, it does not interrupt but intensifies the dramatic situation.

It was not only because of the introduction of passages which called too much attention to themselves as poetry, and could not be dramatically justified, that I found *The Family Reunion* defective: there were two weaknesses which came to strike me as more serious still. The first was that I had taken far too much of the strictly limited time allowed to a dramatist, in presenting a situation, and not left myself enough time, or provided myself with enough material, for developing it in action. I had written what was, on the whole, a good first act; except that for a first act it was much too long. When the curtain rises again, the audience is expecting, as it has a right to expect, that something is going to happen. Instead, it finds itself treated to a further exploration of the background: in other words, to what ought to have been given much earlier if at all. The beginning of the second act presents much the most difficult problem to producer and cast: for the audience's attention is beginning to wander. And then, after what must seem to the audience an interminable time of preparation, the conclusion comes so abruptly that we are, after all, unready for it. This was an elementary fault in mechanics.

But the deepest flaw of all, was in a failure of adjustment between the Greek story and the modern situation. I should either have stuck closer to Aeschylus or else taken a great deal more liberty with his myth. One evidence of this is the appearance of those ill-fated figures, the Furies. They must, in future, be omitted from the cast, and be understood to be visible only to certain of my characters, and not to the audience. We tried every possible manner of presenting them. We put them on the stage, and they looked like uninvited guests who had strayed in from a fancy dress ball. We concealed them behind gauze, and they suggested a still out of a Walt Disney film. We made them dimmer, and they looked like shrubbery just outside the window. I have seen other expedients tried: I have seen them signalling from across the garden, or swarming on to the stage like a football team, and they are never right. They never succeed in being either Greek goddesses or modern spooks. But their failure is merely a symptom of the failure to adjust the ancient with the modern.

A more serious evidence is that we are left in a divided frame of mind, not knowing whether to consider the play the tragedy of the mother or the salvation of the son. The two situations are not reconciled. I find a confirmation of this in the fact that my sympathies now have come to be all with the mother, who seems to me, except perhaps for the chauffeur, the only complete human being in the play; and my hero now strikes me as an insufferable prig.

Well, I had made some progress in learning how to write the first act of a play, and I had – the one thing of which I felt sure – made a good deal of progress in finding a form of versification and an idiom which would serve all my purposes, without recourse to prose, and be capable of unbroken transition between the most intense speech and the most relaxed dialogue. You will understand, after my making these criticisms of *The Family Reunion*, some of the errors that I endeavoured to avoid in designing *The Cocktail Party*. To begin with, no chorus, and no ghosts. I was still inclined to go to a Greek dramatist for my theme, but I was determined to do so merely as a point of departure, and to conceal the origins so well that nobody would identify them until I pointed them out myself. In this at least I have been successful; for no one of my acquaintance (and no dramatic critics) recognized the source of my story in the *Alcestis* of Euripides. In fact, I have had to go into detailed explanation to convince them – I mean, of course, those who were familiar with the plot of that play – of the genuineness of the inspiration. But those who were at first disturbed by the eccentric behaviour of my unknown guest, and his apparently intemporate habits and tendency to burst into song, have found some consolation after I have called their attention to the behaviour of Heracles in Euripides' play.

In the second place, I laid down for myself the ascetic rule to avoid poetry which could not stand the test of strict dramatic utility: with such success, indeed, that it is perhaps an open question whether there is any poetry in the play at all. And finally, I tried to keep in mind that in a play, from time to time, something should happen; that the audience should be kept in the constant expectation that something is going to happen; and that, when it does happen, it should be different, but not too different, from what the audience had been led to expect.

I have not yet got to the end of my investigation of the weaknesses of this play, but I hope and expect to find more than those of which I am yet aware. I say 'hope' because while one can never repeat a success, and therefore must always try to find something different, even if less popular, to do, the desire to write something which will be free of the defects of one's last work is a very powerful and useful incentive. I am aware that the last act of my play only just escapes, if indeed it does escape, the accusation of being not a last act but an epilogue; and I am determined to do something different, if I can, in this respect. I also believe that while the self-education of a poet trying to write for the theatre seems to require a long period of disciplining his poetry, and putting it, so to speak, on a very thin diet in order to adapt it to the needs of the stage he may find that later, when (and if) the understanding of theatrical technique has become second nature, he can dare to make more liberal use of poetry and take greater liberties with ordinary colloquial speech. I base this belief on the evolution of Shakespeare, and on some study of the language in his late plays.

In devoting so much time to an examination of my own plays, I have, I believe, been animated by a better motive than egotism. It seems to me that if we are to have a poetic drama, it is more likely to come from poets learning how to write plays, than from skilful prose dramatists learning to write poetry. That some poets can learn how to write plays, and write good ones, may be only a hope, but I believe a not unreasonable hope; but that a man who has started by writing successful prose plays should then learn how to write good poetry, seems to me extremely unlikely. And, under present-day conditions, and until the verse play is recognized by the larger public as a possible source of entertainment, the poet is likely to get his first opportunity to work for the stage only after making some sort or reputation for himself as the author of other kinds of verse. I have therefore wished to put on record, for what it may be worth to others, some account of the difficulties I have encountered, and the mistakes into which I have fallen, and the weaknesses I have had to try to overcome.

I should not like to close without attempting to set before you, though only in dim outline, the ideal towards which poetic drama should strive. It is an unattainable ideal: and that is why it interests me, for it provides an incentive towards further experiment and exploration, beyond any goal which there is prospect of attaining. It is a function of all art to give us some perception of an order in life, by imposing an order upon it. The painter works by selection, combination, and emphasis among the elements of the visible world; the musician in the world of sound. It seems to me that beyond the nameable, classifiable emotions and motives of our conscious life when directed towards action – the part of life which prose drama is wholly adequate to express – there is a fringe of indefinite extent, of feeling which we can only detect, so to speak, out of the corner of the eye and can never completely focus; of feeling of which we are only aware in a kind of temporary detachment from action. There are great prose dramatists – such as Ibsen and Chekhov – who have at times done things of which I would not otherwise have supposed prose to be capable, but who seem to me, in spite of their success, to have been hampered in expression by writing in prose. This peculiar range of sensibility can be expressed by dramatic poetry, at its moments of greatest intensity. At such moments, we touch the border of those feelings which only music can express.

We can never emulate music, because to arrive at the condition of music would be the annihilation of poetry, and especially of dramatic poetry. Nevertheless, I have before my eyes a kind of mirage of the perfection of verse drama, which would be a design of human action and words, such as to present at once the two aspects of dramatic and of musical order. It seems to me that Shakespeare achieved this at least in certain scenes – even rather early, for there is the balcony scene of *Romeo and Juliet* – and that this was what he was striving towards in his late plays. To go as far in this direction as it is possible to go, without losing that contact with the ordinary everyday world with which drama must come to terms, seems to me the proper aim of dramatic poetry. For it is ultimately the function of art, in imposing a credible order upon ordinary reality, and thereby eliciting some perception of an order *in* reality, to bring us to a condition of serenity, stillness, and reconciliation; and then leave us, as Virgil left Dante, to proceed toward a region where that guide can avail us no farther.

[1950]

EXPERIMENTATION

THE word 'experimentation' may be applied, and honourably applied, to the work of many poets who develop and change in maturity. As a man grows older, he may turn to new subject-matter, or he may treat the same material in a different way; as we age we both live in a different world, and become different men in the same world. The changes may be expressed by a change of rhythm, of imagery, of form: the true experimenter is not impelled by restless curiosity, or by desire for novelty, or the wish to surprise and astonish, but by the compulsion to find, in every new poem as in his earliest, the right form for feelings over the development of which he has, as a poet, no control.

[From the editor's Introductory Essay to *A Choice of Kipling's Verse*, 1941]

REFLECTIONS ON *VERS LIBRE*

It is assumed that *vers libre* exists. It is assumed that *vers libre* is a school; that it consists of certain theories; that its group or groups of theorists will either revolutionize or demoralize poetry if their attack on the iambic pentameter meets with any success. *Vers libre* does not exist, and it is time that this preposterous fiction followed the *élan vital* and the 80,000 Russians into oblivion.*

When a theory of art passes it is usually found that a groat's worth of art has been bought with a million of advertisement. The theory which sold the wares may be quite false, or it may be confused and incapable of elucidation, or it may never have existed. A mythical revolution will have taken place and will have produced a few works of art which perhaps would be even better if still less of the revolutionary theories clung to them. In modern society such revolutions are almost inevitable. An artist happens upon a method, perhaps quite unreflectingly, which is new in the sense that it is essentially different from that of the second-rate people about him, and different in everything but essentials from that of any of his great predecessors. The novelty meets with neglect; neglect provokes attack; and attack demands a theory. In an ideal state of society one might imagine the good New growing naturally out of the good Old, without the need for polemic and theory; this would be a society with a living tradition. In a sluggish society, as actually societies are, tradition is ever lapsing into superstition, and the violent stimulus of novelty is required. This is bad for the artist and his school, who may become circumscribed by their theory and narrowed by their polemic; but the artist can always console himself for his errors in his old age by considering that if he had not fought nothing would have been accomplished.

Vers libre has not even the excuse of a polemic; it is a battle cry

* An allusion to the current delusion, based on rumoured traces of snow in railway carriages, that Russian reinforcements had passed through Great Britain on their way to the Western Front during the first winter of the First World War. [*Editor's note*]

of a freedom, and there is no freedom in art. And as the so-called *vers libre* which is good is anything but 'free', it can better be defended under some other label. Particular types of *vers libre* may be supported on the choice of content, or on the method of handling the content. I am aware that many writers of *vers libre* have introduced such innovations, and that the novelty of their choice and manipulation of material is confused – if not in their own minds, in the minds of many of their readers – with the novelty of the form. But I am not here concerned with imagism, which is a theory about the use of material; I am only concerned with the theory of the verse-form in which imagism is cast. If *vers libre* is a genuine verse-form it will have a positive definition. And I can define it only in negatives: (1) absence of pattern, (2) absence of rhyme, (3) absence of metre.

The third of these qualities is easily disposed of. What sort of a line that would be which would not scan at all I cannot say. Even in the popular American magazines, whose verse columns are now largely given over to *vers libre,* the lines are usually explicable in terms of prosody. Any line can be divided into feet and accents. The simpler metres are a repetition of one combination, perhaps a long and a short, or a short and a long syllable, five times repeated. There is, however, no reason why, within the single line, there should be any repetition; why there should not be lines (as there are) divisible only into feet of different types. How can the grammatical exercise of scansion make a line of this sort more intelligible? Only by isolating elements which occur in other lines, and the sole purpose of doing this is the production of a similar effect elsewhere. But repetition of effect is a question of pattern.

Scansion tells us very little. It is probable that there is not much to be gained by an absolute system of prosody; by the erudite complexities of Swinburnian metre. With Swinburne, once the trick is perceived and the scholarship appreciated, the effect is somewhat diminished. When the unexpectedness, due to the unfamiliarity of the metres to English ears, wears off and is understood, one ceases to look for what one does not find in Swinburne: the inexplicable line with the music which can never be recaptured in other words.

Swinburne mastered his technique, which is a great deal, but he did not master it to the extent of being able to take liberties with it, which is everything. If anything promising for English poetry is hidden in the metres of Swinburne, it probably lies far beyond the point to which Swinburne has developed them. But the most interesting verse which has yet been written in our language has been done either by taking a very simple form, like the iambic pentameter, and constantly withdrawing from it, or taking no form at all, and constantly approximating to a very simple one. It is this contrast between fixity and flux, this unperceived evasion of monotony, which is the very life of verse.

. . . At the beginning of the seventeenth century, and especially in the verse of John Webster who was in some ways a more cunning technician than Shakespeare, one finds the same constant evasion and recognition of regularity. Webster is much freer than Shakespeare, and that his fault is not negligence is evidenced by the fact that it is often at moments of the highest intensity that his verse acquires this freedom. That there is also carelessness I do not deny, but the irregularity of carelessness can be at once detected from the irregularity of deliberation. (In *The White Devil* Brachiano dying, and Cornelia mad, deliberately rupture the bonds of pentameter.)

> *I recover, like a spent taper, for a flash,*
> *And instantly go out.*

> *Cover her face; mine eyes dazzle; she died young.*

> *You have cause to love me, I did enter you in my heart,*
> *Before you would vouchsafe to me for the keys.*

> *This is a vain poetry: but I pray you tell me*
> *If there were proposed me, wisdom, riches, and beauty,*
> *In three several young men, which should I choose?*

These are not lines of carelessness. The irregularity is further enhanced by the use of short lines and the breaking up of lines in dialogue, which alters the quantities. And there are many lines in the drama of this time which are spoilt by regular accentuation.

REFLECTIONS ON 'VERS LIBRE'

I loved this woman in spite of my heart.

[*The Changeling*]

I would have these herbs grow up in his grave.

[*The White Devil*]

Whether the spirit of greatness or of a woman. . . .

[*The Duchess of Malfi*]

The general charge of decadence cannot be preferred. Tourneur and Shirley, who I think will be conceded to have touched nearly the bottom of the decline of tragedy, are much more regular than Webster or Middleton. Tourneur will polish off a fair line of iambics even at the cost of amputating a preposition from its substantive, and in *The Atheist's Tragedy* he has a final 'of' in two lines out of five together.

We may therefore formulate as follows: the ghost of some simple metre should lurk behind the arras in even the 'freest' verse; to advance menacingly as we doze, and withdraw as we rouse. Or, freedom is only truly freedom when it appears against the background of an artificial limitation.

Not to have perceived the simple truth that *some* artificial limitation is necessary except in moments of the first intensity is, I believe, a capital error of even so distinguished a talent as that of Mr E. L. Masters. The *Spoon River Anthology* is not material of the first intensity; it is reflective, not immediate; its author is a moralist, rather than an observer. His material is so near to the material of Crabbe that one wonders why he should have used a different form. Crabbe is, on the whole, the more intense of the two; he is keen, direct, and unsparing. His material is prosaic, not in the sense that it would have been better done in prose, but in the sense of requiring a simple and rather rigid verse-form, and this Crabbe has given it. Mr Masters required a more rigid verse-form, and his epitaphs suffer from the lack of it.

. . . I do not minimize the services of modern poets in exploiting the possibilities of rhymeless verse. They prove the strength of a Movement, the utility of a Theory. What neither Blake nor Arnold

85

could do alone is being done in our time. 'Blank Verse' is the only accepted rhymeless verse in English – the inevitable iambic pentameter. The English ear is (or was) more sensitive to the music of the verse and less dependent upon the recurrence of identical sounds in this metre than in any other. There is no campaign against rhyme. But it is possible that excessive devotion to rhyme has thickened the modern ear. The rejection of rhyme is not a leap at facility; on the contrary, it imposes a much severer strain upon the language. When the comforting echo of rhyme is removed, success or failure in the choice of words, in the sentence structure, in the order, is at once more apparent. Rhyme removed, the poet is at once held up to the standards of prose. Rhyme removed, much ethereal music leaps up from the word, music which has hitherto chirped unnoticed in the expanse of prose. And rhyme forbidden, many Shagpats were unwigged.

And this liberation from rhyme might as well be a liberation *of* rhyme. Freed from its exacting task of supporting lame verse, it could be applied with greater effect where it is most needed. There are often passages in an unrhymed poem where rhyme is wanted for some special effect, for a sudden tightening-up, for a cumulative insistence, or for an abrupt change of mood.

But formal rhymed verse will certainly not lose its place. We only need the coming of a Satirist – no man of genius is rarer – to prove that the heroic couplet has lost none of its edge since Dryden and Pope laid it down. As for the sonnet I am not so sure. But the decay of intricate formal patterns has nothing to do with the advent of *vers libre*. It had set in long before. Only in a closely-knit and homogeneous society, where many men are at work on the same problems, such a society as those which produced the Greek chorus, the Elizabethan lyric, and the Troubadour canzone, will the development of such forms ever be carried to perfection. And as for *vers libre*, we conclude that it is not defined by absence of pattern or absence of rhyme, for other verse is without these; that it is not defined by non-existence of metre, since even the *worst* verse can be scanned; and we conclude that the division between Conservative Verse and *vers libre* does not exist, for there is only good verse, bad verse, and chaos.　　　[From 'Reflections on *Vers Libre*', 1917]

RELEVANCE

PEOPLE are often inclined to disparage poetry which appears to have no bearing on the situation of today; but they are always inclined to ignore that which appears to bear only on the situation of yesterday. A political association may help to give poetry immediate attention: it is in spite of this association that the poetry will be read, if it is read, tomorrow. Poetry is condemned as 'political' when we disagree with the politics; and the majority of readers do not want either imperialism or socialism in verse. But the question is not what is ephemeral, but what is permanent: a poet who appears to be wholly out of touch with his age may still have something very important to say to it; and a poet who has treated problems of his time will not necessarily go out of date. Arnold's 'Stanzas from the Grande Chartreuse' voice a moment of historic doubt, recorded by its most representative mind, a moment which has passed, which most of us have gone beyond in one direction or another: but it represents that moment for ever.

[From the editor's Introductory Essay to *A Choice of Kipling's Verse*, 1941]

'DIFFICULT' POETRY

THE difficulty of poetry (and modern poetry is supposed to be difficult) may be due to one of several reasons. First, there may be personal causes which make it impossible for a poet to express himself in any way but an obscure way; while this may be regrettable, we should be glad, I think, that the man has been able to express himself at all. Or difficulty may be due just to novelty: we know the ridicule accorded in turn to Wordsworth, Shelley and Keats, Tennyson and Browning – but must remark that Browning was the first to be *called* difficult; hostile critics of the earlier poets found them difficult, but called them silly. Or difficulty may be caused by the reader's having been told, or having suggested to himself, that

87

the poem is going to prove difficult. The ordinary reader, when warned against the obscurity of a poem, is apt to be thrown into a state of consternation very unfavourable to poetic receptivity. Instead of beginning, as he should, in a state of sensitivity, he obfuscates his senses by the desire to be clever and to look very hard for something – he doesn't know what – or else by the desire not to be taken in. There is such a thing as stage fright, but what such readers have is pit or gallery fright. The more seasoned reader, he who has reached, in these matters, a state of greater *purity*, does not bother about understanding; not, at least, at first. I know that some of the poetry to which I am most devoted is poetry which I did not understand at first reading; some is poetry which I am not sure I understand yet: for instance, Shakespeare's. And finally, there is the difficulty caused by the author's having left out something which the reader is used to finding; so that the reader, bewildered, gropes about for what is absent, and puzzles his head for a kind of 'meaning' which is not there, and is not meant to be there.

The chief use of the 'meaning' of a poem, in the ordinary sense, may be (for here again I am speaking of some kinds of poetry and not all) to satisfy one habit of the reader, to keep his mind diverted and quiet, while the poem does its work upon him: much as the imaginary burglar is always provided with a bit of nice meat for the house-dog. This is a normal situation of which I approve. But the minds of all poets do not work that way; some of them, assuming that there are other minds like their own, become impatient of this 'meaning' which seems superfluous, and perceive possibilities of intensity through its elimination. I am not asserting that this situation is ideal; only that we must write our poetry as we can, and take it as we find it. It may be that for some periods of society a more relaxed form of writing is right, and for others a more concentrated. I believe that there must be many people who feel, as I do, that the effect of some of the greater nineteenth-century poets is diminished by their bulk. Who now, for the pure pleasure of it, reads Wordsworth, Shelley, and Keats even, certainly Browning and Swinburne and most of the French poets of the century – entire? I by no means believe that the 'long poem' is a thing of the past; but at least there must be more in it for the length than our grandparents seemed to demand; and for us, anything that can be said as well in prose can be said better in prose. And a great deal, in the way of meaning, belongs to prose rather than to poetry. The doctrine of 'Art for Art's sake', a mistaken one, and more advertised than practised, contained this true impulse behind it, that it is a recognition of the error of the poet's trying to do other people's work. But poetry has as much to learn from prose as from other poetry; and I think that an interaction between prose and verse, like the interaction between language and language, is a condition of vitality in literature.

[From *The Use of Poetry and the Use of Criticism*, 1933]

AUDITORY IMAGINATION

WHAT I call the 'auditory imagination' is the feeling for syllable and rhythm, penetrating far below the conscious levels of thought and feeling, invigorating every word; sinking to the most primitive and forgotten, returning to the origin and bringing something back, seeking the beginning and the end. It works through meanings, certainly, or not without meanings in the ordinary sense, and fuses the old and obliterated and the trite, the current, and the new and surprising, the most ancient and the most civilized mentality.

[From *The Use of Poetry and the Use of Criticism*, 1933]

POETIC IMAGERY

ONLY a part of an author's imagery comes from his reading. It comes from the whole of his sensitive life since early childhood. Why, for all of us, out of all that we have heard, seen, felt, in a lifetime, do certain images recur, charged with emotion, rather than others? The song of one bird, the leap of one fish, at a particular place and time, the scent of one flower, an old woman on a German mountain path, six ruffians seen through an open window playing cards at night at a small French railway junction where there was a

89

water-mill:* such memories may have symbolic value, but of what we cannot tell, for they come to represent the depths of feeling into which we cannot peer. We might just as well ask why, when we try to recall visually some period in the past, we find in our memory just the few meagre arbitrarily chosen set of snapshots that we do find there, the faded poor souvenirs of passionate moments.

[From *The Use of Poetry and the Use of Criticism*, 1933]

* Cf. *Journey of the Magi*, by T. S. Eliot, ll. 21–8. [*Editor's note*]

Literary Criticism : Individual Authors

VIRGIL AND DESTINY

FATUM is a word which constantly recurs in the *Aeneid*; a word charged with meaning, and perhaps with more meaning than Virgil himself knew. Our nearest word is 'destiny', and that is a word which means more than we can find any definitions for. It is a word which can have no meaning in a mechanical universe: if that which is wound up must run down, what destiny is there in that? Destiny is not necessitarianism, and it is not caprice: it is something essentially meaningful. Each man has his destiny, though some men are undoubtedly 'men of destiny' in a sense in which most men are not; and Aeneas is egregiously a man of destiny, since upon him the future of the Western World depends. But this is an election which cannot be explained, a burden and responsibility rather than a reason for self-glorification. It merely happens to one man and not to others, to have the gifts necessary in some profound crisis, but he can take no credit to himself for the gifts and the responsibility assigned to him. Some men have had a deep conviction of their destiny, and in that conviction have prospered; but when they cease to act as an instrument, and think of themselves as the active source of what they do, their pride is punished by disaster. Aeneas is a man guided by the deepest conviction of destiny, but he is a humble man who knows that this destiny is something not to be desired and not to be avoided. Of what power is he the servant? Not of the gods, who are themselves merely instruments, and sometimes rebellious ones. The concept of destiny leaves us with a mystery, but it is a mystery not contrary to reason, for it implies that the world, and the course of human history, have meaning.

What then does this destiny, which no Homeric hero shares with Aeneas, mean? For Virgil's conscious mind, and for his contemporary readers, it means the *imperium romanum*. This in itself, as

Virgil saw it, was a worthy justification of history. I think that he had few illusions and that he saw clearly both sides of every question – the case for the loser as well as the case for the winner. Nevertheless even those who have as little Latin as I must remember and thrill at the lines:

> *His ego nec metas rerum, nec tempora pono:*
> *Imperium sine fine dedi ...*
> *Tu regere imperio populos, Romane, memento*
> *(hae tibi erunt artes) pacique imponere morem,*
> *Parcere subiectis et deballare superbos ...*

I say that it was all the end of history that Virgil could be asked to find, and that it was a worthy end. And do you really think that Virgil was mistaken? You must remember that the Roman Empire was transformed into the Holy Roman Empire. What Virgil proposed to his contemporaries was the highest ideal even for an unholy Roman Empire, for any merely temporal empire. We are all, so far as we inherit the civilization of Europe, still citizens of the Roman Empire, and time has not yet proved Virgil wrong when he wrote *nec tempora pono: imperium sine fine dedi*. But, of course, the Roman Empire which Virgil imagined and for which Aeneas worked out his destiny was not exactly the same as the Roman Empire of the legionaries, the proconsuls and governors, the business men and speculators, the demagogues and generals. It was something greater, but something which exists because Virgil imagined it. It remains an ideal, but one which Virgil passed on to Christianity to develop and to cherish.

In the end, it seems to me that the place which Dante assigned to Virgil in the future life, and the role of guide and teacher as far as the barrier which Virgil was not allowed to pass, was not capable of passing, is an exact statement of Virgil's relation to the Christian world. We find the world of Virgil, compared to the world of Homer, to approximate to a Christian world, in the choice, order, and relationship of its values. I have said that this implies no comparison between Homer the poet and Virgil the poet. Neither do I think that it is exactly a comparison between the worlds in which they lived, onsidered apart from the interpretation of these worlds which the poets have given us. It may be merely that we know more about the world of Virgil, and understand it better; and therefore see more clearly how much, in the Roman idea according to Virgil, is due to the shaping hand and the philosophical mind of Virgil himself. For, in the sense in which a poet is a philosopher (as distinct from the sense in which a great poet may embody a great philosophy in great poetry) Virgil is the greatest philosopher of ancient Rome. It is not, therefore, simply that the civilization in which Virgil lived is nearer to the civilization of Christianity than is that of Homer; we can say that Virgil, among classical Latin poets or prose writers, is uniquely near to Christianity. There is a phrase which I have been trying to avoid, but which I now find myself obliged to use: *anima naturaliter Christiana*. Whether we apply it to Virgil is a matter of personal choice; but I am inclined to think that he just falls short : and that is why I said just now that I think Dante has put Virgil in the right place. I will try to give the reason.

I think of another key word, besides *fatum*, which I wish that I could illustrate from Virgil in the same way. What key word can one find in the *Divine Comedy* which is absent from the *Aeneid*? One word of course is *lume*, and all the words expressive of the spiritual significance of light. But this, I think, as used by Dante, has a meaning which belongs only to explicit Christianity, fused with a meaning which belongs to mystical experience. And Virgil is no mystic. The term which one can justifiably regret the lack of in Virgil is *amor*. It is, above all others, the key word for Dante. I do not mean that Virgil never uses it. *Amor* recurs in the *Eclogues* (*amor vincit omnia*). But the loves of the shepherds represent hardly more than a poetic convention. The use of the word *amor* in the *Eclogues* is not illuminated by meanings of the word in the *Aeneid*; in the way in which, for example, we return to Paolo and Francesca with greater understanding of their passion after we have been taken through the circles of love in the *Paradiso*. Certainly, the love of Aeneas and Dido has great tragic force. There is tenderness and pathos enough in the *Aeneid*. But Love is never given, to my mind, the same significance that *pietas* is given; and it is not Love that

93

causes *fatum*, or moves the sun and the stars. Even for intensity o
physical passion, Virgil is more tepid than some other Latin poets
and far below the rank of Catullus. If we are not chilled we at leas
feel ourselves, with Virgil, to be moving in a kind of emotiona
twilight. Virgil was, among all authors of classical antiquity, one fo
whom the world made sense, for whom it had order and dignity, an
for whom, as for no one before his time except the Hebrew prophets
history had meaning. But he was denied the vision of the man wh
could say:

> Within its depths I saw ingathered, bound by love in one volume
> the scattered leaves of all the universe.

Legato con amore in un volume.

[From 'Virgil and the Christian World', a broadcast from London,
9 September 1951]

DANTE

THE first [lesson of Dante] is, that of the very few poets of simila
stature there is none, not even Virgil, who has been a more atten
tive student of the *art* of poetry, or a more scrupulous, painstaking
and *conscious* practitioner of the *craft*. Certainly no English poet ca
be compared with him in this respect, for the more conscious crafts
men – and I am thinking primarily of Milton – have been much
more limited poets, and therefore more limited in their craft also
To realize more and more what this means, through the years o
one's life, is itself a moral lesson; but I draw a further lesson from
it which is a moral lesson too. The whole study and practice of Dante
seems to me to teach that the poet should be the servant of his lan
guage, rather than the master of it. This sense of responsibility is
one of the marks of the *classical* poet, in the sense of 'classical' which
I have tried to define elsewhere, in speaking of Virgil.* Of some
great poets, and of some great English poets especially, one can say
that they were privileged by their genius to *abuse* the English lan

* *What is a Classic?* 1945. The Presidential Address to the Virgil Society
16 October 1945. [*Editor's note*]

94

guage, to develop an idiom so peculiar and even eccentric, that it could be of no use to later poets. Dante seems to me to have a place in Italian literature which, in this respect, only Shakespeare has in ours; that is, they give body to the soul of the language, conforming themselves, the one more and the other less consciously, to what they divined to be its possibilities. And Shakespeare himself takes liberties which only his genius justifies; liberties which Dante, with an equal genius, does not take. To pass on to posterity one's own language, more highly developed, more refined, and more precise than it was before one wrote it, that is the highest possible achievement of the poet as poet. Of course, a really supreme poet makes poetry also more difficult for his successors, but the simple fact of his supremacy, and the price literature must pay, for having a Dante or a Shakespeare, is that it can have only *one*. Later poets must find something else to do, and be content if the things left to do are lesser things. But I am not speaking of what a supreme poet, one of those few without whom the current speech of a people with a great language would not be what it is, does for later poets, or of what he prevents them from doing, but of what he does for everybody after him who speaks that language, whose mother tongue it is, whether they are poets, philosophers, statesmen, or railway porters.

That is one lesson: that the great master of a language should be the great servant of it. The second lesson of Dante – and it is one which no other poet, in any language known to me, can teach – is the lesson of *width of emotional range*. Perhaps it could be best expressed under the figure of the spectrum, or of the gamut. Employing this figure, I may say that the great poet should not only perceive and distinguish more clearly than other men, the colours or sounds within the range of ordinary vision or hearing; he should perceive vibrations beyond the range of ordinary men, and be able to make men see and hear more at each end than they could ever see or hear without his help. We have for instance in English literature great religious poets, but they are, by comparison with Dante, *specialists*. That is all they can do. And Dante, because he could do everything else, is for that reason the greatest 'religious' poet, though to call

95

him a 'religious poet' would be to abate his universality. The *Divine Comedy* expresses everything in the way of emotion, between depravity's despair and the beatific vision, that man is capable of experiencing. It is therefore a constant reminder to the poet, of the obligation to explore, to find words for the inarticulate, to capture those feelings which people can hardly even feel, because they have no words for them; and at the same time, a reminder that the explorer beyond the frontiers of ordinary consciousness will only be able to return and report to his fellow-citizens, if he has all the time a firm grasp upon the realities with which they are already acquainted.

These two achievements of Dante are not to be thought of as separate or separable. The task of the poet, in making people comprehend the incomprehensible, demands immense resources of language; and in developing the language, enriching the meaning of words and showing how much words can do, he is making possible a much greater range of emotion and perception for other men, because he gives them the speech in which more can be expressed.

[From 'A Talk on Dante', delivered at the Italian Institute, London, 4 July 1950]

THE PATTERN OF SHAKESPEARE

THE standard set by Shakespeare is that of a continuous development from first to last, a development in which the choice both of theme and of dramatic and verse technique in each play seems to be determined increasingly by Shakespeare's state of feeling, by the particular stage of his emotional maturity at the time. What is 'the whole man' is not simply his greatest or maturest achievement, but the whole pattern formed by the sequence of plays; so that we may say confidently that the full meaning of any one of his plays is not in itself alone, but in that play in the order in which it was written, in its relation to all of Shakespeare's other plays, earlier and later: we must know all of Shakespeare's work in order to know any of it. No other dramatist of the time approaches anywhere near to this perfection of pattern, of pattern superficial and profound; but the measure in which dramatists and poets approximate to this unity in a lifetime's work, is one of the measures of major poetry and drama.

[From 'John Ford', 1932]

THE UNITY OF SHAKESPEARE

IN Elizabethan and Jacobean drama, and even in the comedy of Congreve and Wycherley, there is almost no analysis of the particular society of the times, except in so far as it records the rise of the City families, and their ambition to ally themselves with needy peerages and to acquire country estates. Even that rise of the City, in *Eastward Hoe* and *Michaelmas Term*, is treated lightly as a foible of the age, and not as a symptom of social decay and change. It is indeed in the lack of this sense of a 'changing world', of corruptions and abuses peculiar to their own time, that the Elizabethan and Jacobean dramatists are blessed. We feel that they believed in their own age, in a way in which no nineteenth- or twentieth-century writer of the greatest seriousness has been able to believe in his age. And accepting their age, they were in a position to concentrate their attention, to their respective abilities, upon the common characteristics of humanity in all ages, rather than upon the differences. We can partly criticize their age through our study of them, but they did not so criticize it themselves. In the work of Shakespeare as a whole, there is to be read the profoundest, and indeed one of the most sombre studies of humanity that has ever been made in poetry; though it is in fact so comprehensive that we cannot qualify it as a whole as either glad or sorry. We recognize the same assumption of permanence in his minor fellows. Dante held it also, and the great Greek dramatists. In periods of unsettlement and change we do not observe this: it was a changing world which met the eyes of Lucian or of Petronius. But in the kind of analysis in which Shakespeare was supreme the other Elizabethan and Jacobean dramatists differed only in degree and in comprehensiveness.

For the age in which Shakespeare lived and the age into which his influence extended after his death, it must be his work, and his work as a whole, that is our criterion. The whole of Shakespeare's work is *one* poem; and it is the poetry of it in this sense, not the poetry of isolated lines and passages or the poetry of the single figures which he created, that matters most. A man might, hypothetically, compose any number of fine passages or even of whole poems which would each give satisfaction, and yet not be a great poet, unless we felt them to be united by one significant, consistent, and developing personality. Shakespeare is the one, among all his contemporaries, who fulfils these conditions; and the nearest to him is Marlowe. Jonson and Chapman have the consistency, but a far lower degree of significant development; Middleton and Webster take a lower place than these; the author of *The Revenger's Tragedy*, whether we call him Tourneur or Middleton or another, accomplishes all that can be accomplished within the limits of a single play. But in all these dramatists there is the essential, as well as the superficies, of poetry; they give the pattern, or we may say the undertone, of the personal emotion, the personal drama, and struggle, which no biography, however full and intimate, could give us; which nothing can give us but our experience of the plays themselves.

[From 'John Ford', 1932]

HAMLET

FEW critics have ever admitted that *Hamlet* the play is the primary problem, and Hamlet the character only secondary. And Hamlet the character has had an especial temptation for that most dangerous type of critic: the critic with a mind which is naturally of the creative order, but which through some weakness in creative power exercises itself in criticism instead. These minds often find in Hamlet a vicarious existence for their own artistic realization. Such a mind had Goethe, who made of Hamlet a Werther; and such had Coleridge, who made of Hamlet a Coleridge; and probably neither of these men in writing about Hamlet remembered that his first business was to study a work of art. The kind of criticism that Goethe and Coleridge produced, in writing of Hamlet, is the most misleading kind possible. For they both possessed unquestionable critical insight, and both make their critical aberrations the more plausible by the substitution – of their own Hamlet for Shakespeare's – which their creative gift effects. We should be thankful that Walter Pater did not fix his attention on this play.

Two writers of our time, J. M. Robertson and Professor Stoll, have issued small books which can be praised for moving in the other direction. Mr Stoll performs a service in recalling to our attention the labours of the critics of the seventeenth and eighteenth centuries,* observing that:

> They knew less about psychology than more recent Hamlet critics, but they were nearer in spirit to Shakespeare's art; and as they insisted on the importance of the effect of the whole rather than on the importance of the leading character, they were nearer, in their old-fashioned way, to the secret of dramatic art in general.

Qua work of art, the work of art cannot be interpreted; there is nothing to interpret; we can only criticize it according to standards, in comparison to other works of art; and for 'interpretation' the chief task is the presentation of relevant historical facts which the reader is not assumed to know. Mr Robertson points out, very pertinently, how critics have failed in their 'interpretation' of *Hamlet* by ignoring what ought to be very obvious: that *Hamlet* is a stratification, that it represents the efforts of a series of men, each making what he could out of the work of his predecessors. The *Hamlet* of Shakespeare will appear to us very differently if, instead of treating the whole action of the play as due to Shakespeare's design, we perceive his *Hamlet* to be superposed upon much cruder material which persists even in the final form.

We know that there was an older play by Thomas Kyd, that extraordinary dramatic (if not poetic) genius who was in all probability the author of two plays so dissimilar as *The Spanish Tragedy* and *Arden of Feversham*; and what this play was like we can guess from three clues: from *The Spanish Tragedy* itself, from the tale of

* I have never, by the way, seen a cogent refutation of Thomas Rymer's objections to *Othello*. [*Author's note*]

Belleforest upon which Kyd's *Hamlet* must have been based, and from a version acted in Germany in Shakespeare's lifetime which bears strong evidence of having been adapted from the earlier, not from the later, play. From these three sources it is clear that in the earlier play the motive was a revenge motive simply; that the action or delay is caused, as in *The Spanish Tragedy*, solely by the difficulty of assassinating a monarch surrounded by guards; and that the 'madness' of Hamlet was feigned in order to escape suspicion, and successfully. In the final play of Shakespeare, on the other hand, there is a motive which is more important than that of revenge, and which explicitly 'blunts' the latter; the delay in revenge is unexplained on grounds of necessity or expediency; and the effect of the 'madness' is not to lull but to arouse the king's suspicion. The alteration is not complete enough, however, to be convincing. Furthermore, there are verbal parallels so close to *The Spanish Tragedy* as to leave no doubt that in places Shakespeare was merely *revising* the text of Kyd. And finally there are unexplained scenes – the Polonius–Laertes and the Polonius–Reynaldo scenes – for which there is little excuse; these scenes are not in the verse style of Kyd, and not beyond doubt in the style of Shakespeare. These Mr Robertson believes to be scenes in the original play of Kyd reworked by a third hand, perhaps Chapman, before Shakespeare touched the play. And he concludes, with very strong show of reason, that the original play of Kyd was, like certain other revenge plays, in two parts of five acts each. The upshot of Mr Robertson's examination is, we believe, irrefragable: that Shakespeare's *Hamlet*, so far as it is Shakespeare's, is a play dealing with the effect of a mother's guilt upon her son, and that Shakespeare was unable to impose this motive successfully upon the 'intractable' material of the old play.

Of the intractability there can be no doubt. So far from being Shakespeare's masterpiece, the play is most certainly an artistic failure. In several ways the play is puzzling, and disquieting as is none of the others. Of all the plays it is the longest and is possibly the one on which Shakespeare spent most pains; and yet he has left in it superfluous and inconsistent scenes which even hasty revision should have noticed. The versification is variable. Lines like

> *But, look, the morn, in russet mantle clad,*
> *Walks o'er the dew of yon high eastern hill,*

are of the Shakespeare of *Romeo and Juliet*. The lines in Act V. Sc. ii,

> *Sir, in my heart there was a kind of fighting*
> *That would not let me sleep . . .*
> *Up from my cabin,*
> *My sea-gown scarf'd about me, in the dark*
> *Grop'd I to find out them: had my desire;*
> *Finger'd their packet . . .*

are of his quite mature. Both workmanship and thought are in an unstable position. We are surely justified in attributing the play, with that other profoundly interesting play of 'intractable' material and astonishing versification, *Measure for Measure*, to a period of crisis, after which follow the tragic successes which culminate in *Coriolanus*. *Coriolanus* may be not as 'interesting' as *Hamlet*, but it is, with *Antony and Cleopatra*, Shakespeare's most assured artistic success. And probably more people have thought *Hamlet* a work of art because they found it interesting, than have found it interesting because it is a work of art. It is the 'Mona Lisa' of literature.

The grounds of *Hamlet*'s failure are not immediately obvious. Mr Robertson is undoubtedly correct in concluding that the essential emotion of the play is the feeling of a son towards a guilty mother:

'[Hamlet's] tone is that of one who has suffered tortures on the score of his mother's degradation. . . . The guilt of a mother is an almost intolerable motive for drama, but it had to be maintained and emphasized to supply a psychological solution, or rather a hint of one.'

This, however, is by no means the whole story. It is not merely the 'guilt of a mother' that cannot be handled as Shakespeare handled the suspicion of Othello, the infatuation of Antony, or the pride of Coriolanus. The subject might conceivably have expanded into a tragedy like these, intelligible, self-complete, in the sunlight. *Hamlet*, like the sonnets, is full of some stuff that the writer could not drag to light, contemplate, or manipulate into art. And when we search for this feeling, we find it, as in the sonnets, very difficult to localize. You cannot point to it in the speeches; indeed, if you examine the two famous soliloquies you see the versification of Shakespeare, but a content which might be claimed by another, perhaps by the author of *The Revenge of Bussy d'Ambois*, Act V. Sc. i. We find Shakespeare's *Hamlet* not in the action, not in any quotations that we might select, so much as in an unmistakable tone which is unmistakably not in the earlier play.

The only way of expressing emotion in the form of art is by finding an 'objective correlative'; in other words, a set of objects, a situation, a chain of events which shall be the formula of that *particular* emotion; such that when the external facts, which must terminate in sensory experience, are given, the emotion is immediately evoked. If you examine any of Shakespeare's more successful tragedies, you will find this exact equivalence; you will find that the state of mind of Lady Macbeth walking in her sleep has been communicated to you by a skilful accumulation of imagined sensory impressions; the words of Macbeth on hearing of his wife's death strike us as if, given the sequence of events, these words were automatically released by the last event in the series. The artistic 'inevitability' lies in this complete adequacy of the external to the emotion; and this is precisely what is deficient in *Hamlet*. Hamlet (the man) is dominated by an emotion which is inexpressible, because it is in *excess* of the facts as they appear. And the supposed identity of Hamlet with his author is genuine to this point: that Hamlet's bafflement at the absence of objective equivalent to his feelings is a prolongation of the bafflement of his creator in the face of his artistic problem. Hamlet is up against the difficulty that his disgust is occasioned by his mother, but that his mother is not an adequate equivalent for it; his disgust envelops and exceeds her. It is thus a feeling which he cannot understand; he cannot objectify it, and it therefore remains to poison life and obstruct action. None of the possible actions can satisfy it; and nothing that Shakespeare can do with the plot can express Hamlet for him. And it must be noticed that the very nature of the *données* of the problem precludes objective equivalence. To have heightened the criminality of Gertrude would have been to provide the formula for a totally different emotion in Hamlet; it is just *because* her character is so negative and insignificant that she arouses in Hamlet the feeling which she is incapable of representing.

The 'madness' of Hamlet lay to Shakespeare's hand; in the earlier play a simple ruse, and to the end, we may presume, understood as a ruse by the audience. For Shakespeare it is less than madness and more than feigned. The levity of Hamlet, his repetition of phrase, his puns, are not part of a deliberate plan of dissimulation, but a form of emotional relief. In the character Hamlet it is the buffoonery of an emotion which can find no outlet in action; in the dramatist it is the buffoonery of an emotion which he cannot express in art. The intense feeling, ecstatic or terrible, without an object or exceeding its object, is something which every person of sensibility has known; it is doubtless a subject of study for pathologists. It often occurs in adolescence: the ordinary person puts these feelings to sleep, or trims down his feelings to fit the business world; the artist keeps them alive by his ability to intensify the world to his emotions. The Hamlet of Laforgue is an adolescent; the Hamlet of Shakespeare is not, he has not that explanation and excuse. We must simply admit that here Shakespeare tackled a problem which proved too much for him. Why he attempted it at all is an insoluble puzzle; under compulsion of what experience he attempted to express the inexpressibly horrible, we cannot ever know. We need a great many facts in his biography; and we should like to know whether, and when, and after or at the same time as what personal experience, he read Montaigne, II. xii, *Apologie de Raimond Sebond*. We should have, finally, to know something which is by hypothesis unknowable, for we assume it to be an experience which, in the manner indicated, exceeded the facts. We should have to understand things which Shakespeare did not understand himself.

[1919]

POSTSCRIPT

I was once under censure for suggesting that in *Hamlet* Shakespeare was dealing with 'intractable material': my words were even interpreted as maintaining that *Coriolanus* is a greater play than *Hamlet*. I am not very much interested in deciding which play of Shakespeare is greater than which other; because I am more and more interested, not in one play or another, but in Shakespeare's work as a whole. I do not think it any derogation to suggest that Shakespeare did not always succeed; such a suggestion would imply a very narrow view of success. His success must always be reckoned in understanding of what he attempted; and I believe that to admit his partial failures is to *approach* the recognition of his real greatness more closely than to hold that he was always granted plenary inspiration. I do not pretend that I think *Measure for Measure*, or *Troilus and Cressida*, or *All's Well That Ends Well*, to be a wholly 'successful' play; but if any one of Shakespeare's plays were omitted we should not be able to understand the rest as well as we do. In such plays, we must consider not only the degree of unification of all the elements into a 'unity of sentiment', but the quality and kind of emotion to be unified, and the elaborateness of the pattern of unification.

[From *The Use of Poetry and the Use of Criticism*, 1933]

BEN JONSON

THE immediate appeal of Jonson is to the mind; his emotional tone is not in the single verse, but in the design of the whole. But not many people are capable of discovering for themselves the beauty which is only found after labour; and Jonson's industrious readers have been those whose interest was historical and curious, and those who have thought that in discovering the historical and curious interest they had discovered the artistic value as well. When we say that Jonson requires study, we do not mean study of his classical scholarship or of seventeenth-century manners. We mean intelligent saturation in his work as a whole; we mean that, in order to enjoy him at all, we must get to the centre of his work and his temperament, and that we must see him unbiased by time, as a contemporary. And to see him as a contemporary does not so much require

the power of putting ourselves into seventeenth-century London as
it requires the power of setting Jonson in our London.

[From 'Ben Jonson', 1919]

THE METAPHYSICAL POETS

THE phrase 'metaphysical poetry' has long done duty as a term of
abuse, or as the label of a quaint and pleasant taste. The question
is to what extent the so-called metaphysicals formed a school
(in our own time we should say a 'movement'), and how far this
so-called school or movement is a digression from the main
current.

Not only is it extremely difficult to define metaphysical poetry,
but difficult to decide what poets practise it and in which of their
verses. The poetry of Donne (to whom Marvell and Bishop King
are sometimes nearer than any of the other authors) is late Elizabethan, its feeling often very close to that of Chapman. The 'courtly'
poetry is derivative from Jonson, who borrowed liberally from the
Latin; it expires in the next century with the sentiment and witti-
cism of Prior. There is finally the devotional verse of Herbert,
Vaughan, and Crashaw (echoed long after by Christina Rossetti and
Francis Thompson); Crashaw, sometimes more profound and less
sectarian than the others, has a quality which returns through the
Elizabethan period to the early Italians. It is difficult to find any
precise use of metaphor, simile, or other conceit, which is common
to all the poets and at the same time important enough as an element of style to isolate these poets as a group. Donne, and often
Cowley, employs a device which is sometimes considered character-
istically 'metaphysical': the elaboration (contrasted with the con-
densation) of a figure of speech to the furthest stage to which
ingenuity can carry it. Thus Cowley develops the commonplace
comparison of the world to a chess-board through long stanzas (*To
Destiny*), and Donne, with more grace, in *A Valediction*, the comparison of two lovers to a pair of compasses. But elsewhere we find,
instead of the mere explication of the content of a comparison, a

development by rapid association of thought which requires considerable agility on the part of the reader.

> On a round ball
> A workman that hath copies by, can lay
> An Europe, Afrique, and an Asia,
> And quickly make that, which was nothing, All,
>> So doth each teare,
>> Which thee doth weare,
> A globe, yea world by that impression grow,
> Till thy tears mixt with mine doe overflow
> This world, by waters sent from thee, my heaven dissolved so.

Here we find at least two connexions which are not implicit in the first figure, but are forced upon it by the poet: from the geographer's globe to the tear, and the tear to the deluge. On the other hand some of Donne's most successful and characteristic effects are secured by brief words and sudden contrasts:

> A bracelet of bright hair about the bone,

where the most powerful effect is produced by the sudden contrast of associations of 'bright hair' and of 'bone'. This telescoping of images and multiplied associations is characteristic of the phrase of some of the dramatists of the period which Donne knew: not to mention Shakespeare, it is frequent in Middleton, Webster, and Tourneur, and is one of the sources of the vitality of their language.

Johnson, who employed the term 'metaphysical poets', apparently having Donne, Cleveland, and Cowley chiefly in mind, remarks of them that 'the most heterogeneous ideas are yoked by violence together'. The force of this impeachment lies in the failure of the conjunction, the fact that often the ideas are yoked but not united; and if we are to judge of styles of poetry by their abuse, enough examples may be found in Cleveland to justify Johnson's condemnation. But a degree of heterogeneity of material compelled into unity by the operation of the poet's mind is omnipresent in poetry. We need no select for illustration such a line as

> Notre âme est un trois-mâts cherchant son Icarie –

we may find it in some of the best lines of Johnson himself:

> His fate was destined to a barren strand,
> A petty fortress, and a dubious hand;
> He left a name at which the world grew pale,
> To point a moral, or adorn a tale –
>
> (*The Vanity of Human Wishes*)

where the effect is due to a contrast of ideas, different in degree but the same in principle, as that which Johnson mildly reprehended. And in one of the finest poems of the age (a poem which could not have been written in any other age), the *Exequy* of Bishop King, the extended comparison is used with perfect success: the idea and the simile become one, in the passage in which the Bishop illustrates his impatience to see his dead wife, under the figure of a journey:

> Stay for me there; I will not faile
> To meet thee in that hollow Vale.
> And think not much of my delay;
> I am already on the way,
> And follow thee with all the speed
> Desire can make, or sorrows breed.
> Each minute is a short degree,
> And ev'ry houre a step towards thee.
> At night when I betake to rest,
> Next morn I rise nearer my West
> Of life, almost by eight houres sail,
> Than when sleep breath'd his drowsy gale. . . .
> But heark! My Pulse, like a soft Drum
> Beats my approach, tells Thee I come;
> And slow howere my marches be,
> I shall at last sit down by Thee.

(In the last few lines there is that effect of terror which is several times attained by one of Bishop King's admirers, Edgar Poe.) Again, we may justly take these quatrains from Lord Herbert's *Ode*, stanzas which would, we think, be immediately pronounced to be of the metaphysical school:

So when from hence we shall be gone,
 And be no more, nor you, nor I,
 As one another's mystery,
Each shall be both, yet both but one.

This said, in her up-lifted face,
 Her eyes, which did that beauty crown,
 Were like two starrs, that having faln down,
Look up again to find their place:

While such a moveless silent peace
 Did seize on their becalmed sense,
 One would have thought some influence
Their ravished spirits did possess.

There is nothing in these lines (with the possible exception of the stars, a simile not at once grasped, but lovely and justified) which fits Johnson's general observations on the metaphysical poets in his essay on Cowley. A good deal resides in the richness of association which is at the same time borrowed from and given to the word 'becalmed'; but the meaning is clear, the language simple and elegant. It is to be observed that the language of these poets is as a rule simple and pure; in the verse of George Herbert this simplicity is carried as far as it can go – a simplicity emulated without success by numerous modern poets. The *structure* of the sentences, on the other hand, is sometimes far from simple, but this is not a vice; it is a fidelity to thought and feeling. The effect, at its best, is far less artificial than that of an ode by Gray. And as this fidelity induces variety of thought and feeling, so it induces variety of music. We doubt whether, in the eighteenth century, could be found two poems in nominally the same metre, so dissimilar as Marvell's *Coy Mistress* and Crashaw's *Saint Teresa;* the one producing an effect of great speed by the use of short syllables, and the other an ecclesiastical solemnity by the use of long ones:

 Love, thou art absolute sole lord
 Of life and death.

If so shrewd and sensitive (though so limited) a critic as Johnson failed to define metaphysical poetry by its faults, it is worth while to inquire whether we may not have more success by adopting the opposite method: by assuming that the poets of the seventeenth century (up to the Revolution) were the direct and normal development of the precedent age; and, without prejudicing their case by the adjective 'metaphysical', consider whether their virtue was not something permanently valuable, which subsequently disappeared, but ought not to have disappeared. Johnson has hit, perhaps by accident, on one of their peculiarities, when he observes that 'their attempts were always analytic'; he would not agree that, after the dissociation, they put the material together again in a new unity.

It is certain that the dramatic verse of the later Elizabethan and early Jacobean poets expresses a degree of development of sensibility which is not found in any of the prose, good as it often is. If we except Marlowe, a man of prodigious intelligence, these dramatists were directly or indirectly (it is at least a tenable theory) affected by Montaigne. Even if we except also Jonson and Chapman, these two were notably erudite, and were notably men who incorporated their erudition into their sensibility: their mode of feeling was directly and freshly altered by their reading and thought. In Chapman especially there is a direct sensuous apprehension of thought, or a re-creation of thought into feeling, which is exactly what we find in Donne:

> in this one thing, all the discipline
> Of manners and of manhood is contained;
> A man to join himself with th' Universe
> In his main sway, and make in all things fit
> One with that All, and go on, round as it;
> Not plucking from the whole his wretched part,
> And into straits, or into nought revert,
> Wishing the complete Universe might be
> Subject to such a rag of it as he;
> But to consider great Necessity.

We compare this with some modern passage:

No, when the fight begins within himself,
A man's worth something. God stoops o'er his head
Satan looks up between his feet — both tug —
He's left, himself, i' the middle; the soul wakes
And grows. Prolong that battle through his life!

It is perhaps somewhat less fair, though very tempting (as both poets are concerned with the perpetuation of love by offspring), to compare with the stanzas already quoted from Lord Herbert's *Ode* the following from Tennyson:

> *One walked between his wife and child,*
> *With measured footfall firm and mild,*
> *And now and then he gravely smiled.*
> > *The prudent partner of his blood*
> > *Leaned on him, faithful, gentle, good,*
> > *Wearing the rose of womanhood.*
> *And in their double love secure,*
> *The little maiden walked demure,*
> *Pacing with downward eyelids pure.*
> > *These three made unity so sweet,*
> > *My frozen heart began to beat,*
> > *Remembering its ancient heat.*

The difference is not a simple difference of degree between poets. It is something which had happened to the mind of England between the time of Donne or Lord Herbert of Cherbury and the time of Tennyson and Browning; it is the difference between the intellectual poet and the reflective poet. Tennyson and Browning are poets, and they think; but they do not feel their thought as immediately as the odour of a rose. A thought to Donne was an experience; it modified his sensibility. When a poet's mind is perfectly equipped for its work, it is constantly amalgamating disparate experience; the ordinary man's experience is chaotic, irregular, fragmentary. The latter falls in love, or reads Spinoza, and these two experiences have nothing to do with each other, or with the noise of the typewriter or the smell of cooking; in the mind of the poet these experiences are always forming new wholes.

We may express the difference by the following theory: The poets of the seventeenth century, the successors of the dramatists of the sixteenth, possessed a mechanism of sensibility which could devour any kind of experience. They are simple artificial, difficult, or fantastic, as their predecessors were; no less nor more than Dante, Guido Cavalcanti, Guinicelli, or Cino. In the seventeenth century a dissociation of sensibility set in, from which we have never recovered; and this dissociation, as is natural, was aggravated by the influence of the two most powerful poets of the century, Milton and Dryden.* Each of these men performed certain poetic functions so magnificently well that the magnitude of the effect concealed the absence of others. The language went on and in some respects improved; the best verse of Collins, Gray, Johnson, and even Goldsmith satisfies some of our fastidious demands better than that of Donne or Marvell or King. But while the language became more refined, the feeling became more crude. The feeling, the sensibility, expressed in the *Country Churchyard* (to say nothing of Tennyson and Browning) is cruder than that in the *Coy Mistress*.

The second effect of the influence of Milton and Dryden followed from the first, and was therefore slow in manifestation. The sentimental age began early in the eighteenth century, and continued. The poets revolted against the ratiocinative, the descriptive; they thought and felt by fits, unbalanced; they reflected. In one or two passages of Shelley's *Triumph of Life,* in the second *Hyperion,* there are traces of a struggle toward unification of sensibility. But Keats and Shelley died, and Tennyson and Browning ruminated.

After this brief exposition of a theory – too brief, perhaps, to carry conviction – we may ask, what would have been the fate of the 'metaphysical' had the current of poetry descended in a direct line from them, as it descended in a direct line to them? They would not, certainly, be classified as metaphysical. The possible interests of a poet are unlimited; the more intelligent he is the better; the more intelligent he is the more likely that he will have interests : our

* For a reconsideration of this opinion, see p. 131 below. [*Editor's note*]

only condition is that he turn them into poetry, and not merely meditate on them poetically. A philosophical theory which has entered into poetry is established, for its truth or falsity in one sense ceases to matter, and its truth in another sense is proved. The poets in question have, like other poets, various faults. But they were, at best, engaged in the task of trying to find the verbal equivalent for states of mind and feeling. And this means both that they are more mature, and that they wear better, than later poets of certainly not less literary ability.

It is not a permanent necessity that poets should be interested in philosophy, or in any other subject. We can only say that it appears likely that poets in our civilization, as it exists at present, must be *difficult*. Our civilization comprehends great variety and complexity, and this variety and complexity, playing upon a refined sensibility, must produce various and complex results. The poet must become more and more comprehensive, more allusive, more indirect, in order to force, to dislocate if necessary, language into his meaning. Hence we get something which looks very much like the conceit – we get, in fact, a method curiously similar to that of the 'metaphysical poets', similar also in its use of obscure words and of simple phrasing.

> *Ô géraniums diaphanes, guerroyeurs sortilèges,*
> *Sacrilèges monomanes!*
> *Emballages, dévergondages, douches! Ô pressoirs*
> *Des vendanges des grands soirs!*
> *Layettes aux abois,*
> *Thyrses au fond des bois!*
> *Transfusions, représailles,*
> *Relevailles, compresses et l'éternel potion,*
> *Angélus! n'en pouvoir plus*
> *De débâcles nuptiales! de débâcles nuptiales!*

The same poet could write also simply:

> *Elle est bien loin, elle pleure,*
> *Le grand vent se lamente aussi ...*

Jules Laforgue, and Tristan Corbière in many of his poems, are nearer to the 'school of Donne' than any modern English poet. But poets more classical than they have the same essential quality of transmuting ideas into sensations, of transforming an observation into a state of mind.

> Pour l'enfant, amoureux de cartes et d'estampes,
> L'univers est égal à son vaste appétit.
> Ah, que le monde est grand à la clarté des lampes!
> Aux yeux du souvenir que le monde est petit!

In French literature the great master of the seventeenth century – Racine – and the great master of the nineteenth – Baudelaire – are in some ways more like each other than they are like anyone else. The greatest two masters of diction are also the greatest two psychologists, the most curious explorers of the soul. It is interesting to speculate whether it is not a misfortune that two of the greatest masters of diction in our language, Milton and Dryden, triumph with a dazzling disregard of the soul. If we continued to produce Miltons and Drydens it might not so much matter, but as things are it is a pity that English poetry has remained so incomplete. Those who object to the 'artificiality' of Milton or Dryden sometimes tell us to 'look into our hearts and write'. But that is not looking deep enough; Racine or Donne looked into a good deal more than the heart. One must look into the cerebral cortex, the nervous system, and the digestive tracts.

May we not conclude, then, that Donne, Crashaw, Vaughan, Herbert and Lord Herbert, Marvell, King, Cowley at his best, are in the direct current of English poetry, and that their faults should be reprimanded by this standard rather than coddled by antiquarian affection? They have been enough praised in terms which are implicit limitations because they are 'metaphysical' or 'witty', 'quaint' or 'obscure', though at their best they have not these attributes more than other serious poets. On the other hand, we must not reject the criticism of Johnson (a dangerous person to disagree with) without having mastered it, without having assimilated the Johnsonian canons of taste. In reading the celebrated passage in his essay on

Cowley we must remember that by wit he clearly means something more serious than we usually mean today; in his criticism of their versification we must remember in what a narrow discipline he was trained, but also how well trained; we must remember that Johnson tortures chiefly the chief offenders, Cowley and Cleveland. It would be a fruitful work, and one requiring a substantial book, to break up the classification of Johnson and exhibit these poets in all their difference of kind and of degree, from the massive music of Donne to the faint, pleasing tinkle of Aurelian Townshend.

[1921]

THE CAROLINE POETS

OUT of that high style developed from Marlowe through Jonson (for Shakespeare does not lend himself to these genealogies) the seventeenth century separated two qualities: wit and magniloquence. Neither is as simple or as apprehensible as its name seems to imply, and the two are not in practice antithetical; both are conscious and cultivated, and the mind which cultivates one may cultivate the other. The actual poetry, of Marvell, of Cowley, of Milton, and of others, is a blend in varying proportions. And we must be on guard not to employ the terms with too wide a comprehension; for like the other fluid terms with which literary criticism deals, the meaning alters with the age, and for precision we must rely to some degree upon the literacy and good taste of the reader. The wit of the Caroline poets is not the wit of Shakespeare, and it is not the wit of Dryden, the great master of contempt, or of Pope, the great master of hatred, or of Swift, the great master of disgust. What is meant is some quality which is common to the songs in *Comus* and Cowley's 'Anacreontics' and Marvell's 'Horatian Ode'. It is more than a technical accomplishment, or the vocabulary and syntax of an epoch; it is, what we have designated tentatively as wit, a tough reasonableness beneath the slight lyric grace. You cannot find it in Shelley or Keats or Wordsworth; you cannot find more than an echo of it in Landor; still less in Tennyson or Browning; and among contemporaries Yeats is an Irishman and Hardy is a modern English-man – that is to say, Hardy is without it and Yeats is outside of the tradition altogether. On the other hand, as it certainly exists in La Fontaine, there is a large part of it in Gautier. And of the magnilo-quence, the deliberate exploitation of the possibilities of magnifi-cence in language which Milton used and abused, there is also use and even abuse in the poetry of Baudelaire.

Wit is not a quality that we are accustomed to associate with 'Puritan' literature, with Milton or with Marvell. But if so, we are at fault partly in our conception of wit and partly in our generaliza-tions about the Puritans. And if the wit of Dryden or of Pope is not the only kind of wit in the language, the rest is not merely a little merriment or a little levity or a little impropriety or a little epigram. And, on the other hand, the sense in which a man like Marvell is a 'Puritan' is restricted. The persons who opposed Charles I and the persons who supported the Commonwealth were not all of the flock of Zeal-of-the-land Busy or the United Grand Junction Ebenezer Temperance Association. Many of them were gentlemen of the time who merely believed, with considerable show of reason, that govern-ment by a Parliament of gentlemen was better than government by a Stuart; though they were, to that extent, Liberal Practi-tioners, they could hardly foresee the tea-meeting and the Dissi-dence of Dissent. Being men of education and culture, even of travel, some of them were exposed to that spirit of the age which was coming to be the French spirit of the age. This spirit, curiously enough, was quite opposed to the tendencies latent or the forces active in Puritanism; the contest does great damage to the poetry of Milton; Marvell, an active servant of the public, but a lukewarm partisan, and a poet on a smaller scale, is far less injured by it. His line on the statue of Charles II, 'It is such a King as no chisel can mend' may be set off against his criticism of the Great Rebellion: 'Men . . . ought and might have trusted the King'. Marvell, there-fore, more a man of the century than a Puritan, speaks more clearly and unequivocally with the voice of his literary age than does Milton.

[From 'Andrew Marvell', 1921]

WHILE it must be admitted that Milton is a very great poet indeed, it is something of a puzzle to decide in what his greatness consists. On analysis, the marks against him appear both more numerous and more significant than the marks to his credit. As a man, he is antipathetic. Either from the moralist's point of view, or from the theologian's point of view, or from the psychologist's point of view, or from that of the political philosopher, or judging by the ordinary standards of likeableness in human beings, Milton is unsatisfactory. The doubts which I have to express about him are more serious than these. His greatness as a poet has been sufficiently celebrated, though I think largely for the wrong reasons, and without the proper reservations. His misdeeds as a poet have been called attention to, as by Mr Ezra Pound, but usually in passing. What seems to me necessary is to assert at the same time his greatness – in that what he could do well he did better than anyone else has ever done – and the serious charges to be made against him, in respect of the deterioration – the peculiar kind of deterioration – to which he subjected the language.

Many people will agree that a man may be a great artist, and yet have a bad influence. There is more of Milton's influence in the badness of the bad verse of the eighteenth century than of anybody's else: he certainly did more harm than Dryden and Pope, and perhaps a good deal of the obloquy which has fallen on these two poets, especially the latter, because of their influence, ought to be transferred to Milton. But to put the matter simply in terms of 'bad influence' is not necessarily to bring a serious charge: because a good deal of the responsibility, when we state the problem in these terms, may devolve on the eighteenth-century poets themselves for being such bad poets that they were incapable of being influenced except for ill. There is a good deal more to the charge against Milton than this; and it appears a good deal more serious if we affirm that Milton's poetry could *only* be an influence for the worse, upon any poet whatever. It is more serious, also, if we affirm that Milton's bad influence may be traced much farther than the eighteenth century, and much farther than upon bad poets: if we say that it was an influence against which we still have to struggle.

There is a large class of persons, including some who appear in print as critics, who regard any censure upon a 'great' poet as a breach of the peace, as an act of wanton iconoclasm, or even hoodlumism. The kind of derogatory criticism that I have to make upon Milton is not intended for such persons, who cannot understand that it is more important, in some vital respects, to be a *good* poet than to be a *great* poet; and of what I have to say I consider that the only jury of judgement is that of the ablest poetical practitioners of my own time.

The most important fact about Milton, for my purpose, is his blindness. I do not mean that to go blind in middle life is itself enough to determine the whole nature of a man's poetry. Blindness must be considered in conjunction with Milton's personality and character, and the peculiar education which he received. It must also be considered in connexion with his devotion to, and expertness in, the art of music. Had Milton been a man of very keen senses – I mean of *all* the five senses – his blindness would not have mattered so much. But for a man whose sensuousness, such as it was, had been withered early by book-learning, and whose gifts were naturally aural, it mattered a great deal. It would seem, indeed, to have helped him to concentrate on what he could do best.

At no period is the visual imagination conspicuous in Milton's poetry. It would be as well to have a few illustrations of what I mean by visual imagination. From *Macbeth*:

> This guest of summer,
> The temple-haunting martlet, does approve
> By his loved mansionry that the heavens' breath
> Smells wooingly here: no jutty, frieze,
> Buttress, nor coign of vantage, but this bird
> Hath made his pendent bed and procreant cradle:
> Where they most breed and haunt, I have observed
> The air is delicate.

It may be observed that such an image, as well as another familiar quotation from a little later in the same play,

> *Light thickens, and the crow*
> *Makes wing to the rooky wood,*

not only offer something to the eye, but, so to speak, to the common sense. I mean that they convey the feeling of being in a particular place at a particular time. The comparison with Shakespeare offers another indication of the peculiarity of Milton. With Shakespeare, far more than with any other poet in English, the combinations of words offer perpetual novelty; they enlarge the meaning of the individual words joined: thus 'procreant cradle', 'rooky wood'. In comparison, Milton's images do not give this sense of particularity, nor are the separate words developed in significance. His language is, if one may use the term without disparagement, *artificial* and *conventional*.

> *O'er the smooth enamel'd green . . .*

> *. . . paths of this drear wood*
> *The nodding horror of whose shady brows*
> *Threats the forlorn and wandering passenger.*

('Shady brow' here is a diminution of the value of the two words from their use in the line from *Dr Faustus*

> *Shadowing more beauty in their airy brows.*)

The imagery in *L'Allegro* and *Il Penseroso* is all general:

> *While the ploughman near at hand,*
> *Whistles o'er the furrowed land,*
> *And the milkmaid singeth blithe,*
> *And the mower whets his scythe,*
> *And every shepherd tells his tale,*
> *Under the hawthorn in the dale.*

It is not a particular ploughman, milkmaid, and shepherd that Milton sees (as Wordsworth might see them); the sensuous effect of these verses is entirely on the ear, and is joined to the concepts of ploughman, milkmaid, and shepherd. Even in his most mature work, Milton does not infuse new life into the word, as Shakespeare does.

> *The sun to me is dark*
> *And silent as the moon,*
> *When she deserts the night*
> *Hid in her vacant interlunar cave.*

Here *interlunar* is certainly a stroke of genius, but is merely combined with 'vacant' and 'cave', rather than giving and receiving life from them. Thus it is not so unfair, as it might at first appear, to say that Milton writes English like a dead language. The criticism has been made with regard to his involved syntax. But a tortuous style, when its peculiarity is aimed at precision (as with Henry James), is not necessarily a dead one; only when the complication is dictated by a demand of verbal music, instead of by any demand of sense.

> *Thrones, dominations, princedoms, virtues, powers,*
> *If these magnific titles yet remain*
> *Not merely titular, since by decree*
> *Another now hath to himself engrossed*
> *All power, and us eclipsed under the name*
> *Of King anointed, for whom all this haste*
> *Of midnight march, and hurried meeting here,*
> *This only to consult how we may best*
> *With what may be devised of honours new*
> *Receive him coming to receive from us*
> *Knee-tribute yet unpaid, prostration vile,*
> *Too much to one, but double how endured,*
> *To one and to his image now proclaimed?*

With which compare:

> *However, he didn't mind thinking that if Cissy should prove all*
> *that was likely enough their having a subject in common couldn't*
> *but practically conduce; though the moral of it all amounted rather*

*to a portent, the one that Haughty, by the same token, had done
least to reassure him against, of the extent to which the native jungle
harboured the female specimen and to which its ostensible cover,
the vast level of mixed growths stirred wavingly in whatever breeze,
was apt to be identifiable but as an agitation of the latest redundant
thing in ladies' hats.*

This quotation, taken almost at random from *The Ivory Tower*, is
not intended to represent Henry James at any hypothetical 'best',
any more than the noble passage from *Paradise Lost* is meant to be
Milton's hypothetical worst. The question is the difference of intention, in the elaboration of styles both of which depart so far from
lucid simplicity. The sound, of course, is never irrelevant, and the
style of James certainly depends for its effect a good deal on the
sound of a voice, James's own, painfully explaining. But the complication, with James, is due to a determination not to simplify, and
in that simplification lose any of the real intricacies and by-paths of
mental movement; whereas the complication of a Miltonic sentence
is an active complication, a complication deliberately introduced
into what was a previously simplified and abstract thought. The
dark angel here is not *thinking* or conversing, but making a speech
carefully prepared for him; and the arrangement is for the sake of
musical value, not for significance. A straightforward utterance, as
of a Homeric or Dantesque character, would make the speaker very
much more real to us; but reality is no part of the intention. We
have in fact to read such a passage not analytically, to get the poetic
impression. I am not suggesting that Milton has no idea to convey,
which he regards as important: only that the syntax is determined
by the musical significance, by the auditory imagination, rather
than by the attempt to follow actual speech or thought. It is at least
more nearly possible to distinguish the pleasure which arises from
the *noise*, from the pleasure due to other elements, than with the
verse of Shakespeare, in which the auditory imagination and the
imagination of the other senses are more nearly fused, and fused
together with the thought. The result with Milton is, in one sense
of the word, *rhetoric*. That term is not intended to be derogatory.

This kind of 'rhetoric' is not necessarily bad in its influence; and it may be considered bad in relation to the historical life of a language as a whole. I have said elsewhere that the living English which was Shakespeare's became split up into two components one of which was exploited by Milton and the other by Dryden. Of the two, I still think Dryden's development the healthier, because it was Dryden who preserved, so far as it was preserved at all, the tradition of conversational language in poetry: and I might add that it seems to me easier to get back to healthy language from Dryden than it is to get back to it from Milton. For what such a generalization is worth, Milton's influence on the eighteenth century was much more deplorable than Dryden's.

If several very important reservations and exceptions are made, I think that it is not unprofitable to compare Milton's development with that of James Joyce. The initial similarities are strong musical tastes and abilities, followed by musical training, wide and curious knowledge, gift for acquiring languages, and remarkable powers of memory perhaps fortified by defective vision. The important difference is that Joyce's imagination is not naturally of so purely auditory a type as Milton's. In his early work, and at least in part of *Ulysses*, there is visual and other imagination of the highest kind; and I may be mistaken in thinking that the later part of *Ulysses* shows a turning from the visible world to draw rather on the resources of phantasmagoria. In any case, one may suppose that the replenishment of visual imagery during later years has been insufficient; so that what I find in *Work in Progress* is an auditory imagination abnormally sharpened at the expense of the visual. There is still a little to be seen, and what there is to see is worth looking at. And I would repeat that with Joyce this development seems to me largely due to circumstances: whereas Milton may be said never to have seen anything. For Milton, therefore, the concentration on sound was wholly a benefit. Indeed, I find, in reading *Paradise Lost*, that I am happiest where there is least to visualize. The eye is not shocked in his twilit Hell as it is in the Garden of Eden, where I for one can get pleasure from the verse only by the deliberate effort not to visualize Adam and Eve and their surroundings.

I am not suggesting any close parallel between the 'rhetoric' of Milton and the later style of Joyce. It is a different music; and Joyce always maintains some contact with the conversational tone. But it may prove to be equally a blind alley for the future development of the language: being preferable to Milton's, in the respect that it cannot be imitated.

A disadvantage of the rhetorical style appears to be, that a dislocation takes place, through the hypertrophy of the auditory imagination at the expense of the visual and tactile, so that the inner meaning is separated from the surface, and tends to become something occult, or at least without effect upon the reader until fully understood. To extract everything possible from *Paradise Lost*, it would seem necessary to read it in two different ways, first solely for the sound, and second for the sense. The full beauty of his long periods can hardly be enjoyed while we are wrestling with the meaning as well; and for the pleasure of the ear the meaning is hardly necessary, except in so far as certain key-words indicate the emotional tone of the passage. Now Shakespeare, or Dante, will bear innumerable readings, but at each reading all the elements of appreciation can be present. There is no interruption between the surface that these poets present to you and the core. While, therefore, I cannot pretend to have penetrated to any 'secret' of these poets, I feel that such appreciation of their work as I am capable of points in the right direction; whereas I cannot feel that my appreciation of Milton leads anywhere outside of the mazes of sound. That, I feel, would be the matter for a separate study, like that of Blake's prophetic books; it might be well worth the trouble, but would have little to do with my interest in the poetry. So far as I perceive anything, it is a glimpse of a theology that I find in large part repellent, expressed through a mythology which would have better been left in the Book of *Genesis*, upon which Milton has not improved. There seems to me to be a division, in Milton, between the philosopher or theologian and the poet; and, for the latter, I suspect also that this concentration upon the auditory imagination leads to at least an occasional levity. I can enjoy the roll of

> *. . . Cambalu, seat of Cathaian Can*
> *And Samarchand by Oxus, Temir's throne,*
> *To Paquin of Sinaean kings, and thence*
> *To Agra and Lahor of great Mogul*
> *Down to the golden Chersonese, or where*
> *The Persian in Ecbatan sate, or since*
> *In Hispahan, or where the Russian Ksar*
> *In Mosco, or the Sultan in Bizance,*
> *Turchestan-born . . .*

and the rest of it, but I feel that this is not serious poetry, not poetry fully occupied about its business, but rather a solemn game. More often, admittedly, Milton uses proper names in moderation, to obtain the same effect of magnificence with them as does Marlowe – nowhere perhaps better than in the passage from *Lycidas*:

> *Whether beyond the stormy Hebrides,*
> *Where thou perhaps under the whelming tide*
> *Visit'st the bottom of the monstrous world;*
> *Or whether thou to our moist vows deny'd*
> *Sleep'st by the fable of Bellerus old,*
> *Where the great vision of the guarded Mount*
> *Looks toward Namancos and Bayona's hold . . .*

than which, for the single effect of grandeur of sound, there is nothing finer in poetry.

I make no attempt to appraise the 'greatness' of Milton in relation to poets who seem to me more comprehensive and better balanced; it has seemed to me more fruitful for the present to press the parallel between *Paradise Lost* and *Work in Progress*; and both Milton and Joyce are so exalted in their own kinds, in the whole of literature, that the only writers with whom to compare them are writers who have attempted something very different. Our views about Joyce, in any case, must remain at the present time tentative. But there are two attitudes both of which are necessary and right to adopt in considering the work of any poet. One is when we isolate him, when we try to understand the rules of his own game, adopt his own point of view: the other, perhaps less usual, is when we measure him by outside standards, most pertinently by the standards of language and of something called Poetry, in our own language and in the whole history of European literature. It is from the second point of view that my objections to Milton are made: it is from this point of view that we can go so far as to say that, although his work realizes superbly one important element in poetry, he may still be considered as having done damage to the English language from which it has not wholly recovered.

> ['A Note on the Verse of John Milton', contributed to
> *Essays and Studies*, 1936]

MILTON II*

SAMUEL JOHNSON, addressing himself to examine Milton's versification, in the *Rambler* of Saturday, 12 January 1751, thought it necessary to excuse his temerity in writing upon a subject already so fully discussed. In justification of his essay this great critic and poet remarked: 'There are, in every age, new errors to be rectified, and new prejudices to be opposed.' I am obliged to phrase my own apology rather differently. The errors of our own times have been rectified by vigorous hands, and the prejudices opposed by commanding voices. Some of the errors and prejudices have been associated with my own name, and of these in particular I shall find myself impelled to speak; it will, I hope, be attributed to me for modesty rather than for conceit if I maintain that no one can correct an error with better authority than the person who has been held responsible for it. And there is, I think, another justification for my speaking about Milton, besides the singular one which I have just given. The champions of Milton in our time, with one notable exception, have been scholars and teachers. I have no claim to be either: I am aware that my only claim upon your attention, in speaking of Milton or of any other great poet, is by appeal to your curiosity, in the hope that

* The Henriette Hertz Lecture, delivered to the British Academy, 26 March 1947. [*Editor's note*]

you may care to know what a contemporary writer of verse thinks of one of his predecessors.

I believe that the scholar and the practitioner in the field of literary criticism should supplement each other's work. The criticism of the practitioner will be all the better, certainly, if he is not wholly destitute of scholarship; and the criticism of the scholar will be all the better if he has some experience of the difficulties of writing verse. But the orientation of the two critics is different. The scholar is more concerned with the understanding of the masterpiece in the environment of its author: with the world in which that author lived, the temper of his age, his intellectual formation, the books which he had read, and the influences which had moulded him. The practitioner is concerned less with the author than with the poem; and with the poem in relation to his own age. He asks: Of what *use* is the poetry of this poet to poets writing today? Is it, or can it become, a living force in English poetry still unwritten? So we may say that the scholar's interest is in the permanent, the practitioner's in the immediate. The scholar can teach us where we should bestow our *admiration* and *respect*: the practitioner should be able, when he is the right poet talking about the right poet, to make an old master-piece actual, give it contemporary importance, and persuade his audience that it is interesting, exciting, enjoyable, and *active*. I can give only one example of contemporary criticism of Milton, by a critic of the type to which I belong if I have any critical pretensions at all: that is the Introduction to Milton's *English Poems* in the 'World's Classics' series, by the late Charles Williams. It is not a comprehensive essay; it is notable primarily because it provides the best prolegomenon to *Comus* which any modern reader could have; but what distinguishes it throughout (and the same is true of most of Williams's critical writing) is the author's warmth of feeling and his success in communicating it to the reader. In this, so far as I am aware, the essay of Williams is a solitary example.

I think it is useful, in such an examination as I propose to make, to keep in mind some critic of the past, of one's own type, by whom to measure one's opinions: a critic sufficiently remote in time, for his local errors and prejudices to be not identical with one's own. That is why I began by quoting Samuel Johnson. It will hardly be contested that as a critic of poetry Johnson wrote as a practitioner and not as a scholar. Because he was a poet himself, and a good poet, what he wrote about poetry must be read with respect. And unless we know and appreciate Johnson's poetry we cannot judge either the merits or the limitations of his criticism. It is a pity that what the common reader today has read, or has remembered, or has seen quoted, are mostly those few statements of Johnson's from which later critics have vehemently dissented. But when Johnson held an opinion which seems to us wrong, we are never safe in dismissing it without inquiring why he was wrong; he had his own 'errors and prejudices', certainly, but for lack of examining them sympathetically we are always in danger of merely countering error with error and prejudice with prejudice. Now Johnson was, in his day, very much a modern: he was concerned with how poetry should be written in his own time. The fact that he came towards the end, rather than the beginning of a style, the fact that his time was rapidly passing away, and that the canons of taste which he observed were about to fall into desuetude, does not diminish the interest of his criticism. Nor does the likelihood that the development of poetry in the next fifty years will take quite different directions from those which to me seem desirable to explore, deter me from asking the questions that Johnson implied: How should poetry be written now? and what place does the answer to this question give to Milton? And I think that the answers to these questions may be different now from the answers that were correct twenty-five years ago.

There is one prejudice against Milton, apparent on almost every page of Johnson's *Life of Milton*, which I imagine is still general: we, however, with a longer historical perspective, are in a better position than was Johnson to recognize it and to make allowance for it. This is a prejudice which I share myself: an antipathy towards Milton the man. Of this in itself I have nothing further to say: all that is necessary is to record one's awareness of it. But this prejudice is often involved with another, more obscure: and I do not think that Johnson had disengaged the two in his own mind. The fact is simply that the Civil War of the seventeenth century, in which

Milton is a symbolic figure, has never been concluded. The Civil War is not ended: I question whether any serious civil war ever does end. Throughout that period English society was so convulsed and divided that the effects are still felt. Reading Johnson's essay one is always aware that Johnson was obstinately and passionately of another party. No other English poet, not Wordsworth, or Shelley, lived through or took sides in such momentous events as did Milton; of no other poet is it so difficult to consider the poetry simply as poetry, without our theological and political dispositions, conscious and unconscious, inherited or acquired, making an unlawful entry. And the danger is all the greater because these emotions now take different vestures. It is now considered grotesque, on political grounds, to be of the party of King Charles; it is now, I believe, considered equally grotesque, on moral grounds, to be of the party of the Puritans; and to most persons today the religious views of both parties may seem equally remote. Nevertheless, the passions are unquenched, and if we are not very wide awake their smoke will obscure the glass through which we examine Milton's poetry. Something has been done, certainly, to persuade us that Milton was never really of any party, but disagreed with everyone. Mr Wilson Knight, in *Chariot of Wrath*, has argued that Milton was more a monarchist than a republican, and not in any modern sense a 'democrat'. And Professor Saurat has produced evidence to show that Milton's theology was highly eccentric, and as scandalous to Protestants as to Catholics – that he was, in fact, a sort of Christadelphian, and perhaps not a very orthodox Christadelphian at that; while on the other hand Mr C. S. Lewis has opposed Professor Saurat by skilfully arguing that Milton, at least in *Paradise Lost*, can be acquitted of heresy even from a point of view so orthodox as that of Mr Lewis himself. On these questions I hold no opinion: it is probably beneficial to question the assumption that Milton was a sound Free Churchman and member of the Liberal Party; but I think that we still have to be on guard against an unconscious partisanship if we aim to attend to the poetry for the poetry's sake.

So much for our prejudices. I come next to the positive objection to Milton which has been raised in our own time, that is to say, the charge that he is an unwholesome influence. And from this I shall proceed to the permanent strictures of reproof (to employ a phrase of Johnson's) and, finally, to the grounds on which I consider him a great poet and one whom poets today might study with profit.

For a statement of the *generalized* belief in the unwholesomeness of Milton's influence I turn to Mr Middleton Murry's critique of Milton in his *Heaven and Earth* – a book which contains chapters of profound insight, interrupted by passages which seem to me intemperate. Mr Murry approaches Milton after his long and patient study of Keats; and it is through the eyes of Keats that he sees Milton.

Keats [Mr Murry writes], *as a poetic artist, second to none since Shakespeare, and Blake, as a prophet of spiritual values unique in our history, both passed substantially the same judgement on Milton: 'Life to him would be death to me.' And whatever may be our verdict on the development of English poetry since Milton, we must admit the justice of Keats's opinion that Milton's magnificence led nowhere. 'English must be kept up,' said Keats. To be influenced beyond a certain point by Milton's art, he felt, dammed the creative flow of the English genius in and through itself. In saying this, I think, Keats voiced the very inmost of the English genius. To pass under the spell of Milton is to be condemned to imitate him. It is quite different with Shakespeare. Shakespeare baffles and liberates; Milton is perspicuous and constricts.*

This is a very confident affirmation, and I criticize it with some diffidence because I cannot pretend to have devoted as much study to Keats, or to have as intimate an understanding of his difficulties, as Mr Murry. But Mr Murry seems to me here to be trying to transform the predicament of a particular poet with a particular aim at a particular moment in time into a censure of timeless validity. He appears to assert that the liberative function of Shakespeare and the constrictive menace of Milton are permanent characteristics of these two poets. 'To be influenced beyond a certain point' by any one master is bad for any poet; and it does not matter whether that influence is Milton's or another's; and as we cannot anticipate where that point will come, we might be better advised to call it an *uncertain* point. If it is not good to remain under the spell of Milton, is it good to remain under the spell of Shakespeare? It depends partly upon what genre of poetry you are trying to develop. Keats wanted to write an epic, and he found, as might be expected, that the time had not arrived at which another English epic, comparable in grandeur to *Paradise Lost*, could be written. He also tried his hand at writing plays: and one might argue that *King Stephen* was more blighted by Shakespeare than *Hyperion* by Milton. Certainly, *Hyperion* remains a magnificent fragment which one re-reads; and *King Stephen* is a play which we may have read once, but to which we never return for enjoyment. Milton made a great epic impossible for succeeding generations; Shakespeare made a great poetic drama impossible; such a situation is inevitable, and it persists until the language has so altered that there is no danger, because no possibility, of imitation. Anyone who tries to write poetic drama, even today, should know that half of his energy must be exhausted in the effort to escape from the constricting toils of Shakespeare: the moment his attention is relaxed, or his mind fatigued, he will lapse into bad Shakespearian verse. For a long time after an epic poet like Milton, or a dramatic poet like Shakespeare, nothing can be done. Yet the effort must be repeatedly made; for we can never know in advance when the moment is approaching at which a new epic, or a new drama, will be possible; and when the moment does draw near it may be that the genius of an individual poet will perform the last mutation of idiom and versification which will bring that new poetry into being.

I have referred to Mr Murry's view of the bad influence of Milton as generalized, because it is implicitly the whole personality of Milton that is in question: not specifically his beliefs, or his language or versification, but the beliefs as realized in that particular personality, and his poetry as the expression of it. By the *particular* view of Milton's influence as bad, I mean that view which attends to the language, the syntax, the versification, the imagery. I do not suggest that there is here a complete difference of subject-matter: it is the difference of approach, the difference of the focus of interest, between the philosophical critic and the literary critic. An incapacity for the abstruse, and an interest in poetry which is primarily a technical interest, dispose my mind towards the more limited and perhaps more superficial task. Let us proceed to look at Milton's influence from this point of view, that of the writer of poetry in our own time.

The reproach against Milton, that his technical influence has been bad, appears to have been made by no one more positively than by myself. I find myself saying, as recently as 1936, that this charge against Milton

*appears a good deal more serious if we affirm that Milton's poetry could only be an influence for the worse, upon any poet whatever. It is more serious, also, if we affirm that Milton's bad influence may be traced much farther than the eighteenth century, and much farther than upon bad poets: if we say that it was an influence against which we still have to struggle.**

In writing these sentences I failed to draw a threefold distinction, which now seems to me of some importance. There are three separate assertions implied. The first is, that an influence has been bad in the past: this is to assert that good poets, in the eighteenth or nineteenth century, would have written better if they had not submitted themselves to the influence of Milton. The second assertion is, that the contemporary situation is such that Milton is a master whom we should avoid. The third is, that the influence of Milton, or of any particular poet, can be *always* bad, and that we can predict that wherever it is found at any time in the future, however remote, it will be a bad influence. Now, the first and third of these assertions I am no longer prepared to make, because, detached from the second, they do not appear to me to have any meaning.

For the first, when we consider one great poet of the past, and one or more other poets, upon whom we say he has exerted a bad influence, we must admit that the responsibility, if there be any, is rather with the poets who were influenced than with the poet whose work exerted the influence. We can, of course, show that certain

* See pp. 116–17 above. [*Editor's note*]

tricks or mannerisms which the imitators display are due to conscious or unconscious imitation and emulation, but that is a reproach against their injudicious choice of a model and not against their model itself. And we can never prove that any particular poet would have written better poetry if he had escaped that influence. Even if we assert, what can only be a matter of faith, that Keats would have written a very great epic poem if Milton had not preceded him, is it sensible to repine for an unwritten masterpiece, in exchange for one which we possess and acknowledge? And as for the remote future, what can we affirm about the poetry that will be written then, except that we should probably be unable to understand or to enjoy it, and that therefore we can hold no opinion as to what 'good' and 'bad' influences will *mean* in that future? The only relation in which the question of influence, good and bad, is significant, is the relation to the immediate future. With that question I shall engage at the end. I wish first to mention another reproach against Milton, that represented by the phrase 'dissociation of sensibility'.

I remarked many years ago, in an essay on Dryden,* that:

In the seventeenth century a dissociation of sensibility set in, from which we have never recovered; and this dissociation, as is natural, was due to the influence of the two most powerful poets of the century, Milton and Dryden.

The longer passage from which this sentence is taken is quoted by Dr Tillyard in his *Milton*. Dr Tillyard makes the following comment:

Speaking only of what in this passage concerns Milton, I would say that there is here a mixture of truth and falsehood. Some sort of dissociation of sensibility in Milton, not necessarily undesirable, has to be admitted; but that he was responsible for any such dissociation in others (at least till this general dissociation had inevitably set in) is untrue.

* The essay, in fact, was on the 'Metaphysical Poets', and was written for *The Times Literary Supplement* in 1921. See p. 105 above. [*Editor's note*]

I believe that the general affirmation represented by the phrase 'dissociation of sensibility' (one of the two or three phrases of my coinage – like 'objective correlative'* – which had a success in the world astonishing to their author) retains some validity; but I now incline to agree with Dr Tillyard that to lay the burden on the shoulders of Milton and Dryden was a mistake. If such a dissociation did take place, I suspect that the causes are too complex and too profound to justify our accounting for the change in terms of literary criticism. All we can say is, that something like this did happen; that it had something to do with the Civil War; that it would even be unwise to say it was caused by the Civil War, but that it is a consequence of the same causes which brought about the Civil War; that we must seek the causes in Europe, not in England alone; and for what these causes were, we may dig and dig until we get to a depth at which words and concepts fail us.

Before proceeding to take up the case against Milton, as it stood for poets twenty-five years ago – the second, and only significant meaning of 'bad influence' – I think it would be best to consider what permanent strictures of reproof may be drawn: those censures which, when we make them, we must assume to be made by enduring laws of taste. The essence of the permanent censure of Milton is, I believe, to be found in Johnson's essay. This is not the place in which to examine certain particular and erroneous judgements of Johnson; to explain his condemnation of *Comus* and *Samson* by his applying dramatic canons which to us seem inapplicable; or to condone his dismissal of the versification of *Lycidas* by the specialization, rather than the absence, of his sense of rhythm. Johnson's most important censure of Milton is contained in three paragraphs, which I must ask leave to quote in full.

Throughout all his greater works [says Johnson] *there prevails an uniform peculiarity of* diction, *a mode and cast of expression which bears little resemblance to that of any former writer; and which is so far removed from common use, that an unlearned reader, when he first opens the book, finds himself surprised by a new language.*

* See p. 102 above. [*Editor's note*]

This novelty has been, by those who can find nothing wrong with Milton, imputed to his laborious endeavours after words suited to the grandeur of his ideas. Our language, *says Addison,* sank under him. *But the truth is, that both in prose and in verse, he had formed his style by a perverse and pedantic principle. He was desirous to use English words with a foreign idiom. This in all his prose is discovered and condemned; for there judgement operates freely, neither softened by the beauty, nor awed by the dignity of his thoughts; but such is the power of his poetry, that his call is obeyed without resistance, the reader feels himself in captivity to a higher and nobler mind, and criticism sinks in admiration.*

Milton's style was not modified by his subject; what is shown with greater extent in Paradise Lost *may be found in* Comus. *One source of his peculiarity was his familiarity with the Tuscan poets; the disposition of his words is, I think, frequently Italian; perhaps sometimes combined with other tongues. Of him at last, may be said what Johnson said of Spenser, that he* wrote no language, *but has formed what Butler called a* Babylonish dialect, *in itself harsh and barbarous, but made by exalted genius and extensive learning the vehicle of so much instruction and so much pleasure, that, like other lovers, we find grace in its deformity.*

This criticism seems to me substantially true: indeed, unless we accept it, I do not think we are in the way to appreciate the peculiar greatness of Milton. His style is not a *classic* style, in that it is not the elevation of a *common* style, by the final touch of genius, to greatness. It is, from the foundation, and in every particular, a personal style, not based upon common speech, or common prose, or direct communication of meaning. Of some great poetry one has difficulty in pronouncing just what it is, what infinitesimal touch, that has made all the difference from a plain statement which anyone could make; the slight transformation which, while it leaves a plain statement a plain statement, has always the maximal, never the minimal, alteration of ordinary language. Every distortion of construction, the foreign idiom, the use of a word in a foreign way or with the meaning of the foreign word from which it is derived rather than the accepted meaning in English, every idiosyncrasy is a particular act of violence which Milton has been the first to commit. There is no cliché, no poetic diction in the derogatory sense, but a perpetual sequence of original acts of lawlessness. Of all modern writers of verse, the nearest analogy seems to me to be Mallarmé, a much smaller poet, though still a great one. The personalities, the poetic theories of the two men could not have been more different; but in respect of the violence which they could do to language, and justify, there is a remote similarity. Milton's poetry is poetry at the farthest possible remove from prose; his prose seems to me too near to half-formed poetry to be good prose.

To say that the work of a poet is at the farthest possible remove from prose would once have struck me as condemnatory: it now seems to me simply, when we have to do with a Milton, the precision of its peculiar greatness. As a poet, Milton seems to me probably the greatest of all eccentrics. His work illustrates no general principles of good writing; the only principles of writing that it illustrates are such as are valid only for Milton himself to observe. There are two kinds of poet who can ordinarily be of use to other poets. There are those who suggest, to one or another of their successors, something which they have not done themselves, or who provoke a different way of doing the same thing: these are likely to be not the greatest, but smaller, imperfect poets with whom later poets discover an affinity. And there are the great poets from whom we can learn negative rules: no poet can teach another to write well, but some great poets can teach others some of the things to avoid. They teach us what to avoid, by showing us what great poetry can do without – how *bare* it can be. Of these are Dante and Racine. But if we are ever to make use of Milton we must do so in quite a different way. Even a small poet can learn something from the study of Dante, or from the study of Chaucer: we must perhaps wait for a great poet before we find one who can profit from the study of Milton.

I repeat that the remoteness of Milton's verse from ordinary speech, his invention of his own poetic language, seems to me one of the marks of his greatness. Other marks are his sense of structure, both in the general design of *Paradise Lost* and *Samson*, and in his syntax; and finally, and not least, his inerrancy, conscious or unconscious, in writing so as to make the best display of his talents, and the best concealment of his weaknesses.

The appropriateness of the subject of *Samson* is too obvious to expatiate upon: it was probably the one dramatic story out of which Milton could have made a masterpiece. But the complete suitability of *Paradise Lost* has not, I think, been so often remarked. It was surely an intuitive perception of what he could not do, that arrested Milton's project of an epic on King Arthur. For one thing, he had little interest in, or understanding of, individual human beings. In *Paradise Lost* he was not called upon for any of that understanding which comes from an affectionate observation of men and women. Such an interest in human beings was not required – indeed its *absence* was a necessary condition – for the creation of his figures of Adam and Eve. These are not a man and woman such as any we know: if they were, they would not be Adam and Eve. They are the original *Man* and *Woman*, not types, but prototypes: if they were not set apart from ordinary humanity they would not be Adam and Eve. They have the general characteristics of men and women, such that we can recognize, in the temptation and the fall, the first motions of the faults and virtues, the abjection and the nobility, of all their descendants. They have ordinary humanity to the right degree, and yet are not, and should not be, ordinary mortals. Were they more particularized they would be false, and if Milton had been more interested in humanity, he could not have created them. Other critics have remarked upon the exactness, without defect or exaggeration, with which Moloch, Belial, and Mammon, in the second book, speak according to the particular sin which each represents. It would not be suitable that the infernal powers should have, in the human sense, characters, for a character is always mixed; but in the hands of an inferior manipulator, they might easily have been reduced to *humours*.

The appropriateness of the material of *Paradise Lost* to the genius and the limitations of Milton, is still more evident when we consider the visual imagery. I have already remarked, in a paper written some years ago,* on Milton's weakness of visual observation, a weakness which I think was always present – the effect of his blindness may have been rather to strengthen the compensatory qualities than to increase a fault which was already present. Mr Wilson Knight, who has devoted close study to recurrent imagery in poetry, has called attention to Milton's propensity towards images of engineering and mechanics; to me it seems that Milton is at his best in imagery suggestive of vast size, limitless space, abysmal depth, and light and darkness. No theme and no setting, other than that which he chose in *Paradise Lost*, could have given him such scope for the kind of imagery in which he excelled, or made less demand upon those powers of visual imagination which were in him defective.

Most of the absurdities and inconsistencies to which Johnson calls attention, and which, so far as they can justly be isolated in this way, he properly condemns, will I think appear in a more correct proportion if we consider them in relation to this general judgement. I do not think that we should attempt to *see* very clearly any scene that Milton depicts: it should be accepted as a shifting phantasmagory. To complain, because we first find the arch-fiend 'chain'd on the burning lake', and in a minute or two see him making his way to the shore, is to expect a kind of consistency which the world to which Milton has introduced us does not require.

This limitation of visual power, like Milton's limited interest in human beings, turns out to be not merely a negligible defect, but a positive virtue, when we visit Adam and Eve in Eden. Just as a higher degree of characterization of Adam and Eve would be unsuitable, so a more vivid picture of the earthly Paradise would have been less paradisiacal. For a greater definiteness, a more detailed account of flora and fauna, could only have assimilated Eden to the landscapes of earth with which we are familiar. As it is, the impression of Eden which we retain, is the most suitable, and is that which Milton was most qualified to give: the impression of *light* – a daylight and a starlight, a light of dawn and of dusk, the light which,

* See p. 116 above. [*Editor's note*]

remembered by a man in his blindness, has a supernatural glory unexperienced by men of normal vision.

We must, then, in reading *Paradise Lost*, not expect to see clearly; our sense of sight must be blurred, so that our *hearing* may become more acute. *Paradise Lost*, like *Finnegan's Wake* (for I can think of no work which provides a more interesting parallel: two great books by blind musicians, each writing a language of his own based upon English), makes this peculiar demand for a readjustment of the reader's mode of apprehension. The emphasis is on the sound, not the vision, upon the word, not the idea; and in the end it is the unique versification that is the most certain sign of Milton's intellectual mastership.

On the subject of Milton's versification, so far as I am aware, little enough has been written. We have Johnson's essay in the *Rambler*, which deserves more study than it has received, and we have a short treatise by Robert Bridges on *Milton's Prosody*. I speak of Bridges with respect, for no poet of our time has given such close attention to prosody as he. Bridges catalogues the systematic irregularities which give perpetual variety to Milton's verse, and I can find no fault with his analysis. But however interesting these analyses are, I do not think that it is by such means that we gain an appreciation of the peculiar rhythm of a poet. It seems to me also that Milton's verse is especially refractory to yielding up its secrets to examination of the single line. For his verse is not formed in this way. It is the period, the sentence, and still more the paragraph, that is the unit of Milton's verse; and emphasis on the line structure is the minimum necessary to provide a counter-pattern to the period structure. It is only in the period that the wave-length of Milton's verse is to be found: it is his ability to give a perfect and unique pattern to every paragraph, such that the full beauty of the line is found in its context, and his ability to work in larger musical units than any other poet – that is to me the most conclusive evidence of Milton's supreme mastery. The peculiar feeling, almost a physical sensation of a breathless leap, communicated by Milton's long periods, and by his alone, is impossible to procure from rhymed verse. Indeed, this mastery is more conclusive evidence of his intellectual power, than is his grasp of any *ideas* that he borrowed or invented. To be able to control so many words at once is the token of a mind of most exceptional energy.

It is interesting at this point to recall the general observations upon blank verse, which a consideration of *Paradise Lost* prompted Johnson to make towards the end of his essay.

The music of the English heroic lines strikes the ear so faintly, that it is easily lost, unless all the syllables of every line cooperate together; this cooperation can only be obtained by the preservation of every verse unmingled with another as a distinct system of sounds; and this distinctness is obtained and preserved by the artifice of rhyme. The variety of pauses, so much boasted by the lovers of blank verse, changes the measures of an English poet to the periods of a declaimer; and there are only a few skilful and happy readers of Milton, who enable their audience to perceive where the lines end or begin. Blank verse, said an ingenious critic, seems to be verse only to the eye.

Some of my audience may recall that this last remark, in almost the same words, was often made, a literary generation ago, about the 'free verse' of the period: and even without this encouragement from Johnson it would have occurred to my mind to declare Milton to be the greatest master of free verse in our language. What is interesting about Johnson's paragraph, however, is that it represents the judgement of a man who had by no means a deaf ear, but simply a *specialized* ear, for verbal music. Within the limits of the poetry of his own period, Johnson is a very good judge of the relative merits of several poets as writers of blank verse. But on the whole, the blank verse of his age might more properly be called unrhymed verse; and nowhere is this difference more evident than in the verse of his own tragedy *Irene:* the phrasing is admirable, the style elevated and correct, but each line cries out for a companion to rhyme with it. Indeed, it is only with labour, or by occasional inspiration, or by submission to the influence of the older dramatists, that the blank verse of the nineteenth century succeeds in making the absence of rhyme inevitable and right, with the rightness of Milton. Even

Johnson admitted that he could not wish that Milton had been a rhymer. Nor did the nineteenth century succeed in giving to blank verse the flexibility which it needs if the tone of common speech, talking of the topics of common intercourse, is to be employed; so that when our more modern practitioners of blank verse do not touch the sublime, they frequently approach the ridiculous. Milton perfected non-dramatic blank verse and at the same time imposed limitations, very hard to break, upon the use to which it may be put if its greatest musical possibilities are to be exploited.

I come at last to compare my own attitude, as that of a poetical practitioner perhaps typical of a generation twenty-five years ago, with my attitude today. I have thought it well to take matters in the order in which I have taken them to discuss first the censures and detractions which I believe to have permanent validity, and which were best made by Johnson, in order to make clearer the causes, and the justification, for hostility to Milton on the part of poets at a particular juncture. And I wished to make clear those excellences of Milton which particularly impress me, before explaining why I think that the study of his verse might at last be of benefit to poets.

I have on several occasions suggested that the important changes in the idiom of English verse which are represented by the names of Dryden and Wordsworth, may be characterized as successful attempts to escape from a poetic idiom which had ceased to have a relation to contemporary speech. This is the sense of Wordsworth's Prefaces. By the beginning of the present century another revolution in idiom – and such revolutions bring with them an alteration of metric, a new appeal to the ear – was due. It inevitably happens that the young poets engaged in such a revolution will exalt the merits of those poets of the past who offer them example and stimulation, and depreciate the merits of poets who do not stand for the qualities which they are zealous to realize. This is not only inevitable, it is right. It is even right, and certainly inevitable, that their practice, still more influential than their critical pronouncements, should attract their own readers to the poets by whose work they have been influenced. Such influence has certainly contributed to the taste, if we can distinguish the *taste* from the *fashion*, for Donne. I do not think that any modern poet, unless in a fit of irresponsible peevishness, has ever denied Milton's consummate powers. And it must be said that Milton's diction is not a poetic diction in the sense of being a debased currency: when he violates the English language he is imitating nobody, and he is inimitable. But Milton does, as I have said, represent poetry at the extreme limit from prose; and it was one of our tenets that verse should have the virtues of prose, that diction should become assimilated to cultivated contemporary speech, before aspiring to the elevation of poetry. Another tenet was that the subject-matter and the imagery of poetry should be extended to topics and objects related to the life of a modern man or woman; that we were to seek the non-poetic, to seek even material refractory to transmutation into poetry, and words and phrases which had not been used in poetry before. And the study of Milton could be of no help: it was only a hindrance.

We cannot, in literature, any more than in the rest of life, live in a perpetual state of revolution. If every generation of poets made it their task to bring poetic diction up to date with the spoken language, poetry would fail in one of its most important obligations. For poetry should help, not only to refine the language of the time, but to prevent it from changing too rapidly: a development of language at too great a speed would be a development in the sense of a progressive deterioration, and that is our danger today. If the poetry of the rest of this century takes the line of development which seems to me, reviewing the progress of poetry through the last three centuries, the right course, it will discover new and more elaborate patterns of a diction now established. In this search it might have much to learn from Milton's extended verse structure; it might also avoid the danger of a *servitude* to colloquial speech and to current jargon. It might also learn that the music of verse is strongest in poetry which has a definite meaning expressed in the properest words. Poets might be led to admit that a knowledge of the literature of their own language, with a knowledge of the literature and the grammatical construction of other languages, is a very valuable part of the poet's equipment. And they might, as I have already hinted, devote some study to Milton as, outside the theatre, the greatest master in our language of freedom within form. A study of *Samson* should sharpen anyone's appreciation of the justified irregularity, and put him on guard against the pointless irregularity. In studying *Paradise Lost* we come to perceive that the verse is continuously animated by the departure from, and return to, the regular measure; and that, in comparison with Milton, hardly any subsequent writer of blank verse appears to exercise any freedom at all. We can also be led to the reflection that a monotony of unscannable verse fatigues the attention even more quickly than a monotony of exact feet. In short, it now seems to me that poets are sufficiently removed from Milton, and sufficiently liberated from his reputation, to approach the study of his work without danger, and with profit to their poetry and to the English language.

[*Milton*, 1947]

THE *PENSÉES* OF PASCAL

IT might seem that about Blaise Pascal, and about the two works on which his fame is founded, everything that there is to say had been said. The details of his life are as fully known as we can expect to know them; his mathematical and physical discoveries have been treated many times; his religious sentiment and his theological views have been discussed again and again; and his prose style has been analysed by French critics. But Pascal is one of those writers who will be and and who must be studied afresh by men in every generation. It is not he who changes, but we who change. It is not our knowledge of him that increases, but our world that alters and our attitudes towards it. The history of human opinions of Pascal and of men of his stature is a part of the history of humanity. That indicates his permanent importance.

The few facts of Pascal's life which need to be recalled in examining the *Pensées*, are as follows. He was born at Clermont in Auvergne in 1623. His family were people of substance of the upper middle class. His father was a government official, who was able to leave, when he died, a sufficient patrimony to his one son and his two daughters. In 1631 the father moved to Paris, and a few years later took up another government post at Rouen. Wherever he lived, the elder Pascal seems to have mingled with some of the best society, and with men of eminence in science and the arts. Blaise was educated entirely by his father at home. He was exceedingly precocious, indeed excessively precocious, for his application to studies in childhood and adolescence impaired his health and is held responsible for his death at thirty-nine. Prodigious though not incredible stories are preserved, especially of his precocity in mathematics. His mind was active rather than accumulative; he showed from his earliest years that disposition to find things out for himself, which has characterized the infancy of Clerk Maxwell and other scientists. Of his later discoveries in physics there is no need for mention here; it must only be remembered that he counts as one of the greatest physicists and mathematicians of all time; and that his discoveries were made during the years when most scientists are still apprentices.

The elder Pascal, Étienne, was a sincere Christian. About 1646 he fell in with some representatives of the religious revival within the Church which has become known as Jansenism – after Jansenius, Bishop of Ypres, whose theological work is taken as the origin of the movement. This period is usually spoken of as the movement of Pascal's 'first conversion'. The word 'conversion', however, is too forcible to be applied at this point to Blaise Pascal himself. The family had always been devout, and the younger Pascal, though absorbed in his scientific work, never seems to have been afflicted with infidelity. His attention was then directed, certainly, to religious and theological matters; but the term 'conversion' can only be applied to his sisters – the elder, already Madame Périer, and particularly the younger, Jacqueline, who at that time conceived a vocation for the religious life. Pascal himself was by no means disposed to renounce the world. After the death of the father in 1650 Jacqueline, a young woman of remarkable strength and beauty of character, wished to take her vows as a sister of Port-Royal, and for some time her wish remained unfulfilled owing to the opposition of her brother. His objection was on the purely worldly ground that she wished to make over her patrimony to the Order; whereas while she lived with him, their combined resources made it possible for him to live more nearly on a scale of expense congenial to his tastes. He liked, in fact, not only to mix with the best society, but to keep a coach and horses – six horses is the number at one time attributed to his carriage. Though he had no legal power to prevent his sister from disposing of her property as she elected the amiable Jacqueline shrank from doing so without her brother's willing approval. The Mother Superior, Mère Angélique – herself an eminent personage in the history of this religious movement – finally persuaded the young novice to enter the order without the satisfaction of bringing her patrimony with her; but Jacqueline remained so distressed by this situation that her brother finally relented.

So far as is known, the worldly life enjoyed by Pascal during this period can hardly be qualified as 'dissipation', and certainly not as 'debauchery'. Even gambling may have appealed to him chiefly as affording a study of mathematical probabilities. He appears to have led such a life as any cultivated intellectual man of good position and independent means might lead and consider himself a model of probity and virtue. Not even a love-affair is laid at his door, though he is said to have contemplated marriage. But Jansenism, as represented by the religious society of Port-Royal, was morally a Puritan movement within the Church, and its standards of conduct were at least as severe as those of any Puritanism in England or America. The period of fashionable society in Pascal's life is, however, of great importance in his development. It enlarged his knowledge of men and refined his tastes; he became a man of the world and never lost what he had learnt; and when he turned his thoughts wholly towards religion, his worldly knowledge was a part of his composition which is essential to the value of his work.

Pascal's interest in society did not distract him from scientific research; nor did this period occupy much space in what is a very short and crowded life. Partly his natural dissatisfaction with such a life, once he had learned all it had to teach him, partly the influence of his saintly sister Jacqueline, partly increasing suffering as his health declined, directed him more and more out of the world and to thoughts of eternity. And in 1654 occurs what is called his 'second conversion', but which might be called his conversion simply.

He made a note of his mystical experience, which he kept always about him, and which was found, after his death, sewn into the coat which he was wearing. The experience occurred on 23 November 1654, and there is no reason to doubt its genuineness unless we choose to deny all mystical experience. Now, Pascal was not a mystic, and his works are not to be classified amongst mystical writings; but what can only be called mystical experience happens to many men who do not become mystics. The work which he undertook soon after, the *Lettres écrites à un provincial*, is a masterpiece of religious controversy at the opposite pole from mysticism. We know quite well that he was at the time when he received his illumination from God in extremely poor health; but it is a commonplace that some forms of illness are extremely favourable, not only to religious illumination, but to artistic and literary composition. A piece of writing meditated, apparently without progress, for months or years, may suddenly take shape and word; and in this state long passages may be produced which require little or no retouch. I have no good word to say for the cultivation of automatic writing as the model of literary composition; I doubt whether these moments *can* be cultivated by the writer; but he to whom this happens assuredly has the sensation of being a vehicle rather than a maker. No masterpiece can be produced whole by such means: but neither does even the higher form of religious inspiration suffice for the religious life; even the most exalted mystic must return to the world, and use his reason to employ the results of his experience in daily life. You may call it communion with the Divine, or you may call it a temporary crystallization of the mind. Until science can teach us to reproduce such phenomena at will, science cannot claim to have explained them; and they can be judged only by their fruits.

From that time until his death, Pascal was closely associated with the society of Port-Royal which his sister Jacqueline, who predeceased him, had joined as a *religieuse*; the society was then fighting for its life against the Jesuits. Five propositions, judged by a committee of cardinals and theologians at Rome to be heretical, were found to be put forward in the work of Jansenius; and the society of Port-Royal, the representative of Jansenism among communities, suffered a blow from which it never revived. It is not the place here to review the bitter controversy and conflict; the best account, from the point of view of a critic of genius who took no side, who was neither Jansenist nor Jesuit, Christian nor infidel, is that in the great book of Sainte-Beuve, *Port-Royal*. And in this book the parts devoted to Pascal himself are among the most brilliant pages of crticism that Sainte-Beuve ever wrote. It is sufficient to notice that the next occupation of Pascal, after his conversion, was to write these eighteen *Letters*, which as prose are of capital importance in the foundation of French classical style, and which as polemic are surpassed by none, not by Demosthenes, or Cicero, or Swift. They have the limitation of all polemic and forensic: they persuade, they seduce, they are unfair. But it is also unfair to assert that, in these *Letters to a Provincial*, Pascal was attacking the Society of Jesus in itself. He was attacking rather a particular school of casuistry which relaxed the requirements of the Confessional; a school which certainly flourished amongst the Society of Jesus, at that time, and of which the Spaniards Escobar and Molina are the most eminent authorities. He undoubtedly abused the art of quotation, as a polemical writer is likely to do; but there were abuses for him to abuse; and he did the job thoroughly. His *Letters* must not be called theology. Academic theology was not a department in which Pascal was versed; when necessary, the fathers of Port-Royal came to his aid. The *Letters* are the work of one of the finest mathematical minds of any time, and of a man of the world who addressed, not theologians, but the world in general – all of the cultivated and many of the less cultivated of the French laity; and with this public they made an astonishing success.

During this time Pascal never wholly abandoned his scientific interests. Though in his religious writings he composed slowly and painfully, and revised often, in matters of mathematics his mind seemed to move with consummate natural ease and grace. Discoveries and inventions sprang from his brain without effort; among the minor devices of this later period, the first omnibus service in Paris is said to owe its origin to his inventiveness. But rapidly failing health, and absorption in the great work he had in mind, left him little time and energy during the last two years of his life.

The plan of what we call the *Pensées* formed itself about 1660. The completed book was to have been a carefully constructed defence of Christianity, a true Apology and a kind of Grammar of Assent, setting forth the reasons which will convince the intellect. As I have indicated before Pascal was not a theologian, and on dogmatic theology had recourse to his spiritual advisers. Nor was he indeed a systematic philosopher. He was a man with an immense genius for science, and at the same time a natural psychologist and moralist. As he was a great literary artist, his book would have been also his own spiritual autobiography; his style, free from all diminishing idiosyncrasies, was yet very personal. Above all, he was a man of strong passions; and his intellectual passion for truth was reinforced by his passionate dissatisfaction with human life unless a spiritual explanation could be found.

We must regard the *Pensées* as merely the first notes for a work which he left far from completion; we have, in Sainte-Beuve's words, a tower of which the stones have been laid on each other, but not cemented, and the structure unfinished. In early years his memory had been amazingly retentive of anything that he wished to remember; and had it not been impaired by increasing illness and pain, he probably would not have been obliged to set down these notes at all. But taking the book as it is left to us, we still find that it occupies a unique place in the history of French literature and in the history of religious meditation.

To understand the method which Pascal employs, the reader must be prepared to follow the process of the mind of the intelligent believer. The Christian thinker – and I mean the man who is trying consciously and conscientiously to explain to himself the sequence which culminates in faith, rather than the public apologist – proceeds by rejection and elimination. He finds the world to be so and so; he finds its character inexplicable by any non-religious theory: among religions he finds Christianity, and Catholic Christianity, to account most satisfactorily for the world and especially for the moral world within; and thus, by what Newman calls 'powerful and concurrent' reasons, he finds himself inexorably committed to the dogma of the Incarnation. To the unbeliever, this method seems disingenuous and perverse: for the unbeliever is, as a rule, not so greatly troubled to explain the world to himself, nor so greatly distressed by its disorder; nor is he generally concerned (in modern terms) to 'preserve values'. He does not consider that if certain emotional states, certain developments of character, and what in the highest sense can be called 'saintliness' are inherently and by inspection known to be good, then the satisfactory explanation of the world must be an explanation which will admit the 'reality' of these values. Nor does he consider such reasoning admissible; he would, so to speak, trim his values according to his cloth, because to him such values are of no great value. The unbeliever starts from the other end, and as like as not with the question: Is a case of human parthenogenesis credible? and this he would call going straight to the heart of the matter. Now Pascal's method is, on the whole, the method natural and right for the Christian; and the opposite method is that taken by Voltaire. It is worth while to remember that Voltaire, in his attempt to refute Pascal, has given once and for all the type of such refutation; and that later opponents of Pascal's Apology for the Christian Faith have contributed little beyond psychological irrelevancies. For Voltaire has presented, better than anyone since, what is the unbelieving point of view; and in the end we must all choose for ourselves between one point of view and another.

I have said above that Pascal's method is 'on the whole' that of the typical Christian apologist; and this reservation was directed at Pascal's belief in miracles, which plays a larger part in his construction than it would in that, at least, of the modern Catholic. It would seem fantastic to accept Christianity because we first believe the Gospel miracles to be true, and it would seem impious to accept it primarily because we believe more recent miracles to be true; we accept the miracles, or some miracles, to be true because we believe the Gospel of Jesus Christ: we found our belief in the miracles on the Gospel, not our belief in the Gospel on the miracles.

But it must be remembered that Pascal had been deeply impressed by a contemporary miracle, known as the miracle of the Holy Thorn: a thorn reputed to have been preserved from the Crown of Our Lord was pressed upon an ulcer which quickly healed. Sainte-Beuve, who as a medical man felt himself on solid ground, discusses fully the possible explanation of this apparent miracle. It is true that the miracle happened at Port-Royal, and that it arrived opportunely to revive the depressed spirits of the community in its political afflictions; and it is likely that Pascal was the more inclined to believe a miracle which was performed upon his beloved sister. In any case, it probably led him to assign a place to miracles, in his study of faith, which is not quite that which we should give to them ourselves.

Now the great adversary against whom Pascal set himself, from the time of his first conversations with M. de Saci at Port-Royal, was Montaigne. One cannot destroy Pascal, certainly; but of all authors Montaigne is one of the least destructible. You could as well dissipate a fog by flinging hand-grenades into it. For Montaigne is a fog, a gas, a fluid, insidious element. He does not reason, he insinuates, charms, and influences; or if he reasons, you must be prepared for his having some other design upon you than to convince you by his argument. It is hardly too much to say that Montaigne is the most essential author to know, if we would understand the course of French thought during the last 300 years. In every way, the influence of Montaigne was repugnant to the men of Port-Royal. Pascal studied him with the intention of demolishing him. Yet, in the *Pensées*, at the very end of his life, we find passage after passage, and the slighter they are the more significant, almost 'lifted' out of Montaigne, down to a figure of speech or a word. The parallels are most often with the long essay of Montaigne called *Apologie de Raymond Sebond* – an astonishing piece of writing upon which Shakespeare also probably drew in *Hamlet*.* Indeed by the time a man knew Montaigne well enough to attack him, he would already be thoroughly infected by him.

It would, however, be grossly unfair to Pascal, to Montaigne, and indeed to French literature, to leave the matter at that. It is no

* See p. 103 above. [*Editor's note*]

diminution of Pascal, but only an aggrandizement of Montaigne. Had Montaigne been an ordinary life-sized sceptic, a small man like Anatole France, or even a greater man like Renan, or even like the greatest sceptic of all, Voltaire, this 'influence' would be to the discredit of Pascal; but if Montaigne had been no more than Voltaire, he could not have affected Pascal at all. The picture of Montaigne which offers itself first to our eyes, that of the original and independent solitary 'personality', absorbed in amused analysis of himself, is deceptive. Montaigne's is no *limited* Pyrrhonism, like that of Voltaire, Renan, or France. He exists, so to speak, on a plane of numerous concentric circles, the most apparent of which is the small inmost circle, a personal puckish scepticism which can be easily aped if not imitated. But what makes Montaigne a very great figure is that he succeeded, God knows how – for Montaigne very likely did not know that he had done it – it is not the sort of thing that men *can* observe about themselves, for it is essentially bigger than the individual's consciousness – he succeeded in giving expression to the scepticism of *every* human being. For every man who thinks and lives by thought must have his own scepticism, that which stops at the question, that which ends in denial, or that which leads to faith and which is somehow integrated into the faith which transcends it. And Pascal, as the type of one kind of religious believer, which is highly passionate and ardent, but passionate only through a powerful and regulated intellect, is in the first sections of his unfinished Apology for Christianity facing unflinchingly the demon of doubt which is inseparable from the spirit of belief.

There is accordingly something quite different from an influence which would prove Pascal's weakness; there is a real affinity between his doubt and that of Montaigne; and through the common kinship with Montaigne Pascal is related to the noble and distinguished line of French moralists, from La Rochefoucauld down. In the honesty with which they face the *données* of the actual world this French tradition has a unique quality in European literature, and in the seventeenth century Hobbes is crude in comparison.

Pascal is a man of the world among ascetics, and an ascetic among men of the world; he had the knowledge of worldliness and the passion of asceticism, and in him the two are fused into an individual whole. The majority of mankind is lazy-minded, incurious, absorbed in vanities, and tepid in emotion, and is therefore incapable of either much doubt or much faith; and when the ordinary man calls himself a sceptic or an unbeliever, that is ordinarily a simple pose, cloaking a disinclination to think anything out to a conclusion. Pascal's disillusioned analysis of human bondage is sometimes interpreted to mean that Pascal was really and finally an unbeliever, who, in his despair, was incapable of enduring reality and enjoying the heroic satisfaction of the free man's worship of nothing. His despair, his disillusion, are, however, no illustration of personal weakness; they are perfectly objective, because they are essential moments in the progress of the intellectual soul; and for the type of Pascal they are the analogue of the drought, the dark night, which is an essential stage in the progress of the Christian mystic. A similar despair, when it is arrived at by a diseased character or an impure soul, may issue in the most disastrous consequences though with the most superb manifestations; and thus we get *Gulliver's Travels*; but in Pascal we find no such distortion; his despair is in itself more terrible than Swift's, because our heart tells us that it corresponds exactly to the facts and cannot be dismissed as mental disease; but it was also a despair which was a necessary prelude to, and element in, the joy of faith.

I do not wish to enter any further than necessary upon the question of the heterodoxy of Jansenism; and it is no concern of this essay whether the Five Propositions condemned at Rome were really maintained by Jansenius in his book *Augustinus*, or whether we should deplore or approve the consequent decay (indeed with some persecution) of Port-Royal. It is impossible to discuss the matter without becoming involved as a controversialist either for or against Rome. But in a man of the type of Pascal – and the type always exists – there is, I think, an ingredient of what may be called Jansenism of temperament, without identifying it with the Jansenism of Jansenius and of other devout and sincere but not immensely gifted doctors. It is accordingly needful to state in brief what the dangerous doctrine of Jansenius was, without advancing too far into theological refinements. It is recognized in Christian theology – and indeed on a lower plane it is recognized by all men in affairs of daily life – that free-will of the natural effort and ability of the individual man and also supernatural *grace*, a gift accorded we know not quite how, are both required, in cooperation, for salvation. Though numerous theologians have set their wits at the problem, it ends in a mystery which we can perceive but not finally decipher. At least, it is obvious that, like any doctrine, a slight excess or deviation to one side or the other will precipitate a heresy. The Pelagians, who were refuted by St Augustine, emphasized the efficacy of human effort and belittled the importance of supernatural grace. The Calvinists emphasized the degradation of man through Original Sin, and considered mankind so corrupt that the will was of no avail; and thus fell into the doctrine of predestination. It was upon the doctrine of grace according to St Augustine that the Jansenists relied; and the *Augustinus* of Jansenius was presented as a sound exposition of the Augustinian views.

Heresies are never antiquated, because they forever assume new forms. For instance, the insistence upon good works and 'service' which is preached from many quarters, or the simple faith that anyone who lives a good and useful life need have no 'morbid' anxieties about salvation, is a form of Pelagianism. On the other hand, one sometimes hears enounced the view that it will make no real difference if all the traditional religious sanctions for moral behaviour break down, because those who are born and bred to be nice people will always prefer to behave nicely, and those who are not will behave otherwise in any case: and this is surely a form of predestination – for the hazard of being born a nice person or not is as uncertain as the gift of grace.

It is likely that Pascal was attracted as much by the fruits of Jansenism in the life of Port-Royal as by the doctrine itself. This devout, ascetic, thoroughgoing society, striving heroically in the midst of a relaxed and easy-going Christianity, was formed to attract a nature so concentrated, so passionate, and so thoroughgoing as Pascal's. But the insistence upon the degraded and helpless state of man, in Jansenism, is something also to which we must be grateful, for to it we owe the magnificent analysis of human motives and occupations which was to have constituted the early part of his book. And apart from the Jansenism which is the work of a not very eminent bishop who wrote a Latin treatise which is now unread, there is also, so to speak, a Jansenism of the individual biography. A moment of Jansenism may naturally take place, and take place rightly, in the individual; particularly in the life of a man of great and intense intellectual powers, who cannot avoid seeing through human beings and observing the vanity of their thoughts and of their avocations, their dishonesty and self-deception, the insincerity of their emotions, their cowardice, the pettiness of their real ambitions.* Actually, considering that much greater maturity is required for these qualities, than for any mathematical or scientific greatness, how easily his brooding on *the misery of man without God* might have encouraged in him the sin of spiritual pride, the *concupiscence de l'esprit:* and how fast a hold he has of humility!

And although Pascal brings to his work the same powers which he exerted in science, it is not as a scientist that he presents himself. He does not seem to say to the reader: I am one of the most distinguished scientists of the day: I understand many matters which will always be mysteries to you, and through science I have come to the Faith; you therefore who are not initiated into science ought to have faith if I have it. He is fully aware of the difference of subject-matter; and his famous distinction between the *esprit de géométrie* and the *esprit de finesse* is one to ponder over.

En l'un, les principes sont palpables, mais éloignés de l'usage commun; de sorte qu'on a peine à tourner la tête de ce côté-là, manque d'habitude: mais pour peu qu'on l'y tourne, on voit les principes à plein; et il faudrait avoir tout à fait l'esprit faux pour

---

* Cette négligence en une affaire où il s'agit d'eux-mêmes, de leur éternité, de leur tout, m'irrite plus qu'elle ne m'attendrit; elle m'étonne et m'épouvante, c'est un monstre pour moi. Je ne dis pas ceci par le zèle pieux d'une dévotion spirituelle. J'entends au contraire qu'on doit avoir ce sentiment par un principe d'intérêt humain et par un intérêt d'amour-propre: il ne faut pour cela que voir ce que voient les personnes les moins éclairées. *Pensées*, ed. Massis, p. 29. [*Author's note*]

mal raisonner sur des principes si gros qu'il est presque impossible qu'ils échappent.

Mais dans l'esprit de finesse, les principes sont dans l'usage commun et devant les yeux de tout le monde. On n'a que faire de tourner la tête, ni de se faire violence; il n'est question que d'avoir bonne vue, mais il faut l'avoir bonne; car les principes sont si déliés et en si grand nombre, qu'il est presque impossible qu'il n'en échappe. Or, l'omission d'un principe mène à l'erreur; ainsi, il faut avoir la vue bien nette pour tous les principes, et ensuite l'esprit juste pour ne pas raisonner faussement sur des principes connus.

It is the just combination of the scientist, the *honnête homme*, and the religious nature with a passionate craving for God that makes Pascal unique. He succeeds where Descartes fails; for in Descartes the element of *esprit de géométrie* is excessive. And in a few phrases about Descartes, in the present book, Pascal laid his finger on the place of weakness.

Je ne puis pardonner à Descartes; il aurait bien voulu, dans toute sa philosophie, se pouvoir passer de Dieu; mais il n'a pu s'empêcher de lui faire donner une chiquenaude, pour mettre le monde en mouvement; après cela, il n'a plus que faire de Dieu.

He who reads this book [Pascal's *Pensées*] will observe at once its fragmentary nature; but only after some study will perceive that the fragmentariness lies in the expression more than in the thought. The 'thoughts' cannot be detached from each other and quoted as if each were complete in itself. *Le cœur a ses raisons que la raison ne connaît point,* how often one has heard that quoted, and quoted often to the wrong purpose.* For this is by no means an exaltation of the 'heart' over the 'head', a defence of unreason. The heart, in Pascal's terminology, is itself truly rational if it is truly the heart. For him, in theological matters which seemed to him much larger, more difficult, and more important than scientific matters, the whole personality is involved.

* And those who have quoted *C'est là ma place au soleil* have often forgotten to add *Voilà le commencement et l'image de l'usurpation de toute la terre.* [*Author's note*]

We cannot quite understand any of the parts, fragmentary as they are, without some understanding of the whole. Capital, for instance, is his analysis of the *three orders*: the order of nature, the order of mind, and the order of charity. These three are *discontinuous*; the higher is not implicit in the lower as in an evolutionary doctrine it would be. In this distinction Pascal offers much about which the modern world would do well to think. And indeed, because of his unique combination and balance of qualities, I know of no religious writer more pertinent to our time. The great mystics, like St John of the Cross, are primarily for readers with a special determination of purpose; the devotional writers, such as St François de Sales, are primarily for those who already feel consciously desirous of the love of God; the great theologians are for those interested in theology. But I can think of no Christian writer, not Newman even, more to be commended than Pascal to those who doubt, but who have the mind to conceive, and the sensibility to feel, the disorder, the futility, the meaninglessness, the mystery of life and suffering, and who can only find peace through a satisfaction of the whole being.

[Introduction to Pascal's *Pensées* (Everyman's Library), 1931]

EIGHTEENTH-CENTURY POETRY

IT is as dangerous to generalize about the poetry of the eighteenth century as about that of any other age; for it was, like any other age, an age of transition. We are accustomed to make a rough tri-partite division between the poetry of the age of Pope, the poetry of sentimental philosophizing – Thomson, Young, Cowper – and the early Romantic movement. What really happened is that after Pope there was no one who thought and felt nearly enough like Pope to be able to use his language quite successfully; but a good many second-rate writers tried to write something like it, unaware of the fact that the change of sensibility demanded a change of idiom. Sensibility alters from generation to generation in everybody, whether we will or no; but expression is only altered by a man of genius. A great many second-rate poets, in fact, are second-rate just for this reason, that they have not the sensitiveness and consciousness to perceive that they feel differently from the preceding generation, and therefore must use words differently. In the eighteenth century there are a good many second-rate poets: and mostly they are second-rate because they were incompetent to find a style of writing for themselves, suited to the matter they wanted to talk about and the way in which they apprehended this matter.

In such a period the poets who are still worth reading may be of two kinds: those who, however imperfectly, attempted innovations in idiom, and those who were just conservative enough in sensibility to be able to devise an interesting variation on the old idiom. The originality of Grey and Collins consists in their adaptation of an Augustan style to an eighteenth-century sensibility. The originality of Goldsmith consists in his having the old and the new in such just proportion that there is no conflict; he is Augustan and also sentimental and rural without discordance. Of all the eighteenth-century poets, Johnson is the nearest to a diehard. And of all the eighteenth-century poets, Goldsmith and Johnson deserve fame because they used the form of Pope beautifully, without ever being mere imitators. And from the point of view of the artisan of verse, their kind of originality is as remarkable as any other: indeed, to be original with the *minimum* of alteration, is sometimes more distinguished than to be original with the *maximum* of alteration.

Certain qualities are to be expected of any type of good verse at any time; we may say the qualities which good verse shares with good prose. Hardly any good poet in English has written *bad* prose; and some English poets have been among the greatest of English prose writers. The finest prose writer of Shakespeare's time was, I think, Shakespeare himself; Milton and Dryden were among the greatest prose writers of their times. Wordsworth and Coleridge may be cited, and Keats; and Shelley – not I think in his correspondence, but certainly in his *Defence of Poetry*. This is not a sign of versatility but of unity. For there are qualities essential to good prose which are essential to good verse as well; and we may say positively with Ezra Pound, that verse must be at least as well written as prose. We may even say that the originality of some poets has consisted in their finding a way of saying in verse what no one else had been able to say except in prose written or spoken. Such is the originality of Donne, who, though employing an elaborate metric and an uncommon vocabulary, yet manages to maintain a tone of direct informal address. The talent of Dryden is exactly the same: the difference is only that the speech which he uses is that of a more formal age. Donne makes poetry out of a learned but colloquial dialogue speech, Dryden out of the prose of political oratory; and Pope out of the most polished drawing-room manner. And of Goldsmith and Johnson we can say the same; their verse is poetry partly because it has the virtues of good prose.

Those who condemn or ignore *en bloc* the poetry of the eighteenth century on the ground that it is 'prosaic' are stumbling over an uncertainty of meaning of the word 'prosaic' to arrive at exactly the wrong conclusion. One does not need to examine a great deal of the inferior verse of the eighteenth century to realize that the trouble with it is that it is not prosaic enough. We are inclined to use 'prosaic' as meaning not only 'like prose', but as 'lacking poetic beauty' – and the Oxford and every other dictionary give us warrant for such use. Only, we ought to distinguish between poetry which is like *good* prose, and poetry which is like *bad* prose. And even so, I believe more prose is bad because it is like bad poetry, than poetry is bad because it is like bad prose. And to have the virtues of good prose is the first and minimum requirement of good poetry.

If you look at the bad verse of any age, you will find most of it lacking in the virtues of prose. When there is a period of good verse, it has often been preceded by a period in which verse was bad because it was too poetic, too artificial; and it is very commonly followed by such another period. The development of blank verse in the hands of Shakespeare and some of his contemporaries was the work of adapting a medium which to begin with was almost intractably poetic, so that it could carry the burdens and exhibit the subtleties of prose; and they accomplished this before prose itself was highly developed. The work of Donne, in a lesser form, was the same. It has prose virtues, and the heavy toil of his minor imitators was wholly to degrade the idiom of Donne into a lifeless verse convention. Speech meanwhile was changing, and Dryden appeared to cleanse the language of verse and once more bring it back to the prose order. For this reason he is a great poet.

The idiom of the Augustan age could not last, for the age itself could not last. But so positive was the culture of that age, that for many years the ablest writers were still naturally in sympathy with it; and it crushed a number of smaller men who felt differently but did not dare to face the fact, and who poured their new wine – always thin, but sometimes of good flavour – into the old bottles. Yet the influence of Dryden and Pope over the middle of the eighteenth century is by no means so great, or so noxious, as has been supposed. A good part of the dreariest verse of the time is written under the shadow of Milton.

> *Far in the watery waste, where his broad wave*
> *From world to world the vast Atlantic rolls,*
> *On from the piny shores of Labrador*
> *To frozen Thule east, her airy height*
> *Aloft to heaven remotest Kilda lifts.*
>
> [Mallet: *Amyntor and Theodora*]

> *Thus far of beauty and the pleasing forms*
> *Which man's untutored fancy, from the scenes*
> *Imperfect of this ever changing world*
> *Creates; and views, enamoured.*
>
> [Akenside: *Pleasures of the Imagination*]

But besides this Miltonic stuff, which is respectable only because Cowper, Thomson, and Young made this line the vehicle for reflection and for observation of nature which prepared the way for Wordsworth; and besides the innumerable Odes, of which none but Gray's and Collins's are remembered, there was a considerable output of five foot couplets of which one can only say that this form of verse is hardly more unsuitable for what the man had to say than any other would have been. Of such is the *Botanic Garden* and its competitors.

Who that beholds the summer's glistening swarms,
Ten thousand thousand gaily gilded forms,
In violent dance of mixed rotation play,
Bask in the beam, and beautify the day.

[Brooke: *Universal Beauty*]

This is decadence. The eighteenth century in English verse is not, after Pope, Swift, Prior, and Gay, an age of courtly verse. It seems more like an age of retired country clergymen and schoolmasters. It is cursed with a Pastoral convention – Collins's Eclogues are bad enough, and those of Shenstone consummately dull – and a ruminative mind. And it is intolerably poetic. Instead of working out the proper form for its matter, when it has any, and informing verse with prose virtues, it merely applies the magniloquence of Milton or the neatness of Pope to matter which is wholly unprepared for it; so that what the writers have to say always appears surprised at the way in which they choose to say it.

In this rural, pastoral, meditative age Johnson is the most alien figure. Goldsmith is more a poet of his time, with his melting sentiment just saved by the precision of his language. But Johnson remains a townsman, if certainly not a courtier; a student of mankind not of natural history; a great prose writer; with no tolerance of swains and milkmaids. He has more in common in spirit with Crabbe than with any of his contemporaries; at the same time he is the last Augustan. He is in no way an imitator of Dryden or Pope; very close to them in idiom, he gives his verse a wholly personal stamp....

In one way, Johnson goes back to an earlier tradition; however inferior as satires Marston's or even Hall's may be to Johnson's, they are surely much nearer to the spirit of Juvenal than are those of Dryden or Pope. Dryden is, in the modern sense, humorous and witty; Pope is, in the modern sense, witty though not humorous; Johnson, neither humorous nor witty in this sense, has yet 'the proper wit of poetry', as the seventeenth century and the Augustan age had it also. I can better expose this by a few quotations than by a definition.

There mark what ills the scholar's life assail,
Toil, envy, want, the patron, and the jail.

Condemned a needy supplicant to wait,
While ladies interpose, and slaves debate.

Fate never wounds more deep the generous heart,
Than when a blockhead's insult point the dart.

Some fiery fop, with new commission vain,
Who sleeps on brambles till he kills his man;
Some frolick drunkard, reeling, from a feast,
Provokes a broil, and stabs you for a jest.

The precision of such verse gives, I think, an immense satisfaction to the reader; he has said what he wanted to say, with that urbanity which contemporary verse would do well to study; and the satisfaction I get from such lines is what I call the *minimal* quality of poetry. There is much greater poetry than Johnson's; but after all, how little, how very little, good poetry there is anyway. And the kind of satisfaction these lines give me is something that I must have, at least, from any poetry in order to like it. . . .

Those who demand of poetry a day-dream, or a metamorphosis of their own feeble desires and lusts, or what they believe to be 'intensity' of passion, will not find much in Johnson. He is like Pope and Dryden, Crabbe and Landor, a poet for those who want poetry and not something else, some stay for their own vanity.

[From an Introductory Essay to Johnson's
London: A Poem and *The Vanity of Human Wishes*, 1930]

BLAKE

If one follows Blake's mind through the several stages of his poetic development it is impossible to regard him as a naïf, a wild man, a wild pet for the supercultivated. The strangeness is evaporated, the peculiarity is seen to be the peculiarity of all great poetry: something which is found (not everywhere) in Homer and Aeschylus and

Dante and Villon, and profound and concealed in the work of Shakespeare – and also in another form in Montaigne and in Spinoza. It is merely a peculiar honesty, which, in a world too frightened to be honest, is peculiarly terrifying. It is an honesty against which the whole world conspires, because it is unpleasant. Blake's poetry has the unpleasantness of great poetry. Nothing that can be called morbid or abnormal or perverse, none of the things which exemplify the sickness of an epoch or a fashion, has this quality; only those things which, by some extraordinary labour of simplification, exhibit the essential sickness or strength of the human soul. And this honesty never exists without great technical accomplishment. The question about Blake the man is the question of the circumstances that concurred to permit this honesty in his work, and what circumstances define its limitations. The favouring conditions probably include these two : that, being early apprenticed to a manual occupation, he was not compelled to acquire any other education in literature than he wanted, or to acquire it for any other reason than that he wanted it; and that, being a humble engraver, he had no journalistic–social career open to him.

There was, that is to say, nothing to distract him from his interests or to corrupt these interests: neither the ambitions of parents or wife, nor the standards of society, nor the temptations of success; nor was he exposed to imitation of himself or of anyone else. These circumstances – not his supposed inspired and untaught spontaneity – are what make him innocent.

The *Songs of Innocence and of Experience*, and the poems from the Rossetti manuscript, are the poems of a man with a profound interest in human emotions, and a profound knowledge of them. The emotions are presented in an extremely simplified, abstract form. This form is one illustration of the eternal struggle of art against education, of the literary artist against the continuous deterioration of language.

It is important that the artist should be highly educated in his own art; but his education is one that is hindered rather than helped by the ordinary processes of society which constitute education for the ordinary man. For these processes consist largely in the acquisition of impersonal ideas which obscure what we really are and feel, what we really want, and what really excites our interest. It is of course not the actual information acquired, but the conformity which the accumulation of knowledge is apt to impose, that is harmful. Tennyson is a very fair example of a poet almost wholly encrusted with opinion, almost wholly merged into his environment. Blake, on the other hand, knew what interested him, and he therefore presents only the essential, only, in fact, what can be presented, and need not be explained. And because he was not distracted, or frightened, or occupied in anything but exact statements, he understood. He was naked, and saw man naked, and from the centre of his own crystal. To him there was no more reason why Swedenborg should be absurd than Locke. He accepted Swedenborg, and eventually rejected him, for reasons of his own. He approached everything with a mind unclouded by current opinions. There was nothing of the superior person about him. This makes him terrifying.

*

We have the same respect for Blake's philosophy (and perhaps for that of Samuel Butler) that we have for an ingenious piece of home-made furniture: we admire the man who has put it together out of the odds and ends about the house. England has produced a fair number of these resourceful Robinson Crusoes; but we are not really so remote from the Continent, or from our own past, as to be deprived of the advantages of culture if we wish them.

We may speculate, for amusement, whether it would not have been beneficial to the north of Europe generally, and to Britain in particular, to have had a more continuous religious history. The local divinities of Italy were not wholly exterminated by Christianity, and they were not reduced to the dwarfish fate which fell upon our trolls and pixies. The latter, with the major Saxon deities, were perhaps no great loss in themselves, but they left an empty place; and perhaps our mythology was further impoverished by the divorce from Rome. Milton's celestial and infernal regions are large but insufficiently furnished apartments filled by heavy conversation; and one remarks about the Puritan mythology its thinness. And about

Blake's supernatural territories, as about the supposed ideas that dwell there, we cannot help commenting on a certain meanness of culture. They illustrate the crankiness, the eccentricity, which frequently affects writers outside of the Latin traditions, and which such a critic as Arnold should certainly have rebuked. And they are not essential to Blake's inspiration.

Blake was endowed with a capacity for considerable understanding of human nature, with a remarkable and original sense of language and the music of language, and a gift of hallucinated vision. Had these been controlled by a respect for impersonal reason, for common sense, for the objectivity of science, it would have been better for him. What his genius required, and what it sadly lacked, was a framework of accepted and traditional ideas which would have prevented him from indulging in a philosophy of his own, and concentrated his attention upon the problems of the poet. Confusion of thought, emotion, and vision is what we find in such a work as *Also Sprach Zarathustra*; it is eminently not a Latin virtue. The concentration resulting from a framework of mythology and theology and philosophy is one of the reasons why Dante is a classic, and Blake only a poet of genius. The fault is perhaps not with Blake himself, but with the environment which failed to provide what such a poet needed; perhaps the circumstances compelled him to fabricate, perhaps the poet required the philosopher and mythologist; although the conscious Blake may have been quite unconscious of the motives.

[From 'William Blake', 1920]

COLERIDGE

COLERIDGE was one of those unhappy persons – Donne, I suspect, was such another – of whom one might say, that if they had not been poets, they might have made something of their lives, might even have had a career; or conversely, that if they had not been interested in so many things, crossed by such diverse passions, they might have been great poets. It was better for Coleridge, as poet, to read books of travel and exploration than to read books of metaphysics and political economy. He did genuinely want to read books of metaphysics and political economy, for he had a certain talent for such subjects. But for a few years he had been visited by the Muse (I know of no poet to whom this hackneyed metaphor is better applicable) and thenceforth was a haunted man; for anyone who has ever been visited by the Muse is thenceforth haunted. He had no vocation for the religious life, for there again somebody like a Muse, or a much higher being, is to be invoked; he was condemned to know that the little poetry he had written was worth more than all he could do with the rest of his life. The author of *Biographia Literaria* was already a ruined man. Sometimes, however, to be a 'ruined man' is itself a vocation.

[From *The Use of Poetry and the Use of Criticism*, 1933]

WORDSWORTH

It would appear that the revolution effected by Wordsworth was very far-reaching indeed. He was not the first poet to present himself as the inspired prophet, nor indeed is this quite Wordsworth's case. Blake may have pretended, and with some claim, to have penetrated mysteries of heaven and hell, but no claim that Blake might make seems to descend upon the 'poet' in general; Blake simply had the visions, and made use of poetry to set them forth. Scott, and Byron in his more popular works, were merely society entertainers. Wordsworth is really the first, in the unsettled state of affairs in his time, to annex new authority for the poet, to meddle with social affairs, and to offer a new kind of religious sentiment which it seemed the peculiar prerogative of the poet to interpret. Since Matthew Arnold made his Selections from Wordsworth's poetry, it has become a commonplace to observe that Wordsworth's true greatness as poet is independent of his opinions, of his theory of diction or of his nature-philosophy, and that it is found in poems in which he has no ulterior motive whatever. I am not sure that this critical eclecticism cannot go too far; that we can judge and enjoy a man's poetry while leaving wholly out of account all of the things for which he cared deeply, and on behalf of which he turned his poetry to account. If we dismiss Wordsworth's interests and beliefs, just how much, I wonder, remains? To retain them, or to keep them in mind instead of deliberately extruding them in preparation for enjoying his poetry, is that not necessary to appreciate how great a poet Wordsworth really is? Consider, for instance, one of the very finest poets of the first part of the nineteenth century: Landor. He is an undoubted master of verse and prose; he is the author of at least one long poem which deserves to be much more read than it is; but his reputation has never been such as to bring him into comparison with Wordsworth or with either of the younger poets with whom we have now to deal. It is not only by reason of a handful of poems or a number of isolated lines expressive of deeper emotion than that of which Landor was capable, that we give Wordsworth his place; there is something integral about such greatness, and something significant in his place in the pattern of history, with which we have to reckon. And in estimating for ourselves the greatness of a poet we have to take into account also the *history* of his greatness. Wordsworth is an essential part of history; Landor only a magnificent by-product.

[From *The Use of Poetry and the Use of Criticism*, 1933]

ARNOLD

ARNOLD was not a man of vast or exact scholarship, and he had neither walked in hell nor been rapt to heaven; but what he did know, of books and men, was in its way well-balanced and well-marshalled. After the prophetic frenzies of the end of the eighteenth and the beginning of the nineteenth century, he seems to come to us saying: 'This poetry is very fine, it is opulent and careless, it is sometimes profound, it is highly original; but you will never establish and maintain a tradition if you go on in this haphazard way. There are minor virtues which have flourished better at other times and in other countries: these you must give heed to, these you must apply, in your poetry, in your prose, in your conversation and your way of living; else you condemn yourselves to enjoy only fitful and transient bursts of literary brilliance, and you will never as a people, a nation, a race, have a fully formed tradition and personality.' However well-nourished we may be on previous literature and previous culture, we cannot afford to neglect Arnold.

I have elsewhere tried to point out some of Arnold's weaknesses when he ventured into departments of thought for which his mind was unsuited and ill-equipped. In philosophy and theology he was an undergraduate; in religion a Philistine. It is a pleasanter task to define a man's limitations within the field in which he is qualified; for there, the definition of limitation may be at the same time a precision of the writer's excellences. Arnold's poetry has little technical interest. It is academic poetry in the best sense; the best fruit which can issue from the promise shown by the prize-poem. When he is not simply being himself, he is most at ease in a master's gown: 'Empedocles on Etna' is one of the finest academic poems ever written. He tried other robes which become him less well; I cannot but think of 'Tristram and Iseult' and 'The Forsaken Merman' as charades. 'Sohrab and Rustum' is a fine piece, but less fine than *Gebir*; and in the classical line Landor, with a finer ear, can beat Arnold every time. But Arnold is a poet to whom one readily returns. It is a pleasure, certainly after associating with the riff-raff of the early part of the century, to be in the company of a man *qui sait se conduire*, but Arnold is something more than an agreeable Professor of Poetry. With all his fastidiousness and superciliousness and officiality, Arnold is more intimate with us than Browning, more intimate than Tennyson ever is except at moments, as in the passionate flights in *In Memoriam*. He is the poet and critic of a period of false stability. All his writing in the kind of *Literature and Dogma* seems to me a valiant attempt to dodge the issue, to mediate between Newman and Huxley; but his poetry, the best of it, is too honest to employ any but his genuine feelings of unrest, loneliness, and dissatisfaction. Some of his limitations are manifest enough. In his essay on 'The Study of Poetry' he has several paragraphs on Burns, and for an Englishman and an Englishman of his time, Arnold understands Burns very well. Perhaps I have a partiality for small oppressed nationalities like the Scots that makes Arnold's patronizing manner irritate me; and certainly I suspect Arnold of helping to fix the wholly mistaken notion of Burns as a singular untutored English dialect poet, instead of as a decadent representative of a great alien tradition. But he says (taking occasion to rebuke the country in which Burns lived) that 'no one can deny that it is of advantage to a poet to deal with a beautiful world'; and this remark strikes me as betraying a limitation. It is an advantage to mankind in general to live in a beautiful world; that no one can doubt. But for the poet is it so important? We mean all sorts of things, I know, by Beauty. But the essential advantage for a poet is not to have a beautiful world with which to deal: it is to be able to see beneath both beauty and ugliness; to see the boredom, and the horror, and the glory.

[From *The Use of Poetry and the Use of Criticism*, 1933]

TENNYSON'S *IN MEMORIAM*

TENNYSON is a great poet, for reasons that are perfectly clear. He has three qualities which are seldom found together except in the greatest poets: abundance, variety, and complete competence. We therefore cannot appreciate his work unless we read a good deal of it. We may not admire his aims: but whatever he sets out to do, he succeeds in doing, with a mastery which gives us the sense of confidence that is one of the major pleasures of poetry. His variety of metrical accomplishment is astonishing. Without making the mistake of trying to write Latin verse in English, he knew everything about Latin versification that an English poet could use; and he said of himself that he thought he knew the quantity of the sounds of every English word except perhaps *scissors*. He had the finest ear of any English poet since Milton. He was the master of Swinburne; and the versification of Swinburne, himself a classical scholar, is often crude and sometimes cheap in comparison with Tennyson's. Tennyson extended very widely the range of active metrical forms in English: in *Maud* alone the variety is prodigious. But innovation in metric is not to be measured solely by the width of the deviation from accepted practice. It is a matter of the historical situation: at some moments a more violent change may be necessary than at others. The problem differs at every period. At some times, a violent revolution may be neither possible nor desirable; at such times, a change which may appear very slight is the change which the important poet will make. The innovation of Pope, after Dryden, may not seem very great; but it is the mark of the master to be able to make small changes which will be highly significant, as at another time to make radical changes, through which poetry will curve back again to its norm.

*

The reading of long poems is not nowadays much practised: in the age of Tennyson it appears to have been easier. For a good many long poems were not only written but widely circulated; and the level was high: even the second-rate long poems of that time, like *The Light of Asia*, are better worth reading than most long modern novels. But Tennyson's long poems are not long poems in quite the same sense as those of his contemporaries. They are very different in kind from *Sordello* or *The Ring and the Book*, to name the greatest by the greatest of his contemporary poets. *Maud* and *In Memoriam* are each a series of poems, given form by the greatest lyrical resourcefulness that a poet has ever shown. The *Idylls of the King* have merits and defects similar to those of *The Princess*. An idyll is a 'short poem descriptive of some picturesque scene or incident'; in choosing the name Tennyson perhaps showed an appreciation of his limitations. For his poems are always descriptive, and always picturesque; they are never really narrative. The *Idylls of the King* are no different in kind from some of his early poems; the 'Morte d'Arthur' is in fact an early poem. *The Princess* is still an idyll, but an idyll that is too long. Tennyson's versification in this poem is as masterly as elsewhere: it is a poem which we must read, but which we excuse ourselves from reading twice. And it is worth while recognizing the reason why we return again and again, and are always stirred by the lyrics which intersperse it, and which are among the greatest of all poetry of their kind, and yet avoid the poem itself. It is not, as we may think while reading, the outmoded attitude towards the relations of the sexes, the exasperating views on the subjects of matrimony, celibacy, and female education, that makes us recoil from *The Princess*. We can swallow the most antipathetic doctrines if we are given an exciting narrative. But for narrative Tennyson had no gift at all. For a static poem, and a moving poem, on the same subject, you have only to compare his 'Ulysses' with the condensed and intensely exciting narrative of that hero in the XXVIth Canto of Dante's *Inferno*. Dante is telling a story. Tennyson is only stating an elegiac mood. The very greatest poets set before you real men talking, carry you on in real events moving. Tennyson could not tell a story at all. It is not that in *The Princess* he tried to tell a story and failed: it is rather that an idyll protracted to such length becomes unreadable. So *The Princess* is a dull poem; one of the poems of which we may say that they are beautiful but dull.

But in *Maud* and in *In Memoriam*, Tennyson is doing what every conscious artist does, turning his limitations to good purpose. *Maud* consists of a few very beautiful lyrics, such as 'O let the solid ground', 'Birds in the high Hall garden', and 'Go not, happy day', around which the semblance of a dramatic situation has been constructed with the greatest metrical virtuosity. The whole situation is unreal; the ravings of the lover on the edge of insanity sound false, and fail, as do the bellicose bellowings, to make one's flesh creep with sincerity. It would be foolish to suggest that Tennyson ought to have gone through some experience similar to that described: for a poet with dramatic gifts, a situation quite remote from his personal experience may release the strongest emotion. And I do not believe for a moment that Tennyson was a man of mild feelings or weak passions. There is no evidence in his poetry that he knew the experience of violent passion for a woman; but there is plenty of evidence of emotional intensity and violence – but of emotion so deeply suppressed, even from himself, as to tend rather towards the blackest melancholia than towards dramatic action. And it is emotion which, so far as my reading of the poems can discover, attained no ultimate clear purgation. I should reproach Tennyson not for mildness, or tepidity, but rather for lack of serenity.

> *Of love that never found his earthly close,*
> *What sequel?*

The fury of *Maud* is shrill rather than deep, though one feels in every passage what exquisite adaptation of metre to the mood Tennyson is attempting to express. I think that the effect of feeble violence, which the poem as a whole produces, is the result of a fundamental error of form. A poet can express his feelings as fully through a dramatic, as through a lyrical form; but *Maud* is neither one thing nor the other, just as *The Princess* is more than an idyll, and less than a narrative. In *Maud*, Tennyson neither identifies himself with the lover, nor identifies the lover with himself: consequently the real feelings of Tennyson, profound and tumultuous as they are, never arrive at expression.

It is, in my opinion, in *In Memoriam*, that Tennyson finds full expression. Its technical merit alone is enough to ensure its perpetuity. While Tennyson's technical competence is everywhere masterly and satisfying, *In Memoriam* is the most unapproachable of all his poems. Here are 132 passages, each of several quatrains in the same form, and never monotony or repetition. And the poem has to be comprehended as a whole. We may not memorize a few passages, we cannot find a 'fair sample'; we have to comprehend the whole of a poem which is essentially the length that it is. We may choose to remember:

> *Dark house, by which once more I stand*
> *Here in the long unlovely street,*
> *Doors, where my heart was used to beat*
> *So quickly, waiting for a hand,*

> *A hand that can be clasp'd no more —*
> *Behold me, for I cannot sleep,*
> *And like a guilty thing I creep*
> *At earliest morning to the door.*

He is not here; but far away
The noise of life begins again,
And ghastly thro' the drizzling rain
On the bald street breaks the blank day.

This is great poetry, economical of words, a universal emotion related to a particular place; and it gives me the shudder that I fail to get from anything in *Maud*. But such a passage, by itself, is not *In Memoriam*: *In Memoriam* is the whole poem. It is unique: it is a long poem made by putting together lyrics, which have only the unity and continuity of a diary, the concentrated diary of a man confessing himself. It is a diary of which we have to read every word.

Apparently Tennyson's contemporaries, once they had accepted *In Memoriam*, regarded it as a message of hope and reassurance to their rather fading Christian faith. It happens now and then that a poet by some strange accident expresses the mood of his generation, at the same time that he is expressing a mood of his own which is quite remote from that of his generation. This is not a question of insincerity: there is an amalgam of yielding and opposition below the level of consciousness. Tennyson himself, on the conscious level of the man who talks to reporters and poses for photographers, to judge from remarks made in conversation and recorded in his son's Memoir, consistently asserted a convinced, if somewhat sketchy, Christian belief. And he was a friend of Frederick Denison Maurice – nothing seems odder about that age than the respect which its eminent people felt for each other. Nevertheless, I get a very different impression from *In Memoriam* from that which Tennyson's contemporaries seem to have got. It is of a very much more interesting and tragic Tennyson. His biographers have not failed to remark that he had a good deal of the temperament of the mystic – certainly not at all the mind of the theologian. He was desperately anxious to hold the faith of the believer, without being very clear about what he wanted to believe: he was capable of illumination which he was incapable of understanding. The 'Strong Son of God, immortal Love', with an invocation of whom the poem opens, has only a hazy connexion with the Logos, or the Incarnate God. Tennyson is distressed by the idea of a mechanical universe; he is naturally, in lamenting his friend, teased by the hope of immortality and reunion beyond death. Yet the renewal craved for seems at best but a continuance, or a substitute for the joys of friendship upon earth. His desire for immortality never is quite the desire for Eternal Life; his concern is for the loss of man rather than for the gain of God.

> Shall he,
> Man, her last work, who seem'd so fair,
> Such splendid purpose in his eyes,
> Who roll'd the psalm to wintry skies,
> Who built him fanes of fruitless prayer,
>
> Who trusted God was love indeed
> And love Creation's final law —
> Tho' Nature, red in tooth and claw
> With ravine, shriek'd against his creed —
>
> Who loved, who suffer'd countless ills,
> Who battled for the True, the Just,
> Be blown about the desert dust,
> Or seal'd within the iron hills?

That strange abstraction, 'Nature', becomes a real god or goddess, perhaps more real, at moments, to Tennyson than God ('Are God and Nature then at Strife?'). The hope of immortality is confused (typically of the period) with the hope of the gradual and steady improvement of this world. Much has been said of Tennyson's interest in contemporary science, and of the impression of Darwin. *In Memoriam*, in any case, antedates *The Origin of Species* by several years, and the belief in social progress by democracy antedates it by many more; and I suspect that the faith of Tennyson's age in human progress would have been quite as strong even had the discoveries of Darwin been postponed by fifty years. And after all, there is no logical connexion: the belief in progress being current already, the discoveries of Darwin were harnessed to it:

No longer half-akin to brute,
  For all we thought and loved and did
  And hoped, and suffer'd, is but seed
Of what in them is flower and fruit;

Whereof the man, that with me trod
  This planet, was a noble type
  Appearing ere the times were ripe,
That friend of mine who lives in God,

That God, which ever lives and loves,
  One God, one law, one element,
  And one far-off divine event,
To which the whole creation moves.

These lines show an interesting compromise between the religious attitude and, what is quite a different thing, the belief in human perfectibility; but the contrast was not so apparent to Tennyson's contemporaries. They may have been taken in by it, but I don't think that Tennyson himself was, quite: his feelings were more honest than his mind. There is evidence elsewhere – even in an early poem, 'Locksley Hall', for example – that Tennyson by no means regarded with complacency all the changes that were going on about him in the progress of industrialism and the rise of the mercantile and manufacturing and banking classes; and he may have contemplated the future of England, as his years drew out, with increasing gloom. Temperamentally, he was opposed to the doctrine that he was moved to accept and to praise.

Tennyson's feelings, I have said, were honest; but they were usually a good way below the surface. *In Memoriam* can, I think, justly be called a religious poem, but for another reason than that which made it seem religious to his contemporaries. It is not religious because of the quality of its faith, but because of the quality of its doubt. Its faith is a poor thing, but its doubt is a very intense experience. *In Memoriam* is a poem of despair, but of despair of a religious kind. And to qualify its despair with the adjective 'religious' is to elevate it above most of its derivatives. For *The City of Dread-*

ful Night, and *A Shropshire Lad*, and the poems of Thomas Hardy, are small work in comparison with *In Memoriam*: it is greater than they and comprehends them.

In ending we must go back to the beginning and remember that *In Memoriam* would not be a great poem, or Tennyson a great poet, without the technical accomplishment. Tennyson is the great master of metric as well as of melancholia; I do not think any poet in English has ever had a finer ear for vowel sound, as well as subtler feeling for some moods of anguish:

> *Dear as remember'd kisses after death,*
> *And sweet as those by hopeless fancy feign'd*
> *On lips that are for others; deep as love,*
> *Deep as first love, and wild with all regret.*

And this technical gift of Tennyson's is no slight thing. Tennyson lived in a time which was already acutely time-conscious: a great many things seemed to be happening, railways were being built, discoveries were being made, the face of the world was changing. That was a time busy in keeping up to date. It had, for the most part, no hold on permanent things, on permanent truths about man and God and life and death. The surface of Tennyson stirred about with his time; and he had nothing to which to hold fast except his unique and unerring feeling for the sounds of words. But in this he had something that no one else had. Tennyson's surface, his technical accomplishment, is intimate with his depths: what we most quickly see about Tennyson is that which moves between the surface and the depths, that which is of slight importance. By looking innocently at the surface we are most likely to come to the depths, to the abyss of sorrow. Tennyson is not only a minor Virgil, he is also with Virgil as Dante saw him, a Virgil among the Shades, the saddest of all English poets, among the Great in Limbo, the most instinctive rebel against the society in which he was the most perfect conformist.

Tennyson seems to have reached the end of his spiritual development with *In Memoriam*; there followed no reconciliation, no resolution.

And now no sacred staff shall break in blossom,
No choral salutation lure to light
A spirit sick with perfumes and sweet night,

or rather with twilight, for Tennyson faced neither the darkness nor the light in his later years. The genius, the technical power, persisted to the end, but the spirit had surrendered. A gloomier end than that of Baudelaire: Tennyson had no *singulier avertissement*. And having turned aside from the journey through the dark night, to become the surface flatterer of his own time, he has been rewarded with the despite of an age that succeeds his own in shallowness.

[From the Introduction to *Poems of Tennyson* (Nelson Classics), 1936]

BAUDELAIRE

I

ANYTHING like a just appreciation of Baudelaire has been slow to arrive in England, and still is defective or partial even in France. There are, I think, special reasons for the difficulty in estimating his worth and finding his place. For one thing, Baudelaire was in some ways far in advance of the point of view of his own time, and yet was very much of it, very largely partook of its limited merits, faults, and fashions. For another thing, he had a great part in forming a generation of poets after him; and in England he had what is in a way the misfortune to be first and extravagantly advertised by Swinburne, and taken up by the followers of Swinburne. He was universal, and at the same time confined by a fashion which he himself did most to create. To dissociate the permanent from the temporary, to distinguish the man from his influence, and finally to detach him from the associations of those English poets who first admired him, is no small task. His comprehensiveness itself makes difficulty, for it tempts the partisan critic, even now, to adopt Baudelaire as the patron of his own beliefs.

It is the purpose of this essay to affirm the importance of Baudelaire's prose works. This is to see Baudelaire as something more than the author of the *Fleurs du mal*, and consequently to revise somewhat our estimate of that book. Baudelaire came into vogue at a time when 'Art for Art's sake' was a dogma. The care which he took over his poems and the fact that, contrary to the fluency of his time, both in France and England, he restricted himself to this one volume, encouraged the opinion that Baudelaire was an artist exclusively for art's sake. The doctrine does not, of course, really apply to anybody; no one applied it less than Pater, who spent many years, not so much in illustrating it, as in expounding it as a *theory of life*, which is not the same thing at all. But it was a doctrine which did affect criticism and appreciation, and which did obstruct a proper judgement of Baudelaire. He is in fact a greater man than was imagined, though perhaps not such a perfect poet.

Baudelaire has, I believe, been called a fragmentary Dante, for what that description is worth. It is true that many people who enjoy Dante enjoy Baudelaire; but the differences are as important as the similarities. Baudelaire's inferno is very different in quality and significance from that of Dante. Truer, I think, would be the description of Baudelaire as a later and more limited Goethe. As we begin to see him now, he represents his own age in somewhat the same way as that in which Goethe represents an earlier age. As a critic of the present generation, Mr Peter Quennell has recently said in his book, *Baudelaire and the Symbolists*:

He had enjoyed a sense of his own age, *had recognized its pattern while the pattern was yet incomplete, and – because it is only our misapprehension of the present which prevents our looking into the immediate future, our ignorance of today and of its real as apart from its spurious tendencies and requirements – had anticipated many problems, both on the aesthetic and on the moral plane, in which the fate of modern poetry is still concerned.*

Now the man who has this sense of his age is hard to analyse. He is exposed to its follies as well as sensitive to its inventions; and in Baudelaire, as well as in Goethe, is some of the outmoded nonsense of his time. The parallel between the German poet who has always been the symbol of perfect 'health' in every sense, as well as of universal curiosity, and the French poet who has been the symbol of morbidity in mind and concentrated interest in work, may seem paradoxical. But after this lapse of time the difference between 'health' and 'morbidity' in the two men becomes more negligible; there is something artificial and even priggish about Goethe's healthiness, as there is about Baudelaire's unhealthiness; we have passed beyond both fashions, of health or malady, and they are both merely men with restless, critical, curious minds and the 'sense of the age'; both men who understood and foresaw a great deal. Goethe, it is true, was interested in many subjects which Baudelaire left alone; but by Baudelaire's time it was no longer necessary for a man to embrace such varied interests in order to have the sense of the age; and in retrospect some of Goethe's studies seem to us (not altogether justly) to have been merely dilettante hobbies. The most of Baudelaire's prose writings (with the exception of the translations from Poe, which are of less interest to an English reader) are as important as the most of Goethe. They throw light on the *Fleurs du mal* certainly, but they also expand immensely our appreciation of their author.

It was once the mode to take Baudelaire's Satanism seriously, as it is now the tendency to present Baudelaire as a serious and Catholic Christian. This diversity of opinion needs some discussion. I think that the latter view – that Baudelaire is essentially Christian – is nearer the truth than the former, but it needs considerable reservation. When Baudelaire's Satanism is dissociated from its less creditable paraphernalia, it amounts to a dim intuition of a part, but a very important part, of Christianity. Satanism itself, so far as not merely an affectation, was an attempt to get into Christianity by the back door. Genuine blasphemy, genuine in spirit and not purely verbal, is the product of partial belief, and is as impossible to the complete atheist as to the perfect Christian. It is a way of affirming belief. This state of partial belief is manifest throughout the *Journaux intimes*. What is significant about Baudelaire is his theological innocence. He is discovering Christianity for himself; he is not assuming it as a fashion or weighing social or political reasons, or any other accidents. He is beginning, in a way, at the beginning; and, being a discoverer, is not altogether certain what he is exploring and to what it leads; he might almost be said to be making again, as one man, the effort of scores of generations. His Christianity is rudimentary or embryonic; at best, he has the excesses of a Tertullian (and even Tertullian is not considered wholly orthodox and well-balanced). His business was not to practise Christianity, but – what was much more important for his time – to assert its *necessity*.

Baudelaire's morbidity of temperament cannot, of course, be ignored: and no one who has looked at the work of Crépet or the recent small biographical study of François Porché can forget it. We should be misguided if we treated it as an unfortunate ailment which can be discounted or attempted to detach the sound from the unsound in his work. Without the morbidity none of his work would be possible or significant; his weaknesses can be composed into a larger whole of strength, and this is implied in my assertion that neither the health of Goethe nor the malady of Baudelaire matters in itself: it is what both men made of their endowments that matters. To the eye of the world, and quite properly for all questions of private life, Baudelaire was thoroughly perverse and insufferable: a man with a talent for ingratitude and unsociability, intolerably irritable, and with a mulish determination to make the worst of everything; if he had money, to squander it; if he had friends, to alienate them; if he had any good fortune, to disdain it. He had the pride of the man who feels in himself great weakness and great strength. Having great genius, he had neither the patience nor the inclination, had he had the power, to overcome his weakness; on the contrary, he exploited it for theoretical purposes. The morality of such a course may be a matter for endless dispute; for Baudelaire, it was the way to liberate his mind and give us the legacy and lesson that he has left.

He was one of those who have great strength, but strength merely to *suffer*. He could not escape suffering and could not transcend it, so he *attracted* pain to himself. But what he could do, with that immense passive strength and sensibilities which no pain could impair, was to study his suffering. And in this limitation he is wholly unlike Dante, not even like any character in Dante's Hell. But, on the other hand, such suffering as Baudelaire's implies the possibility of a positive state of beatitude. Indeed, in his way of suffering is already a kind of presence of the supernatural and of the super-human. He rejects always the purely natural and the purely human; in other words, he is neither 'naturalist' nor 'humanist'. Either because he cannot adjust himself to the actual world he has to reject it in favour of Heaven and Hell, or because he has the perception of Heaven and Hell he rejects the present world: both ways of putting it are tenable. There is in his statements a good deal of romantic detritus; *ses ailes de géant l'empêchent de marcher*, he says of the Poet and the Albatross, but not convincingly; but there is also truth about himself and about the world. His *ennui* may of course be explained, as everything can be explained, in psychological or patholo-gical terms; but it is also, from the opposite point of view, a true form of *acedia*, arising from the unsuccessful struggle towards the spiritual life.

II

From the poems alone, I venture to think, we are not likely to grasp what seems to me the true sense and significance of Baudelaire's mind. Their excellence of form, their perfection of phrasing, and their superficial coherence, may give them the appearance of pre-senting a definite and final state of mind. In reality, they seem to me to have the external but not the internal form of classic art. One might even hazard the conjecture that the care for perfection of form, among some of the romantic poets of the nineteenth century, was an effort to support, or to conceal from view, an inner disorder. Now the true claim of Baudelaire as an artist is not that he found a superficial form, but that he was searching for a form of life. In minor form he never indeed equalled Théophile Gautier, to whom he significantly dedicated his poems: in the best of the slight verse of Gautier there is a satisfaction, a balance of inwards and form, which we do not find in Baudelaire. He had a greater technical ability than Gautier, and yet the content of feeling is constantly bursting the receptacle. His apparatus, by which I do not mean his command of words and rhythms, but his stock of imagery (and every poet's stock of imagery is circumscribed somewhere), is not wholly perdurable or adequate. His prostitutes, mulattoes, Jewesses, serpents, cats, corpses form a machinery which has not worn very well; his Poet, or his Don Juan, has a romantic ancestry which is too clearly traceable. Compare with the costumery of Baudelaire the stock of imagery of the *Vita Nuova*, or of Cavalcanti, and you find Baudelaire's does not everywhere wear as well as that of several centuries earlier; compare him with Dante or Shakespeare, for what such a comparison is worth, and he is found not only a much smaller poet, but one in whose work much more that is perishable has entered.

To say this is only to say that Baudelaire belongs to a definite place in time. Inevitably the offspring of romanticism, and by his nature the first counter-romantic in poetry, he could, like anyone else, only work with the materials which were there. It must not be forgotten that a poet in a romantic age cannot be a 'classical' poet except in tendency. If he is sincere, he must express with individual differences the general state of mind – not as a *duty*, but simply because he cannot help participating in it. For such poets, we may expect often to get much help from reading their prose works and even notes and diaries; help in deciphering the discrepancies between head and heart, means and end, materials and ideals.

What preserves Baudelaire's poetry from the fate of most French poetry of the nineteenth century up to his time, and has made him, as M. Valéry has said in a recent introduction to the *Fleurs du mal*, the one modern French poet to be widely read abroad, is not quite easy to conclude. It is partly that technical mastery which can hardly be overpraised, and which has made his verse an inexhaustible study for later poets, not only in his own language. When we read

> *Maint joyau dort enseveli*
> *Dans les ténèbres et l'oubli,*
> *Bien loin des pioches et des sondes;*
> *Mainte fleur épanche à regret*
> *Son parfum doux comme un secret*
> *Dans les solitudes profondes,*

we might for a moment think it a more lucid bit of Mallarmé; and so original is the arrangement of words that we might easily overlook its borrowing from Gray's *Elegy*. When we read

> *Valse mélancolique et langoureux vertige!*

we are already in the Paris of Laforgue. Baudelaire gave to French poets as generously as he borrowed from English and American poets. The renovation of Racine's alexandrine has been mentioned often enough; but its significance should not be over-emphasized, for it sometimes comes near to being a trick. But even without this, Baudelaire's variety and resourcefulness would still be immense.

Furthermore, besides the stock of images which he used that seems already second-hand, he gave new possibilities to poetry in a new stock of imagery of contemporary life.

> *... Au cœur d'un vieux faubourg, labyrinthe fangeux*
> *Où l'humanité grouille en ferments orageux,*
> *On voit un chiffonnier qui vient, hochant la tête,*
> *Buttant, et se cognant aux murs comme un poète.*

This introduces something new, and something universal in modern life. (The last line quoted, which in ironic terseness anticipates Corbière, might be contrasted with the whole poem 'Bénédiction' which begins the volume.) It is not merely in the use of imagery of common life, not merely in the use of imagery of the sordid life of a great metropolis, but in the elevation of such imagery to the *first intensity* – presenting it as it is, and yet making it represent something much more than itself – that Baudelaire has created a mode of release and expression for other men.

This invention of language, at a moment when French poetry in particular was famishing for such invention, is enough to make of Baudelaire a great poet, a great landmark in poetry. Baudelaire is indeed the greatest exemplar in *modern* poetry in any language, for his verse and language is the nearest thing to a complete renovation that we have experienced. But his renovation of an attitude towards life is no less radical and no less important. In his verse, he is now less a model to be imitated or a source to be drained than a reminder of the duty, the consecrated task, of sincerity. From a fundamental sincerity he could not deviate. The superficies of sincerity (as I think has not always been remarked) is not always there. As I have suggested, many of his poems are insufficiently removed from their romantic origins, from Byronic paternity and Satanic fraternity. The 'satanism' of the Black Mass was very much in the air; in exhibiting it Baudelaire is the voice of his time; but I would observe that in Baudelaire, as in no one else, it is redeemed by *meaning something else*. He uses the same paraphernalia, but cannot limit its symbolism even to all that of which he is conscious. Compare him with Huysmans in *À Rebours*, *En route*, and *Là-bas*. Huysmans, who is a first-rate realist of his time, only succeeds in making his diabolism interesting when he treats it externally, when he is merely describing a manifestation of his period (if such it was). His own interest in such matters is, like his interest in Christianity, a petty affair. Huysmans merely provides a document. Baudelaire would not even provide that, if he had been really absorbed in that ridiculous hocus-pocus. But actually Baudelaire is concerned, not with demons, black masses, and romantic blasphemy, but with the real problem of good and evil. It is hardly more than an accident of time that he uses the current imagery and vocabulary of blasphemy. In the middle nineteenth century, the age which (at its best) Goethe had prefigured, an age of bustle, programmes, platforms, scientific progress, humanitarianism, and revolutions which improved nothing, an age of progressive degradation, Baudelaire perceived that what really matters is Sin and Redemption. It is a proof of his honesty that he went as far as he could honestly go and no further. To a mind observant of the post-Voltaire France (*Voltaire ... le prédicateur des concierges*), a mind which saw the world of *Napoléon le petit* more lucidly than did that of Victor Hugo, a mind which at the same time had no affinity for the *Saint-Sulpicerie* of the day, the recognition of the reality of Sin is a New Life; and the possibility of damnation is so immense a relief in a world of electoral reforms, plebiscites, sex reform, and dress reform, that damnation itself is an immediate form of salvation – of salvation from the ennui of modern life, because it at last gives some significance to living. It is this, I believe, that Baudelaire is trying to express; and it is this which separates him from the modernist Protestantism of Byron and Shelley. It is apparently Sin in the Swinburnian sense, but really Sin in the permanent Christian sense, that occupies the mind of Baudelaire.

Yet, as I said, the sense of Evil implies the sense of Good. Here too, Baudelaire apparently confuses, and perhaps did confuse, Evil with its theatrical representations. Baudelaire is not always certain in his notion of the Good. The romantic idea of Love is never quite exorcized, but never quite surrendered to. In 'Le Balcon', which M. Valéry considers, and I think rightly, one of Baudelaire's most beautiful poems, there is all the romantic idea, but something more: the reaching out towards something which cannot be had *in,* but which may be had partly *through,* personal relations. Indeed, in much romantic poetry the sadness is due to the exploitation of the fact that no human relations are adequate to human desires, but also to the disbelief in any further object for human desires than that which, being human, fails to satisfy them. One of the unhappy necessities of human existence is that we have to 'find things out for ourselves'. If it were not so, the statement of Dante would, at least for poets, have done once for all. Baudelaire has all the romantic sorrow, but invents a new kind of romantic nostalgia – a derivative of his nostalgia being the *poésie des départs,* the *poésie des salles d'attente.* In a beautiful paragraph of *Mon cœur mis à nu,* he imagines the vessels lying in harbour as saying: '*Quand partons-nous vers le bonheur?*' and his minor successor Laforgue exclaims: '*Comme ils sont beaux, les trains manqués.*' The poetry of flight – which, in contemporary France, owes a great debt to the poems of Valéry Larbaud's 'A. O. Barnabooth' – is, in its origin in this paragraph of Baudelaire, a dim recognition of the direction of beatitude.

But in the adjustment of the natural to the spiritual, of the bestial to the human, and the human to the supernatural, Baudelaire is a bungler compared with Dante; the best that can be said, and that is a very great deal, is that what he knew he found out for himself. In his book, the *Journaux intimes,* and especially in *Mon cœur mis à nu,* he has a great deal to say of the love of man and woman. One aphorism which has been especially noticed is the following: *'la volupté unique et suprême de l'amour gît dans la certitude de faire le mal.'* This means, I think, that Baudelaire has perceived that what distinguishes the relations of man and woman from the copulation of beasts is the knowledge of Good and Evil (or *moral* Good and Evil which are not natural Good and Bad or Puritan Right and Wrong). Having an imperfect, vague, romantic conception of Good, he was at least able to understand that the sexual act as evil is more digni-fied, less boring, than as the natural, 'life-giving', cheery automatism of the modern world. For Baudelaire, sexual operation is at least something not analogous to Kruschen Salts.

So far as we are human, what we do must be either evil or good;* so far as we do evil or good, we are human; and it is better, in a paradoxical way, to do evil than to do nothing: at least, we exist. It is true to say that the glory of man is his capacity for salvation; it is also true to say that his glory is his capacity for damnation. The worst that can be said of most of our malefactors, from statesmen to thieves, is that they are not men enough to be damned. Baudelaire was man enough for damnation: whether he *is* damned is, of course, another question, and we are not prevented from praying for his repose. In all his humiliating traffic with other beings, he walked secure in this high vocation, that he was capable of a damnation denied to the politicians and the newspaper editors of Paris.

III

Baudelaire's notion of beatitude certainly tended to the wishy-washy; and even in one of the most beautiful of his poems, 'L'Invitation au voyage', he hardly exceeds the *poésie des départs*. And because his vision is here so restricted, there is for him a gap between human love and divine love. His human love is definite and positive, his divine love vague and uncertain: hence his insistence upon the evil of love, hence his constant vituperations of the female. In this there is no need to pry for psychopathological causes, which would be

* 'Know ye not, that to whom ye yield yourselves servants to obey, his servants ye are to whom ye obey; whether of sin unto death, or of obedience unto righteousness?' – Romans vi. 16. [*Author's note*]

irrelevant at best; for his attitude towards women is consistent with the point of view which he had reached. Had he been a woman he would, no doubt, have held the same views about men. He has arrived at the perception that a woman must be to some extent a symbol; he did not arrive at the point of harmonizing his experience with his ideal needs. The complement, and the correction to the *Journaux intimes*, so far as they deal with the relations of man and woman, is the *Vita Nuova*, and the *Divine Comedy*. But – I cannot assert it too strongly – Baudelaire's view of life, such as it is, is objectively apprehensible, that is to say, his idiosyncrasies can partly explain his view of life, but they cannot explain it away. And this view of life is one which has grandeur and which exhibits heroism; it was an evangel to his time and to ours. '*La vraie civilisation*', he wrote, '*n'est pas dans le gaz, ni dans la vapeur, ni dans les tables tournantes. Elle est dans la diminution des traces du péché originel.*' It is not quite clear exactly what *diminution* here implies, but the tendency of his thought is clear, and the message is still accepted by but few. More than half a century later T. E. Hulme left behind him a paragraph which Baudelaire would have approved:

In the light of these absolute values, man himself is judged to be essentially limited and imperfect. He is endowed with Original Sin. While he can occasionally accomplish acts which partake of perfection, he can never himself be perfect. Certain secondary results in regard to ordinary human action in society follow from this. A man is essentially bad, he can only accomplish anything of value by discipline – ethical and political. Order is thus not merely negative, but creative and liberating. Institutions are necessary.

[Introduction to Baudelaire's *Intimate Journals*, 1930]

THOMAS HARDY

THE work of Thomas Hardy represents an interesting example of a powerful personality uncurbed by any institutional attachment or by submission to any objective beliefs: unhampered by any ideas, or even by what sometimes acts as a partial restraint upon inferior writers, the desire to please a large public. He seems to me to have written as nearly for the sake of 'self-expression' as a man well can; and the self which he had to express does not strike me as a particularly wholesome or edifying matter of communication. He was indifferent even to the prescripts of good writing: he wrote sometimes overpoweringly well, but always very carelessly; at times his style touches sublimity without ever having passed through the stage of being good. In consequence of his self-absorption, he makes a great deal of landscape; for landscape is a passive creature which lends itself to an author's mood. Landscape is fitted too for the purposes of an author who is interested not at all in men's minds, but only in their emotions; and perhaps only in men as vehicles for emotions. It is only, indeed, in their emotional paroxysms that most of Hardy's characters come alive. This extreme emotionalism seems to me a symptom of decadence; it is a cardinal point of faith in a romantic age, to believe that there is something admirable in violent emotion for its own sake, whatever the emotion or whatever its object. But it is by no means self-evident that human beings are most real when most violently excited; violent physical passions do not in themselves differentiate men from each other, but rather tend to reduce them to the same state; and the passion has significance only in relation to the character and behaviour of the man at other moments of his life and in other contexts. Furthermore, strong passion is only interesting or significant in strong men; those who abandon themselves without resistance to excitements which tend to deprive them of reason, become merely instruments of feeling and lose their humanity; and unless there is moral resistance and conflict there is no meaning. But as the majority is capable neither of strong emotion nor of strong resistance, it always inclines to admire passion for its own sake, unless instructed to the contrary; and, if somewhat deficient in vitality, people imagine passion to be the surest evidence of vitality. This in itself may go towards accounting for Hardy's popularity.

[From *After Strange Gods*, 1934]

THE generations of poetry in our age seem to cover a span of about twenty years. I do not mean that the best work of any poet is limited to twenty years: I mean that it is about that length of time before a new school or style of poetry appears. By the time, that is to say, that a man is fifty, he has behind him a kind of poetry written by men of seventy, and before him another kind written by men of thirty. That is my position at present, and if I live another twenty years I shall expect to see still another younger school of poetry. One's relation to Yeats, however, does not fit into this scheme. When I was a young man at the university in America, just beginning to write verse, Yeats was already a considerable figure in the world of poetry, and his early period was well defined. I cannot remember that his poetry at that stage made any deep impression upon me. A very young man, who is himself stirred to write, is not primarily critical or even widely appreciative. He is looking for masters who will elicit his consciousness of what he wants to say himself, of the kinds of poetry that is in him to write. The taste of an adolescent writer is intense, but narrow: it is determined by personal needs. The kind of poetry that I needed, to teach me the use of my own voice, did not exist in English at all; it was only to be found in French. For this reason the poetry of the young Yeats hardly existed for me until after my enthusiasm had been won by the poetry of the older Yeats; and by that time – I mean, from 1919 on – my own course of evolution was already determined. Hence, I find myself regarding him, from one point of view, as a contemporary and not a predecessor; and from another point of view, I can share the feelings of younger men, who came to know and admire him by that work from 1919 on, which was produced while they were adolescent.

Certainly, for the younger poets of England and America, I am sure that their admiration for Yeats's poetry has been wholly good. His idiom was too different for there to be any danger of imitation,

---

* From the first Annual Yeats Lecture, delivered to the Friends of the Irish Academy at the Abbey Theatre, Dublin, 30 June 1940. [*Editor's note*]

his opinions too different to flatter and confirm their prejudices. It was good for them to have the spectacle of an unquestionably great living poet, whose style they were not tempted to echo and whose ideas contradicted those in vogue among them. You will not see, in their writing, more than passing evidences of the impression he made, but the work, and the man himself as poet, have been of the greatest significance to them for all that. This may seem to contradict what I have been saying about the kind of poetry that a young poet chooses to admire. But I am really talking about something different. Yeats would not have this influence had he not become a great poet; but the influence of which I speak is due to the figure of the poet himself, to the integrity of his passion for his art and his craft which provided such an impulse for his extraordinary development. When he visited London he liked to meet and talk to younger poets. People have sometimes spoken of him as arrogant and overbearing. I never found him so; in his conversations with a younger writer I always felt that he offered terms of equality, as to a fellow worker, a practitioner of the same mystery. It was, I think, that, unlike many writers, he cared more for poetry than for his own reputation as a poet or his picture of himself as a poet. Art was greater than the artist: and this feeling he communicated to others; which was why younger men were never ill at ease in his company.

This, I am sure, was part of the secret of his ability, after becoming unquestionably the master, to remain always a contemporary. Another is the continual development of which I have spoken. This has become almost a commonplace of criticism of his work. But while it is often mentioned, its causes and its nature have not been often analysed. One reason, of course, was simply concentration and hard work. And behind that is character: I mean the special character of the artist as artist – that is, the force of character by which Dickens, having exhausted his first inspiration, was able in middle age to proceed to such a masterpiece, so different from his early work, as *Bleak House*. It is difficult and unwise to generalize about ways of composition – so many men, so many ways – but it is my experience that towards middle age a man has three choices: to stop writing altogether, to repeat himself with perhaps an increasing skill of virtuosity, or by taking thought to adapt himself to middle age and find a different way of working. Why are the later long poems of Browning and Swinburne mostly unread? It is, I think, because one gets the essential Browning or Swinburne entire in earlier poems; and in the later, one is reminded of the early freshness which they lack, without being made aware of any compensating new qualities. When a man is engaged in work of abstract thought – if there is such a thing as wholly abstract thought outside of the mathematical and the physical sciences – his mind can mature, while his emotions either remain the same or only atrophy, and it will not matter. But maturing as a poet means maturing as the whole man, experiencing new emotions appropriate to one's age, and with the same intensity as the emotions of youth.

One form, a perfect form, of development is that of Shakespeare, one of the few poets whose work of maturity is just as exciting as that of their early manhood. There is, I think, a difference between the development of Shakespeare and Yeats, which makes the latter case still more curious. With Shakespeare, one sees a slow, continuous development of mastery of his craft of verse, and the poetry of middle age seems implicit in that of early maturity. After the first few verbal exercises you say of each piece of work: 'This is the perfect expression of the sensibility of that stage of his development.' That a poet should develop at all, that he should find something new to say, and say it equally well, in middle age, has always something miraculous about it. But in the case of Yeats the kind of development seems to me different. I do not want to give the impression that I regard his earlier and his later work almost as if they had been written by two different men. Returning to his earlier poems after making a close acquaintance with the later, one sees, to begin with, that in technique there was a slow and continuous development of what is always the same medium and idiom. And when I say development, I do not mean that many of the early poems, for what they are, are not as beautifully written as they could be. There are some, such as 'Who Goes with Fergus?' which are as perfect of their kind as anything in the language. But the best, and the best known of them, have this limitation: that they are as satisfactory in isolation, as 'anthology pieces', as they are in the context of his other poems of the same period.

I am obviously using the term 'anthology piece' in a rather special sense. In any anthology, you find some poems which give you complete satisfaction and delight in themselves, such that you are hardly curious who wrote them, hardly want to look further into the work of that poet. There are others, not necessarily so perfect or complete, which make you irresistibly curious to know more of that poet through his other work. Naturally, this distinction applies only to short poems, those in which a man has only been able to put a part of his mind, if it is a mind of any size. With some such you feel at once that the man who wrote them must have had a great deal more to say, in different contexts, of equal interest. Now among all the poems in Yeats's earlier volumes I find only in a line here or there that sense of a unique personality which makes one sit up in excitement and eagerness to learn more about the author's mind and feelings. The intensity of Yeats's own emotional experience hardly appears. We have sufficient evidence of the intensity of experience of his youth, but it is from the retrospections in some of his later work that we have our evidence.

I have, in early essays, extolled what I called impersonality in art, and it may seem that, in giving as a reason for the superiority of Yeats's later work the greater expression of personality in it, I am contradicting myself. It may be that I expressed myself badly, or that I had only an adolescent grasp of that idea – as I can never bear to re-read my own prose writings, I am willing to leave the point unsettled – but I think now, at least, that the truth of the matter is this. There are two forms of impersonality: that which is natural to the mere skilful craftsman, and that which is more and more achieved by the maturing artist. The first is that of what I have called the 'anthology piece', of a lyric by Lovelace or Suckling, or of Campion, a finer poet than either. The second impersonality is that of the poet who, out of intense and personal experience, is able to express a general truth; retaining all the particularity of his experience, to make of it a general symbol. And the strange thing is that Yeats, having been a great craftsman in the first kind, became a great poet in the second. It is not that he became a different man, for, as I have hinted, one feels sure that the intense experience of youth had been lived through – and indeed, without this early experience he could never have attained anything of the wisdom which appears in his later writing. But he had to wait for a later maturity to find expression of early experience; and this makes him, I think, a unique and especially interesting poet.

Consider the early poem which is in every anthology, 'When you are old and grey and full of sleep', or 'A Dream of Death' in the same volume of 1893. They are beautiful poems, but only craftsman's work, because one does not feel present in them the particularity which must provide the material for the general truth. By the time of the volume of 1904 there is a development visible in a very lovely poem, 'The Folly of Being Comforted', and in 'Adam's Curse'; something is coming through, and in beginning to speak as a particular man he is beginning to speak for man. This is clearer still in the poem 'Peace', in the 1910 volume. But it is not fully evinced until the volume of 1914, in the violent and terrible epistle dedicatory of *Responsibilities*, with the great lines

> *Pardon that for a barren passion's sake,*
> *Although I have come close on forty-nine. . . .*

And the naming of his age in the poem is significant. More than half a lifetime to arrive at this freedom of speech. It is a triumph.

There was much also for Yeats to work out of himself, even in technique. To be a younger member of a group of poets, none of them certainly of anything like his stature, but further developed in their limited path, may arrest for a time a man's development of idiom. Then again, the weight of the pre-Raphaelite prestige must have been tremendous. The Yeats of the Celtic twilight – who seems to me to have been more the Yeats of the pre-Raphaelite twilight – uses Celtic folklore almost as William Morris uses Scandinavian folklore. His longer narrative poems bear the mark of Morris. Indeed, in the pre-Raphaelite phase, Yeats is by no means the least of the pre-Raphaelites. I may be mistaken, and I may be impertinent, but the play, *The Shadowy Waters*, seems to me one of the most perfect expressions of the vague enchanted beauty of that school: yet it strikes me – and this is what may be an impertinence on my part – as the western seas descried through the back window of a house in Kensington, an Irish myth for the Kelmscott Press; and when I try to visualize the speakers in the play, they have the great dim, dreamy eyes of the knights and ladies of Burne-Jones. I think that the phase in which he treated Irish legend in the manner of Rossetti or Morris is a phase of confusion. He did not master this legend until he made it a vehicle for his own creation of character – not, really, until he began to write the *Plays for Dancers*. The point is, that in becoming more Irish, not in subject-matter but in expression, he became at the same time universal.

The points that I particularly wish to make about Yeats's development are two. The first, on which I have already touched, is that to have accomplished what Yeats did in the middle and later years is a great and permanent example – which poets-to-come should study with reverence – of what I have called Character of the Artist: a kind of moral, as well as intellectual, excellence. The second point, which follows naturally after what I have said in criticism of the lack of complete emotional expression in his early work, is that Yeats is pre-eminently the poet of middle age. By this I am far from meaning that he is a poet only for middle-aged readers: the attitude towards him of younger poets who write in English, the world over, is enough evidence to the contrary. Now, in theory, there is no reason why a poet's inspiration or material should fail, in middle age or at any time before senility. For a man who is capable of experience finds himself in a different world in every decade of his life; as he sees it with different eyes, the material of his art is continually renewed. But in fact, very few poets have shown this capacity of adaptation to the years. It requires, indeed, an exceptional honesty and courage to face the change. Most men either cling to the experiences of youth, so that their writing becomes an insincere mimicry of their earlier work, or they leave their passion behind, and write only from the head, with a hollow and wasted virtuosity. There is another and even worse temptation: that of becoming dignified, of becoming public figures with only a public existence – coat-racks hung with decorations and distinctions, doing, saying, and even thinking and feeling only what they believe the public expects of them. Yeats was not that kind of poet: and it is, perhaps, a reason why young men should find his later poetry more acceptable than older men easily can. For the young can see him as a poet who in his work remained in the best sense always young, who even in one sense became young as he aged. But the old, unless they are stirred to something of the honesty with oneself expressed in the poetry, will be shocked by such a revelation of what a man really is and remains. They will refuse to believe that *they* are like that.

I see at this point that I may have given the impression, contrary to my desire and my belief, that the poetry and the plays of Yeats's earlier period can be ignored in favour of his later work. You cannot divide the work of a great poet so sharply as that. Where there is the continuity of such a positive personality and such a single purpose, the later work cannot be understood, or properly enjoyed, without a study and appreciation of the earlier; and the later work again reflects light upon the earlier; and shows us beauty and significance not before perceived. We have also to take account of the historical conditions. As I have said above, Yeats was born into the end of a literary movement, and an English movement at that: only those who have toiled with language know the labour and constancy required to free oneself from such influences – yet, on the other hand, once we are familiar with the older voice, we can hear its individual tones even in his earliest published verse. In my own time of youth there seemed to be no immediate great powers of poetry either to help or to hinder, either to learn from or to rebel against, yet I can understand the difficulty of the other situation, and the magnitude of the task. With the verse play, on the other hand, the situation is reversed, because Yeats had nothing, and we have had Yeats. He started writing plays at a time when the prose play of contemporary life seemed triumphant, with an indefinite future stretching before it; when the comedy of light farce dealt only with certain privileged strata of metropolitan life; and when the serious play tended to be an ephemeral tract on some transient social problem. We can begin to

see now that even the imperfect early attempts he made are probably more permanent literature than the plays of Ibsen or of Shaw;
and that his dramatic work as a whole may prove a stronger defence
against the successful urban Shaftesbury Avenue vulgarity which he
opposed as stoutly as they. Just as, from the beginning, he made and
thought his poetry in terms of speech and not in terms of print, so in
the drama he always meant to write plays to be played and not merely
to be read. He cared, I think, more for the theatre as an organ for
the expression of the consciousness of a people, than as a means
to his own fame or achievement; and I am convinced that it is only
if you serve it in this spirit that you can hope to accomplish anything
worth doing with it. Of course, he had some great advantages, the
recital of which does not rob him of any of his glory: his colleagues,
a people with a natural and unspoilt gift for speech and for acting.
It is impossible to disentangle what he did for the Irish theatre from
what the Irish theatre did for him. From this point of advantage,
the idea of the poetic drama was kept alive when everywhere else it
had been driven underground. I do not know where our debt to
him as a dramatist ends – and in time, it will not end until that
drama itself ends. In his occcasional writings on dramatic topics he
has asserted certain principles to which we must hold fast: such as
the primacy of the poet over the actor, and of the actor over the
scene-painter; and the principle that the theatre, while it need not be
concerned only with 'the people' in the narrow Russian sense, must
be for the people; that to be permanent it must concern itself with
fundamental situations. Born into a world in which the doctrine of
'Art for Art's sake' was generally accepted, and living on into one
in which art has been asked to be instrumental to social purposes, he
held firmly to the right view which is between these, though not in
any way a compromise between them, and showed that an artist,
by serving his art with entire integrity, is at the same time rendering
the greatest service he can to his own nation and to the whole world.

[From 'The Poetry of W. B. Yeats', 1940]

SOCIAL CRITICISM

Social Criticism

WAR

IN face of any naturally horrifying phenomenon like war we must measure the suffering, direct and indirect, against the spiritual good which may come of suffering. We may find that the proportion of futile suffering, and of that kind of suffering which makes men worse rather than better, which abates their human dignity and deadens their sense of responsibility, is far too high; and that the total effect is at best one of futility. What we have to concern ourselves with primarily is the causes in modern society, in our industrial and financial machinery it may be, which bring about the *kind* of war which we have experienced; and to give our adherence to all alterations in that machinery which tend to remove the motives. We do not, I suppose, deny that society is very deeply affected morally and spiritually by material conditions, even by a machinery which it has constructed piecemeal and with short-sighted aims. This is not to accept any doctrine of determinism, for it means no more than that society, and the majority of individuals composing it, are only imperfectly conscious of what they are doing, directed by impure motives and aiming at false goods.

[From 'Catholicism and the International Order', 1934]

THE REFORMATION OF SOCIETY

No scheme for a change of society can be made to appear immediately palatable, except by falsehood, until society has become so desperate that it will accept any change. A Christian society only becomes acceptable after you have fairly examined the alternatives. We might, of course, merely sink into an apathetic decline: without faith, and therefore without faith in ourselves; without a philosophy of life, either Christian or pagan; and without art. Or we might get a 'totalitarian democracy', different but having much in common with other pagan societies, because we shall have changed step by step in order to keep pace with them: a state of affairs in which we shall have regimentation and conformity, without respect for the needs of the individual soul; the puritanism of a hygienic morality in the interest of efficiency; uniformity of opinion through propaganda, and art only encouraged when it flatters the official doctrines of the time. To those who can imagine, and are therefore repelled by, such a prospect, one can assert that the only possibility of control and balance is a religious control and balance; that the only hopeful course for a society which would thrive and continue its creative activity in the arts of civilization, is to become Christian. That prospect involves, at least, discipline, inconvenience, and discomfort: but here as hereafter the alternative to hell is purgatory.

[From *The Idea of a Christian Society*, 1939]

CHURCH AND STATE

To identify any particular form of government with Christianity is a dangerous error: for it confounds the permanent with the transitory, the absolute with the contingent. Forms of government, and of social organization, are in constant process of change, and their operation may be very different from the theory which they are supposed to exemplify. A theory of the State may be, explicitly or implicitly, anti-Christian: it may arrogate rights which only the Church is entitled to claim, or pretend to decide moral questions on which only the Church is qualified to pronounce. On the other hand, a régime may in practice claim either more or less than it professes, and we have to examine its workings as well as its constitution. We have no assurance that a democratic régime might not be as inimical to Christianity in practice, as another might be in theory: and the best government must be relative to the character and the stage of intelligence and education of a particular people in a particular place at a particular time. Those who consider that a discussion of the

nature of a Christian society should conclude by supporting a particular form of political organization, should ask themselves whether
they really believe our form of government to be more important
than our Christianity; and those who are convinced that the present
form of government of Britain is the one most suitable for any
Christian people, should ask themselves whether they are confusing
a Christian society with a society in which individual Christianity
is tolerated.

Our preoccupation with foreign politics during the last few years
has induced a surface complacency rather than a consistent attempt
at self-examination of conscience. Sometimes we are almost persuaded that we are getting on very nicely, with a reform here and
a reform there, and would have been getting on still better, if only
foreign governments did not insist upon breaking all the rules and
playing what is really a different game. What is more depressing still
is the thought that only fear or jealousy of foreign success can alarm
us about the health of our own nation; that only through this anxiety
can we see such things as depopulation, malnutrition, moral deterioration, the decay of agriculture, as evils at all. And what is worst
of all is to advocate Christianity, not because it is true, but because
it might be beneficial. Towards the end of 1938 we experienced a
wave of revivalism which should teach us that folly is not the prerogative of any one political party or any one religious communion,
and that hysteria is not the privilege of the uneducated. The Christianity expressed has been vague, the religious fervour has been a
fervour for democracy. It may engender nothing better than a disguised and peculiarly sanctimonious nationalism, accelerating our
progress towards the paganism which we say we abhor. To justify
Christianity because it provides a foundation of morality, instead of
showing the necessity of Christian morality from the truth of Christianity, is a very dangerous inversion; and we may reflect, that a good
deal of the attention of totalitarian states has been devoted, with a
steadiness of purpose not always found in democracies, to providing
their national life with a foundation of morality – the wrong kind
perhaps, but a good deal more of it. It is not enthusiasm, but dogma,
that differentiates a Christian from a pagan society.

It is very easy for speculation on a possible Christian order in the future to tend to come to rest in a kind of apocalyptic vision of a golden age of virtue. But we have to remember that the Kingdom of Christ on earth will never be realized, and also that it is always being realized; we must remember that whatever reform or revolution we carry out, the result will always be a sordid travesty of what human society should be – though the world is never left wholly without glory. In such a society as I imagine, as in any that is not petrified, there will be innumerable seeds of decay. Any human scheme for society is realized only when the great mass of humanity has become adapted to it; but this adaptation becomes also, insensibly, an adaptation of the scheme itself to the mass on which it operates: the overwhelming pressure of mediocrity, sluggish and indomitable as a glacier, will mitigate the most violent, and depress the most exalted revolution, and what is realized is so unlike the end that enthusiasm conceived, that foresight would weaken the effort.

[From *The Idea of a Christian Society*, 1939]

CHRISTIANITY AND SOCIETY

THE Idea of a Christian Society is one which we can accept or reject; but if we are to accept it, we must treat Christianity with a great deal more *intellectual* respect than is our wont; we must treat it as being for the individual a matter primarily of thought and not of feeling. The consequences of such an attitude are too serious to be acceptable to everybody: for when the Christian faith is not only felt, but thought, it has practical results which may be inconvenient. For to see the Christian faith in this way – and to see it in this way is not necessarily to accept it, but only to understand the real issues – is to see that the difference between the Idea of a Neutral Society (which is that of the society in which we live at present) and the Idea of a Pagan Society (such as the upholders of democracy abominate) is, in the long run, of minor importance. I am not at this moment concerned with the means for bringing a Christian Society into existence; I am not even primarily concerned with making it appear desirable; but I am very much concerned with making clear its difference from the kind of society in which we are now living. Now to understand the society in which he lives, must be to the interest of every conscious thinking person. The current terms in which we describe our society, the contrasts with other societies by which we – of the 'Western Democracies' – eulogize it, only operate to deceive and stupefy us. To speak of ourselves as a Christian Society, in contrast to that of Germany or Russia, is an abuse of terms. We mean only that we have a society in which no one is penalized for the *formal profession* of Christianity; but we conceal from ourselves the unpleasant knowledge of the real values by which we live. We conceal from ourselves, moreover, the similarity of our society to those which we execrate: for we should have to admit, if we recognized the similarity, that the foreigners do better. I suspect that in our loathing of totalitarianism, there is infused a good deal of admiration for its efficiency.

[From *The Idea of a Christian Society*, 1939]

A CHRISTIAN COMMUNITY

FOR the great mass of humanity whose attention is occupied mostly by their direct relation to the soil, or the sea, or the machine, and to a small number of persons, pleasures, and duties, two conditions are required. The first is that, as their capacity for *thinking* about the objects of faith is small, their Christianity may be almost wholly realized in behaviour: both in their customary and periodic religious observances, and in a traditional code of behaviour towards their neighbours. The second is that, while they should have some perception of how far their lives fall short of Christian ideals, their religious and social life should form for them a natural whole, so that the difficulty of behaving as Christians should not impose an intolerable strain. These two conditions are really the same differently stated; they are far from being realized today.

The traditional unit of the Christian Community in England is the parish. I am not here concerned with the problem of how radically this system must be modified to suit a future state of things. The parish is certainly in decay, from several causes of which the least cogent is the division into sects: a much more important reason is urbanization – in which I am including also *sub*-urbanization, and all the causes and effects of urbanization. How far the parish must be superseded will depend largely upon our view of the necessity of accepting the causes which tend to destroy it. In any case, the parish will serve my purpose as an example of a community unit. For this unit must not be solely religious, and not solely social; nor should the individual be a member of two separate, or even overlapping units, one religious and the other social. The unitary community should be religious–social, and it must be one in which all classes, if you have classes, have their centre of interest. That is a state of affairs which is no longer wholly realized except in very primitive tribes indeed.

It is a matter of concern not only in this country, but has been mentioned with concern by the late Supreme Pontiff, speaking not of one country but of all civilized countries, that the masses of the people have become increasingly alienated from Christianity. In an industrialized society like that of England, I am surprised that the people retains as much Christianity as it does. For the great majority of the people – and I am not here thinking of social classes, but of intellectual strata – religion must be primarily a matter of behaviour and habit, must be integrated with its social life, with its business and its pleasures, and the specifically religious emotions must be a kind of extension and sanctification of the domestic and social emotions. Even for the most highly developed and conscious individual, living in the world, a consciously Christian direction of thought and feeling can only occur at particular moments during the day and during the week, and these moments themselves recur in consequence of formed habits; to be conscious, without remission, of a Christian and a non-Christian alternative at moments of choice, imposes a very great strain. The mass of the population, in a Christian society, should not be exposed to a way of life in which there is too sharp and frequent a conflict between what is easy for them or what their circumstances dictate and what is Christian. The compulsion to live in such a way that Christian behaviour is only possible in a restricted number of situations, is a very powerful force against Christianity; for behaviour is as potent to affect belief, as belief to affect behaviour.

I am not presenting any idyllic picture of the rural parish, either present or past, in taking as a norm the idea of a small and mostly self-contained group attached to the soil and having its interests centred in a particular place, with a kind of unity which may be designed, but which also has to grow through generations. It is the idea, or ideal, of a community small enough to consist of a nexus of direct personal relationships, in which all iniquities and turpitudes will take the simple and easily appreciable form of wrong relations between one person and another. But at present not even the smallest community, unless so primitive as to present objectionable features of another kind, is so simplified as this; and I am not advocating any complete reversion to any earlier state of things, real or idealized. The example appears to offer no solution to the problem of industrial, urban, and suburban life which is that of the majority of the population. In its religious organization, we may say that Christendom has remained fixed at the stage of development suitable to a simple agricultural and piscatorial society, and that modern material organization – or if 'organization' sounds too complimentary, we will say 'complication' – has produced a world for which Christian social forms are imperfectly adapted. Even if we agree on this point, there are two simplifications of the problem which are suspect. One is to insist that the only salvation for society is to return to a simpler mode of life, scrapping all the constructions of the modern world that we can bring ourselves to dispense with. This is an extreme statement of the neo-Ruskinian view, which was put forward with much vigour by the late A. J. Penty. When one considers the large amount of determination in social structure, this policy appears Utopian: if such a way of life ever comes to pass, it will be – as may well happen in the long run – from natural causes, and not from the moral will of men. The other alternative is to accept the modern world as it is and simply try to adapt Christian social ideals to it. The latter resolves itself into a mere doctrine of expediency; and is a surrender of the faith that Christianity itself can play any part in shaping social forms. And it does not require a Christian attitude to perceive that the modern system of society has a great deal in it that is inherently bad.

[From *The Idea of a Christian Society*, 1939]

MAN AND HIS ENVIRONMENT

MY local feelings were stirred very sadly by my first view of New England, on arriving from Montreal, and journeying all one day through the beautiful desolate country of Vermont. Those hills had once, I suppose, been covered with primeval forest; the forest was razed to make sheep pastures for the English settlers; now the sheep are gone, and most of the descendants of the settlers; and a new forest appeared blazing with the melancholy glory of October maple and beech and birch scattered among the evergreens; and after this procession of scarlet and gold and purple wilderness you descend to the sordor of the half-dead mill towns of southern New Hampshire and Massachusetts. It is not necessarily those lands which are the most fertile or most favoured in climate that seem to me the happiest, but those in which a long struggle of adaptation between man and his environment has brought out the best qualities of both; in which the landscape has been moulded by numerous generations of one race, and in which the landscape in turn has modified the race to its own character. And those New England mountains seemed to me to give evidence of a human success so meagre and transitory as to be more desperate than the desert.

[From *After Strange Gods*, 1934]

'CHRISTIAN' OR 'PAGAN'

WE are living at present in a kind of doldrums between opposing winds of doctrine, in a period in which one political philosophy has lost its cogency for behaviour, though it is still the only one in which public speech can be framed. This is very bad for the English language; it is this disorder (for which we are all to blame) and not individual insincerity, which is responsible for the hollowness of many political and ecclesiastical utterances. You have only to examine the mass of newspaper leading articles, the mass of political exhortation, to appreciate the fact that good prose cannot be written by a people without convictions. The fundamental objection to fascist doctrine, the one which we conceal from ourselves because it might condemn ourselves as well, is that it is pagan. There are other objections too, in the political and economic sphere, but they are not objections that we can make with dignity until we set our own affairs in order. There are still other objections, to oppression and violence and cruelty, but however strongly we feel, these are objections to means and not to ends. It is true that we sometimes use the word 'pagan', and in the same context refer to ourselves as 'Christian'. But we always dodge the real issue. Our newspapers have done all they could with the red herring of the 'German national religion', an eccentricity which is after all no odder than some cults held in Anglo-Saxon countries: this 'German national religion' is comforting in that it persuades us that *we* have a Christian civilization; it helps to disguise the fact that our aims, like Germany's, are materialistic. And the last thing we should like to do would be to examine the 'Christianity' which, in such contexts as this, we say we keep.

[From *The Idea of a Christian Society*, 1939]

THE STRAIT GATE

THERE is no good in making Christianity easy and pleasant; 'Youth', or the better part of it, is more likely to come to a difficult religion than to an easy one. For some, the intellectual way of approach must be emphasized; there is need of a more intellectual laity. For them and for others, the way of discipline and asceticism must be emphasized; for even the humblest Christian layman can and must live what, in the modern world, is comparatively an ascetic life. Discipline of the emotions is even rarer, and in the modern world still more difficult, than discipline of the mind; some eminent lay preachers of 'discipline' are men who know only the latter. Thought, study, mortification, sacrifice: it is such notions as these that should be impressed upon the young – who differ from the young of other times merely in having a different middle-aged generation behind them. You will never attract the young by making Christianity easy; but a good many can be attracted by finding it difficult: difficult both to the disorderly mind and to the unruly passions.

[From *Thoughts after Lambeth*, 1931]

'PRIVATE RELIGIONS'

I SUSPECT that there is some taint of Original H. G. Wells about most of us in English-speaking countries; and that we enjoy drawing general conclusions from particular disciplines, using our accomplishment in one field as the justification for theorizing about the world in general. It is also a weakness of Anglo-Saxons to like to hold personal and private religions and to promulgate them. And when a scientist gets loose into the field of religion, all that he can do is to give us the impression which his scientific knowledge and thought has produced upon his everyday, and usually commonplace, personal, and private imagination.

[From *Thoughts after Lambeth*, 1931]

CONFORMITY TO NATURE

WE may say that religion, as distinguished from modern paganism, implies a life in conformity with nature. It may be observed that the natural life and the supernatural life have a conformity to each other which neither has with the mechanistic life: but so far has our notion of what is natural become distorted, that people who consider it 'unnatural' and therefore repugnant, that a person of either sex should elect a life of celibacy, consider it perfectly 'natural' that families should be limited to one or two children. It would perhaps be more natural, as well as in better conformity with the Will of God, if there were more celibates and if those who were married had larger families. But I am thinking of 'conformity to nature' in a wider sense than this. We are being made aware that the organization of society on the principle of private profit, as well as public destruction, is leading both to the deformation of humanity by unregulated industrialism, and to the exhaustion of natural resources, and that a good deal of our material progress is a progress for which succeeding generations may have to pay dearly. I need only mention, as an instance now very much before the public eye, the results of 'soil-erosion' – the exploitation of the earth, on a vast scale for two generations, for commercial profit: immediate benefits leading to dearth and desert. I would not have it thought that I condemn a society because of its material ruin, for that would be to make its material success a sufficient test of its excellence; I mean only that a wrong attitude towards nature implies, somewhere, a wrong attitude towards God, and that the consequence is an inevitable doom. For a long enough time we have believed in nothing but the values arising in a mechanized, commercialized, urbanized way of life: it would be as well for us to face the permanent conditions upon which God allows us to live upon this planet. And without sentimentalizing the life of the savage, we might practise the humility to observe, in some of the societies upon which we look down as primitive or backward, the operation of a social–religious–artistic complex which we should emulate upon a higher plane. We have been accustomed to regard 'progress' as always integral; and have yet to learn that it is only by an effort and a discipline, greater than society has yet seen the need of imposing upon itself, that material knowledge and power is gained without loss of spiritual knowledge and power. The struggle to recover the sense of relation to nature and to God, the recognition that even the most primitive feelings should be part of our heritage, seems to me to be the explanation and justification of the life of D. H. Lawrence, and the excuse for his aberrations. But we need not only to learn how to look at the world with the eyes of a Mexican Indian – and I hardly think that Lawrence succeeded –

and we certainly cannot afford to stop there. We need to know how to see the world as the Christian Fathers saw it; and the purpose of reascending to origins is that we should be able to return, with greater spiritual knowledge, to our own situation. We need to recover the sense of religious fear, so that it may be overcome by religious hope.

[From *The Idea of a Christian Society*, 1939]

MODERN EDUCATION

QUESTIONS of education are frequently discussed as if they bore no relation to the social system in which and for which the education is carried on. This is one of the commonest reasons for the unsatisfactoriness of the answers. It is only within a particular social system that a system of education has any meaning. If education today seems to deteriorate, if it seems to become more and more chaotic and meaningless, it is primarily because we have no settled and satisfactory arrangement of society, and because we have both vague and diverse opinions about the kind of society we want. Education is a subject which cannot be discussed in a void: our questions raise other questions, social, economic, financial, political. And the bearings are on more ultimate problems even than these: to know what we want in education we must know what we want in general, we must derive our theory of education from our philosophy of life. The problem turns out to be a religious problem.

The progress (I do not mean the extension) of education for several centuries has been from one aspect a drift, from another aspect a push; for it has tended to be dominated by the idea of *getting on*. The individual wants more education, not as an aid to the acquisition of wisdom but in order to get on; the nation wants more in order to get the better of other nations, the class wants it to get the better of other classes, or at least to hold its own against them. Education is associated therefore with technical efficiency on the one hand, and with rising in society on the other. Education becomes something to which everybody has a 'right', even irrespective of his capacity; and when everyone gets it – by that time, of course, in a diluted and adulterated form – then we naturally discover that education is no longer an infallible means of getting on, and people turn to another fallacy: that of 'education for leisure' – without having revised their notions of 'leisure'. As soon as this precious motive of snobbery evaporates, the zest has gone out of education; if it is not going to mean more money, or more power over others, or a better social position, or at least a steady and respectable job, few people are going to take the trouble to acquire education. For deteriorate it as you may, education is still going to demand a good deal of drudgery. And the majority of people are incapable of enjoying leisure – that is, unemployment *plus* an income and a status of respectability – in any but pretty simple forms – such as balls propelled by hand, by foot, and by engines or tools of various types; in playing cards; or in watching dogs, horses, or other men engage in feats of speed or skill. The uneducated man with an empty mind if he be free from financial anxiety or narrow limitation, and can obtain access to golf-clubs, dance halls, etc., is, for all I can see, as well equipped to fill his leisure contentedly as is the educated man.

[From 'Modern Education and the Classics', 1932]

THE CLASSICS AND THE MAN OF LETTERS

NOT very long ago, an eminent author, in the course of expressing his views about the future of education after this war, went a little out of his way to declare that in the new order there would still be a place for Greek. He qualified this concession, however, by explaining that the study of Greek was a field of scholarship of equal dignity with Egyptology, and several other specialized studies which he named, and that the opportunity to pursue these studies should, in any liberal society, be provided for the few who were particularly drawn to them. I read this in one of the periodicals which are found in the waiting-rooms of certain experts in applied science; and having neglected to make a note of the passage before being summoned to my professional appointment, I cannot quote chapter and verse, and therefore withhold the name of the author. But this statement, made without irony and wholly in a spirit of enlightened generosity, started the train of thought which I propose to continue here. I am grateful to the writer for having suggested to my mind the only possible role in which I can present myself on this occasion.* In my earlier years I obtained, partly by subtlety, partly by effrontery, and partly by accident, a reputation amongst the credulous for learning and scholarship, of which (having no further use for it) I have since tried to disembarrass myself. Better to confess one's weaknesses, when they are certain to be revealed sooner or later, than to leave them to be exposed by posterity: though it is, I have discovered, easier in our times to acquire an undeserved reputation for learning than to get rid of it: but that is neither here nor there. My point is that if I made those claims for the classics which can only be supported by the erudition of the scholar, or those which can only be pleaded by what we now call the education*ist*, I might jeopardize the cause: for there are far better scholars than I, who attach less importance to the study of Latin and Greek than I do, and there are teachers who can demonstrate the impracticability of the studies which I should like to promote. But if I present the defence of the classics merely from the point of view of the man of letters, I am on safer ground: and I think you will agree that the claim to be a man of letters is, after all, a modest pretension. I must, however, begin by explaining why I have used this rather indefinite term, and what I mean by it.

If I were more specific, and spoke of 'the poet', 'the novelist', 'the dramatist', or 'the critic', I should suggest to your minds a number of particular considerations which would distract your attention from the view of literature as a whole which I wish to keep before us in the present context. Take, for instance, the term 'poet' and the objections which it would immediately evoke. We are commonly inclined to assume that the creation of literature, and poetry espe-

* The meeting of the Classical Association at Cambridge on 15 April 1942, when this Presidential Address was delivered. [*Editor's note*]

cially, depends simply upon the unpredictable appearance from time to time of writers of genius; that genius cannot be brought into the world at will, and that when it does appear it is likely to break every rule, that no system of education can foster it, and no system of education can stifle it. If we look at literature as merely a succession of great writers, instead of looking at the literature of one European language as something which forms a significant whole in itself, and a significant part in the literature of Europe, this is the view we are likely to take. Taking this view, we look at each great writer by himself; and looking at him by himself, we are unlikely to believe that he would have been a greater writer, or an inferior writer, if he had had a different kind of education. The defects of a great writer's background are inextricably confused with its advantages; just as the shortcomings of his character are indissolubly associated with his shining virtues, and his material difficulties with his success. Can we regret, for instance, that François Villon did not choose to mix with more respectable society, or that Robert Burns did not have the same schooling as Dr Johnson? The life of a man of genius, viewed in relation to his writing, comes to take a pattern of inevitability, and even his disabilities will seem to have stood him in good stead.

This way of looking at a great poet or novelist or dramatist, is half of the truth: it is what we find when we look at one writer after another, without balancing this point of view by the imaginative grasp of a national literature as a whole. I wanted to make it clear that I do not pretend that a classical education is essential for the writer of genius: and unless I can suggest to your minds that a great literature is more than the sum of a number of great writers, that it has a character of its own, much of my contention will be misunderstood. It is because I do not want to concentrate your attention upon the man of genius that I have used the term 'man of letters'. This includes men of the second or third, or lower ranks as well as the greatest; and these secondary writers provide collectively, and individually in varying degrees, an important part of the environment of the great writer, as well as his first audience, his first appreciators, his first critical correctors – and perhaps his first detractors. The continuity of a literature is essential to its greatness; it is very largely the function of secondary writers to preserve this continuity, and to provide a body of writings which is not necessarily read by posterity, but which plays a great part in forming the link between those writers who continue to be read. This continuity is largely unconscious, and only visible in historical retrospect : I need only refer you for evidence to the monumental, though brief, essay by Professor R. W. Chambers on *The Continuity of English Prose*. And it is within this continuity, and within this environment, that, for my present purpose, individual authors have to be considered. When we look at them in this way, we can see that, among the great, even some of the most formal and correct have been also innovators and even rebels, and that even some of the most revolutionary have carried on the work of those from whose influence they rebelled.

It would be easy, indeed, to muster an army of great names, of men who have become great writers with very little educational advantage. Bunyan and Abraham Lincoln are only two among the names more frequently cited. These men, and others, learned how to use the English language very largely from the English Bible : and it is the tritest commonplace that a knowledge of the Bible, Shakespeare, and Bunyan (I might add the Book of Common Prayer) could teach a man of genius, or a man of first-rate ability short of genius, all that he needs in order to write English well. But I would remark first, that it is by no means irrelevant that the translators of that English Bible were great scholars in their time as well as great stylists; and we have to ask, not merely what had Shakespeare and Bunyan read, but what had the English authors read whose works nourished Shakespeare and Bunyan? And I would remark next, that the education given to Shakespeare, or Bunyan, or Lincoln, would be about the most difficult kind to get today. It would be much more reasonable to expect to find a poet with the learning of a Ben Jonson or a Milton than either a poet or prose writer who had had the advantages of Shakespeare or Bunyan. No schoolmaster could afford the reputation of sending his pupils forth as ill-furnished as these men were. And there is too much to read, for anybody to be expected to master, and to believe in, a few authors; apart from the fact that out of school there is every pressure to write badly, to talk incoherently, and to think confusedly.

It should be apparent at this point, that our primary concern in considering the education of the man of letters, is not the amount of learning which a man acquires, the number of years during which he is subjected to the educational process, or the degree of scholastic distinction which he attains: what is of prime importance is the type of education within which his schooling falls. The most instructive contrast of degree of education within the same type is that provided by Shakespeare and Milton, our two greatest poets. We can say of Shakespeare, that never has a man turned so little knowledge to such great account: we must couple Milton with Dante, in saying that never has a poet possessed of such great learning so completely justified the acquisition of it. Shakespeare's education, what he had of it, belongs in the same tradition as that of Milton: it was essentially a classical education. The significance of a type of education may lie almost as much in what it omits as in what it includes. Shakespeare's classical knowledge appears to have been derived largely from translations. But he lived in a world in which the wisdom of the ancients was respected, and their poetry admired and enjoyed; he was less well educated than many of his colleagues, but his was education of the same kind – and it is almost more important, for a man of letters, that his associates should be well educated than that he should be well educated himself. The standards and the values were there; and Shakespeare himself had that ability, which is not native to everyone, to extract the utmost possible from translations. In these two advantages he had what mattered most.

If Shakespeare's knowledge was fragmentary and second-hand, that of Milton was comprehensive and direct. A lesser poet, with the learning and the tastes of Milton, would have been in danger of becoming a mere pedant in verse. An understanding of Milton's poetry requires some acquaintance with several subjects none of which is very much in favour today; a knowledge of the Bible, not necessarily in Hebrew and Greek, but certainly in English; a knowledge of classical literature, mythology and history of Latin syntax and versification and of Christian theology. Some knowledge of

Latin is necessary, not only for understanding what Milton is talking about, but much more for understanding his style and his music. It is not that Milton's vocabulary is excessively weighted with Latin words: there was more of that in the previous century. An acquaintance with Latin is necessary if we are to understand, and to accept, the involutions of his sentence structure, and if we are to hear the complete music of his verse. The present generation may miss, what we cannot expect from Milton, the colloquial style, the sound of the conversational voice, the range of mood and emotion which requires a more homely diction for its expression; it may sometimes find his syntax tortured. Milton has been reproached, and there is some truth behind the reproach, for writing English like a dead language: I think it was Landor who said so, and Landor is a critic to be treated with respect. Milton's was certainly a style fatal to imitators: that is just as true of the style of James Joyce, and the influence of a great writer upon other writers can neither add to nor detract from his title to honour. The point is that Milton's Latinism is essential to his greatness, and that I have only chosen him as the extreme example of English poetry in general. You may write English poetry without knowing any Latin; I am not so sure whether without Latin you can wholly understand it. I believe, and have said elsewhere, that the rich possibilities of English verse – possibilities still unexhausted – owe much to the variety of racial strains bringing in a variety of speech and verse rhythms; and that English verse also owes much to the fact that Greek for three hundred years, and Latin for longer than that, have gone to its formation. And what I have said of verse can be applied to prose also, though perhaps with less compulsion: can we really enter into the style of Clarendon unless we have at least a smattering of Tacitus, or the style of Gibbon unless we have some awareness of the immense power upon him of the classical and post-classical chroniclers, the patristic and post-patristic theologians, who provided him with his material?

If a classical education is the background for English literature in the past, we are justified in affirming not merely that a good knowledge of Latin (if not of Greek) should be expected of those who teach English literature, but that some knowledge of Latin should be expected of those who study it. This is not quite the direction, however, which I propose to pursue. I am not here concerned with the teaching of literature, but with teaching only in relation to those who are going to write it. For many generations the classics provided the basis of the education of the people from whom the majority of our men of letters have sprung: which is far from saying that the majority of our men of letters have been recruited from any limited social class. This common basis of education has, I believe, had a great part in giving English letters of the past that unity which gives us the right to say that we have not only produced a succession of great writers, but a literature, and a literature which is a distinguished part of a recognizable entity called European Literature. We are then justified in inquiring what is likely to happen, to our language and our literature, when the connexion between the classics and our own literature is completely broken, when the classical scholar is as completely specialized as the Egyptologist, and when the poet or the critic whose mind and taste have been exercised on Latin and Greek literature will be more exceptional than the dramatist who has prepared himself for his task in the theatre by a close study of optical, electrical, and acoustical physics? You have the option of welcoming the change as the dawn of emancipation, or of deploring it as the twilight of literature; but at least you must agree that we might expect it to mark some great difference between the literature of the past and that of the future – perhaps so great as to be the transition from an old language to a new one.

In the past twenty years I have observed what seems to me a deterioration in the middle literary stratum, and notably in the standards and the scholarship which are wanted for literary criticism.

The reasons for such a decline are no doubt complex, and I am not going to suggest that this is all due to the neglect of classical studies, or that a revival of these studies would be enough to stem the current. But the disappearance of any common background of instruction, any common body of literary and historical knowledge, any common acquaintance with the foundations of English literature, has probably made it easier for writers to comply with the pressure of tendencies for which they were not responsible. One function of criticism – I am not thinking of the great critics or the classics of criticism, but rather of the hebdomadary reviewer, formerly anonymous, who has now more often the publicity of signature, though seldom the satisfaction of higher pay – one function of criticism is to act as a kind of cog regulating the rate of change of literary taste. When the cog sticks, and reviewers remain fast in the taste of a previous generation, the machine needs to be ruthlessly dismantled and reassembled; when it slips, and the reviewer accepts novelty as a sufficient criterion of excellence, the machine needs to be stopped and tightened up. The effect of either fault in the machine is to cause a division between those who see no good in anything that is new, and those who see no good in anything else: the antiquation of the old, and the eccentricity and even charlatanism of the new, are both thereby accelerated. The effect of this failure of criticism is to place the serious writer in a dilemma: either to write for too large a public or to write for too small a public. And the curious result of either choice, is to place a premium on the ephemeral. The novelty of a work of imagination which is only popular, and has nothing really new in it, soon wears off: for a later generation will prefer the original to the copy, when both belong to the past. And the novelty of anything that is merely new produces only a momentary shock: the same work will not produce the same shock twice, but must be followed by something newer.

The charge has been brought against the more original literature of our time, that it has been written for a small and exclusive audience – an audience not small and exclusive because it was the best, but because (so it has been alleged) it consisted of perverse, eccentric, or anti-social people with their snobbish parasites. This appears to be an accusation which the most dissimilar groups can concur in bringing: the conservative who regard anything new as anarchic, and the radical who regard anything they do not understand as undemocratic. With the political passions enlisted for the support of these judgements I am not here concerned. My point is that this is a consequence, not of individual aberrancy – though it creates a situation in which the sham can easily pass, for a time and with some readers, as genuine – but of social disintegration: in the literary aspect, of critical decay. It arises from the lack of continuous communication, of the artist with his friends and fellow artists and the small number of keen amateurs of the arts, with a larger public educated in the same way; of taste cultivated upon the literature of the past but ready to accept what is good in the present when that is brought to their notice, and so with the world at large. If an author's first discriminating readers are themselves isolated from the larger world, their influence upon him may be unbalanced: their taste is in danger of yielding to their group prejudice and fancy, and they may easily succumb to the temptation of overvaluing the achievement of their members and favourite authors.

It is one thing to pass these strictures upon the present condition of literature, or to voice forebodings of its diminished future, and quite another to put forward positive suggestions about the type of education most profitable for the man of letters, and the way in which it could be fitted into the general educational scheme. In concern with education we are attentive to the problems of the child and the adolescent; very largely to the average or the mediocre child; very largely to the child whose educational opportunities have heretofore been meagre. When we think of the larger pattern we are apt to think (quite rightly) in terms of the production of good citizens. The question I leave with you is the question whether we think the maintenance of the greatness of our literature a matter of sufficient importance to be taken account of, in our educational planning, at all? and even if we agree about its importance, whether education can take any responsibility for it? The answer may be, No. But the question must be asked, and the answer must not be a hasty answer. The right answer can only come after some very hard thinking, and thinking with very wide scope, by many people. I would not dissimulate the difficulty. The problem of training an adequate supply of good scientists, in various departments, is one very much with us; it is, I imagine, one much more readily capable of solution than is my problem. But I do not think that it would seem so much more soluble, were it not that we all recognize, under the pressure of material evidence, its necessity; and I think that agreement on the importance of a problem makes the solution of it much more likely.

I can see that the proper training of a man with the scientific bent, even now when the ramifications of the sciences are so extensive and the knowledge to be assimilated in any branch of science so vast, is more readily susceptible of precise determination. So, for that matter, is the training for any other art than that of letters. The painter, the sculptor, the architect, the musician, though they may have more difficulty in scraping a living, or in combining the pursuit of their art with an unrelated stipendiary job, all have a much more definite technique to master than that of the writer. Their essential training is more technical; the subjects which they must learn are more clearly indicated; and they do not need that varied general culture without which the man of letters is ill-equipped. Another difference, not unconnected with the foregoing, is that literary ability does not, with any certainty, manifest itself so early, or with such precise confidence of its goal, as does a bent towards another art. A desire to express oneself in verse (or so my experience inclines me to believe) is a trait of the majority of Anglo-Saxons of both sexes at some stage of their development: it may even persist long after the lack of vocation is patent to everyone except the authors themselves. When a schoolboy composes good verses, we are justified in expecting that he will, in later life, excel in some pursuit or other – but that pursuit may take him very far from poetry or letters – it may lead toward the bar or the episcopal bench. The true literary mind is likely to develop slowly; it needs a more comprehensive and more varied diet, a more miscellaneous knowledge of facts, a greater experience of men and of ideas, than the kind required for the practice of the other arts. If therefore presents a more baffling educational problem. In saying this, I am not arrogating any pre-eminence for the art of letters itself: I am merely pointing out a difference in the preparation.

I should like to make clear at this point that there are several arguments in favour of the classical education with which, however cogent and sufficient, I am not here concerned. Into the question whether all children, whatever their destination, should be taught elementary Latin, and perhaps Greek – the question whether it is desirable, and then whether it is practicable – I shall not venture.

I would only remark that the question of the age up to which all children should have the same education, and the question of the common element in all education up to a later stage, is a very important one even from the point of view of the man of letters: for upon this depends the possibility of a general audience, the possibility both of the author's being able to communicate with people in all walks of life, and of their being able to understand each other. I would also observe in passing, that to postpone the introduction to Latin to the age at which a boy appears to be more gifted for languages than for other studies is to postpone it too long – apart from my belief that it would be most desirable for everyone to possess some knowledge of Latin even if none of Greeek. I am not here interested, however, in the advocacy of the study of these two languages as 'mental discipline'. I think that the defence of any study purely as 'discipline' in the modern sense can be maintained too obstinately: I have, for instance, heard compulsory chapel defended, by an unbeliever, on the ground that it was good for boys to have a duty which they disliked so much. The defence of 'discipline' in the abstract, the belief that any 'mental discipline' carried out in the right way and far enough will produce an abstract 'educated man', seems to have some relation to the egalitarian tendencies of the nineteenth century which extended to subjects of study the same ideal of equality held for the human beings who might study them. A *disciple*, at any rate, is surely a willing pupil, and one who attaches himself to a master voluntarily, because he believes in the value of the subject which the master professes and believes that that master is qualified to give him the initiation he wants. Discipleship, that is, starts by a valuation – by the desire to attain to some particular knowledge or proficiency, not by the desire for training in the abstract followed by the judgement that this subject of study will provide it. For my purpose it is the value of the subject that is in question, not the incidental and necessary 'discipline' by which its command is attained. And as I am not considering discipline in the abstract, so I am not considering 'education' in the abstract, or the somewhat barren question of the definition of the abstract 'educated man'.

For my purposes, also, the distinction between 'vocational' and 'cultural' education is of little use: apart from the disadvantage that 'vocational' is apt to connote merely a salary and a pension, and 'cultural' to connote an 'education for leisure' which is either a refined hedonism or a skill to practise harmless hobbies. The writer, *qua* writer, seldom draws a salary, and he has no problem of occupying a supposed leisure. Everything may be grist to his mill, and the more knowledge of every kind that he can assimilate the better: the serious distinction, for him, is between the subjects which he should be taught, and the subjects which he should acquire by himself. His business is communication through language; when he is an imaginative writer, he is engaged in the most difficult form of communication, where precision is of the utmost importance, a precision which cannot be given beforehand but has to be found in every new phrase. In order to understand language in the way in which the man of letters should understand it, we must know the various purposes for which language has been used; and that involves some knowledge of the subjects for the communication of which men have used language in the past: notably of history, for you cannot understand the literature of the past without some knowledge of the conditions under which it was written, and the sort of people who wrote it; of logic, for that is an investigation of the anatomy of thought in language; of philosophy, for that is the attempt to use language in the most abstract way possible.

Into this already formidable programme we have to introduce at some stage at least one modern foreign language as well as our own language and the classics. It should be a major language with a parallel development to our own, and with a flourishing contemporary literature; for we are greatly helped to develop objectivity of taste if we can appreciate the work of foreign authors, living in the same world as ourselves, and expressing their vision of it in another great language. The possession of several foreign languages is of course better than of one alone; but it is impossible to understand the language, the literature, and the people of more than one foreign country equally well. In our time, the most important foreign language for the man of letters, has been French: and I need not remind you that for French a knowledge of Latin is still more important, and a knowledge of Greek hardly less important, than for English. For a man of very exceptional linguistic ability, who was not already sunk beneath the burden of the acquirements I recommend, I believe that an acquaintance with some great and more remote language might be a very valuable addition; Hebrew suggests itself, but both for extreme difference of structure and intellectual dignity a very good choice would be Chinese: but to mention this is to scan the very horizon of possibility.

All these branches of learning have to be acquired through teachers; and there does not appear to be much space left in the curriculum for scientific subjects. I am assuming however that my excellent man of letters will have had (what I did not attain) enough training at school in the language of mathematics not to be completely baffled when he attempts, by himself, to understand the general significance of some scientific discovery. The only reason of universal applicability, why he could not acquire more detailed scientific knowledge in his formal education, is the very obvious one that there was not time: for I have allowed for some hours to be spent in eating, sleeping, social ritual, conviviality, worship, athletic activities, and physical training. It is most desirable that he should be able, throughout his life, to take an interest in subjects in which he has not been trained; for, as I have suggested, to a person of some power of imagination almost anything can be of use. It is sometimes suggested that the wonders of science provide nourishment for the imagination. I am sure they can; but I think a distinction should be drawn between the imagination of a great scientist, arriving at a discovery on the basis of observed phenomena, the significance of which had escaped other equally well trained and informed scientists, and the imagination of a Lucretius, or even a Shelley, informing their scientific knowledge with an emotional life with which the scientist, as such, has no concern.

I have not, as you see, been urging the claims of 'cultural', or general, education against specialized; for in its way, the education of the man of letters must be itself specialized and 'vocational'. But we have to face one more difficulty. I have made clear that I am not

attempting to legislate for the man of genius, but for the environment of men of letters into which he will be born or find his way.
But on the other hand you cannot draw a sharp line between the
man of letters and his audience, between the critic in print and the
critic in conversation. Nobody suffers more from being limited to
the society of his own profession than does the writer: it is still
worse when his audience is composed chiefly of other writers or
would-be writers. He needs a small public of substantially the same
education as himself, as well as the same tastes; a larger public with
some common background with him; and finally he should have
something in common with everyone who has intelligence and sensibility and can read his language. The problem of the survival of
English literature, therefore, brings us to the problem of the need
for unity in education, the need for some unification which will not
be to the detriment of any of the branches of learning and investigation, scientific or humanistic. This problem, so much greater than
any problem of administration, organization, or curricular devices,
because it is a spiritual problem, because its solution involves not
merely planning, but *growing* a pattern of values, is so vast a problem that it is not one for the educational specialist alone, but for all
who are concerned with the structure of society. It is one with which
I have no more to do here than to show my awareness of it. My only
contribution is to proclaim that the future of English Literature
will be deeply affected by the way in which we solve or fail to solve
this problem.

My particular thesis has been that the maintenance of classical
education is essential to the maintenance of the continuity of English
Literature. How, and by what adaptation to the necessary, the desirable, and the inevitable, the place for the classics in education is
to be found is not a subject on which I have the right to claim your
attention. But I am sure that this is one important line of defence
of the classics. The standards of the highest scholarship have to be
kept up, and the work of research honoured: it is necessary that the
prestige of the great scholars should not be allowed to dwindle. That
there will continue to be a place for the great scholar — without
whom the whole fabric of classical education crumbles — I do not

doubt: what is less certain is that in the future he will be discovered young enough to be given the proper training; and that he will be allowed any greater role than that of preparing a few younger men to carry on his work, without prospect of wider influence. The second group is that of non-professional scholarship and of scholarship in other fields in which an accurate knowledge of the classical languages is, or should be required; it includes not only the theologians and the historians, but the clergy and ministry, the teachers of modern language and literature, and the literary critics. For the last of these, certainly, it should hardly be enough that he should have spent some years at school in acquiring the languages, if he never afterwards opens a text: he must have the literature accessible and operative in his taste and judgements; he must be able to enjoy it. But the maintenance of these types of scholarship is not enough or even possible unless some knowledge of the civilizations of Greece and Rome, some respect for their achievements, some understanding of their historical relation to our own, and some *translation* can be cultivated among a very much larger number of people: among those who (like myself) have not remembered enough to read the originals with ease, and among those who have never studied the languages at all. A limited preserve of scholarship will be ineffectual unless a much wider respect for, and appreciation of the relevance of, the subject-matter of this scholarship can be disseminated amongst those who will never be given the first-hand knowledge.

My assertions about the dependence of English Literature upon the Latin and Greek literatures, will, I am aware, have no persuasive influence whatever upon several classes of people. There are those who do not believe that literature is a matter of any great importance, and those who, while conceding a certain value to the literature of the past, do not consider it of great importance that English Literature should continue to take a front rank. There are those who acknowledge the importance of literature, but do not believe that one type of education or another will make much difference to its further survival. There are those who, immersed perhaps in the immense difficulties of providing some sort of education or other to the whole of the nation, consider this extra problem less urgent, or complain that they have so many other things to think of that it is more than can be coped with. And finally, there are those who want so new a world that they even welcome the prospect of a breach of continuity. And in many minds, no doubt, all of these attitudes can co-exist in a half-formed state; now one, now another, presenting itself in consciousness.

To attempt to confute all these objections would be an impertinence in the present company, and some of them come much more within the province of those who have had life-long experience of the classroom and the council chamber. My appeal can only address itself to those who already accept the contention that the preservation of a living literature is more than a matter of interest only to amateurs of verse and readers of novels; and who see in it the preservation of developed speech, and of civilization against barbarism. They will be those also who appreciate the need, if the present chaos is ever to be reduced to order, of something more than an administrative or an economic unification – the need of a cultural unification in diversity of Europe; and who believe that a new unity can only grow on the old roots : the Christian Faith, and the classical languages which Europeans inherit in common. These roots are, I think, inextricably intertwined. I should not care to risk the heresy, upon which some religious–political writers have appeared to verge, of regarding Christianity as a European, rather than a universal Faith : I do not wish to be accused of inventing a new heresy to the effect that salvation depends upon getting a first in classics. But the culture of Europe, such as it is, is a Christian culture; and conversely, the traditional religious faith of Europe, including Britain, cannot preserve its intellectual vigour unless a high standard of Latin and Greek scholarship is maintained amongst its teachers. But these considerations are beyond the mandate which I have assumed for this occasion. And I do not wish to leave you with the impression that I am asking too much of formal education, either in the sphere of religion or in that of literature : I am quite aware that an educational system cannot of itself bring about either great faith or great literature : it is truer to say that our education is not so much the generator of our culture as the offspring of it. But those who care for the preservation, the extension, and the advancement of our culture cannot fail to interest themselves, however unqualified they may be to pass judgement, in our classical heritage.

[*The Classics and the Man of Letters*, 1942]

THE DECAY OF THE MUSIC-HALL

THE middle classes, in England as elsewhere, under democracy, are morally dependent upon the aristocracy, and the aristocracy are subordinate to the middle class, which is gradually absorbing and destroying them. The lower class still exists; but perhaps it will not exist for long. In the music-hall comedians they find the expression and dignity of their own lives; and this is not found in the most elaborate and expensive revue. In England, at any rate, the revue expresses almost nothing. With the decay of the music-hall, with the encroachment of the cheap and rapid-breeding cinema, the lower classes will tend to drop into the same state of protoplasm as the bourgeoisie. The working man who went to the music-hall and saw Marie Lloyd and joined in the chorus was himself performing part of the act; he was engaged in that collaboration of the audience with the artist which is necessary in all art and most obviously in dramatic art. He will now go to the cinema, where his mind is lulled by continuous senseless music and continuous action too rapid for the brain to act upon, and will receive, without giving, in that same listless apathy with which the middle and upper classes regard any entertainment of the nature of art. He will also have lost some of his interest in life. Perhaps this will be the only solution. In an interesting essay in the volume of *Essays on the Depopulation of Melanesia*, the psychologist W. H. R. Rivers adduced evidence which has led him to believe that the natives of that unfortunate archipelago are dying out principally for the reason that the 'Civilization' forced upon them has deprived them of all interest in life. They are dying from pure boredom. When every theatre has been replaced by 100 cinemas, when every musical instrument has been replaced by 100 gramophones, when every horse has been replaced by 100 cheap motor-cars, when electrical ingenuity has made it possible for every child to hear its bedtime stories from a loud-speaker, when applied science has done everything possible with the materials on this earth to make life as interesting as possible, it will not be surprising if the population of the entire civilized world rapidly follows the fate of the Melanesians.

[From 'Marie Lloyd', 1923]

SOCIETY AND THE ARTS

WHAT are the most fruitful social conditions for the production of works of the first order, philosophical, literary, or in the other arts, is perhaps one of those topics of controversy more suitable for conversation than for writing about. There may perhaps be no one set of conditions most suitable for the efflorescence of all these activities; it is equally possible that the necessary conditions may vary from one country and civilization to another. The régime of Louis XIV or of the Tudors and Stuarts could hardly be called libertarian; on the other hand, the rule of authoritarian governments in our time does not appear conducive to a renascence of the arts. Whether the arts flourish best in a period of growth and expansion, or in one of decay, is a question that I cannot answer. A strong and even tyrannous government may do no harm, so long as the sphere of its control is strictly limited; so long as it limits itself to restricting the liberties, without attempting to influence the minds, of its subjects; but a régime of unlimited demagogy appears to be stultifying. I must restrict my consideration to the position of the arts in our present society, and to what it should be in such a future society as I envisage.

It may be that the conditions unfavourable to the arts today lie too deep and are too extensive to depend upon the differences between one form of government and another; so that the prospect before us is either of slow continuous decay or of sudden extinction. You cannot, in any scheme for the reformation of society, aim directly at a condition in which the arts will flourish: these activities are probably by-products for which we cannot deliberately arrange the conditions. On the other hand, their decay may always be taken as a symptom of some social ailment to be investigated. The future of art and thought in a democratic society does not appear any brighter than any other, unless democracy is to mean something very different from anything actual. It is not that I would defend a moral censorship: I have always expressed strong objections to the suppression of books possessing, or even laying claim to literary merit. But what is more insidious than any censorship, is the steady influence which operates silently in any mass society organized for profit, for the depression of standards of art and culture. The increasing organization of advertisement and propaganda – or the influencing of masses of men by any means except through their intelligence – is all against them. The economic system is against them; the chaos of ideals and confusion of thought in our large-scale mass education is against them; and against them also is the disappearance of any class of people who recognize public and private responsibility of patronage of the best that is made and written. At a period in which each nation has less and less 'culture' for its own consumption, all are making furious efforts to export their culture, to impress upon each other their achievements in arts which they are ceasing to cultivate or understand. And just as those who should be the intellectuals regard theology as a special study, like numismatics or heraldry, with which they need not concern themselves, and theologians observe the same indifference to literature and art, as special studies which do not concern *them*, so our political classes regard both fields as territories of which they have no reason to be ashamed of remaining in complete ignorance. Accordingly the more serious authors have a limited, and even provincial audience, and the more popular write for an illiterate and uncritical mob.

[From *The Idea of a Christian Society*, 1939]

THE CRITERION*

In starting *The Criterion*, I had the aim of bringing together the best in new thinking and new writing in its time, from all the countries of Europe that had anything to contribute to the common good. Of course it was designed primarily for English readers, and therefore all foreign contributions had to appear in an English translation. There may be a function for reviews published in two or more languages, and in two or more countries simultaneously. But even such reviews, searching all Europe for contributions, must contain some pieces of translation, if they are to be read by everybody. And they cannot take the place of those periodicals which appear in each country and which are intended primarily for the readers in that country. So my review was an ordinary English periodical, only of international scope. I sought, therefore, first to find out who were the best writers, unknown or little known outside of their own country, whose work deserved to be known more widely. Second, I tried to establish relations with those literary periodicals abroad, the aims of which corresponded most nearly to my own. I mention, as instances, the *Nouvelle Revue française* (then edited by Jacques Rivière, and subsequently by Jean Paulhan), the *Neue Rundschau*, the *Neue Schweizer Rundschau*, the *Revista de Occidente* in Spain, *Il Convegno* and others in Italy. These connexions developed very satisfactorily, and it was no fault of any of the editors concerned, if they subsequently languished. I am still of the opinion, twenty-three years after I began, and seven years after I ended, that the existence of such a network of independent reviews, at least one in every capital of Europe, is necessary for the transmission of ideas – and to make possible the circulation of ideas while they are still fresh. The editors of such reviews, and if possible the more regular contributors, should be able to get to know each other personally, to visit each other, to entertain each other, and to exchange ideas in conversa-

* *The Criterion* was founded by T. S. Eliot and edited by him, from the first issue, in October 1922, to the last, in January 1939. [*Editor's note*]

tion. In any one such periodical, of course, there must be much that will be of interest only to readers of its own nation and language. But their cooperation should continually stimulate that circulation of influence of thought and sensibility, between nation and nation in Europe, which fertilizes and renovates from abroad the literature of each one of them. And through such cooperation, and the friendships between men of letters which ensue from it, should emerge into public view those works of literature which are not only of local, but of European significance.

The Criterion had, I believe, a definite character and cohesion, although its contributors were men holding the most diverse political, social, and religious views. I think also that it had a definite congeniality with the foreign periodicals with which it associated itself. The question of a writer's political, social, or religious views simply did not enter into our calculations, or into those of our foreign colleagues. What the common basis was, both at home and abroad, is not easy to define. In those days it was unnecessary to formulate it; at the present time it becomes impossible to formulate. I should say that it was a common concern for the highest standards both of thought and expression, that it was a common curiosity and openness of mind to new ideas. The ideas with which you did not agree, the opinions which you could not accept, were as important to you as those which you found immediately acceptable. You examined them without hostility, and with the assurance that you could learn from them. In other words, we could take for granted an interest, a delight, in ideas for their own sake, in the free play of intellect. And I think that also, among our chief contributors and colleagues, there was something which was not so much a consciously held belief, but an unconscious assumption. Something which had never been doubted, and therefore had no need to rise to the conscious level of affirmation. It was the assumption that there existed an international fraternity of men of letters, within Europe: a bond which did not replace, but was perfectly compatible with, national loyalties, religious loyalties, and differences of political philosophy. And that it was our business not so much to make any particular ideas prevail, as to maintain intellectual activity on the highest level.

[From the second of three broadcast talks to Germany in 1946 on 'The Unity of European Culture'. Reprinted as an Appendix in *Notes towards the Definition of Culture*, 1948]

A VALEDICTION

FOR this immediate future, perhaps for a long way ahead, the continuity of culture may have to be maintained by a very small number of people indeed – and these not necessarily the best equipped with worldly advantages. It will not be the large organs of opinion, or the old periodicals; it must be the small and obscure papers and reviews, those which hardly are read by anyone but their own contributors, that will keep critical thought alive, and encourage authors of original talent. I wish that a periodical could be sold like admission to a theatre, at a varying scale of prices; for just as the majority of the more critical and appreciative part of the public is often to be found in the cheaper seats, so I suspect that the price at which *The Criterion* has had to be published is prohibitive to most of the readers who are qualified to appreciate what is good in it, and to criticize what is faulty.

In the present state of public affairs – which has induced in myself a depression of spirits so different from any other experience of fifty years as to be a new emotion – I no longer feel the enthusiasm necessary to make a literary review what it should be. This is not to suggest that I consider literature to be at this time, or at any time, a matter of indifference. On the contrary, I feel that it is all the more essential that authors who are concerned with that small part of 'literature' which is really creative – and seldom immediately popular – should apply themselves sedulously to their work, without abatement or sacrifice of their artistic standards on any pretext whatsoever.

[From 'Last Words', *The Criterion*, January 1939]

THE term *culture* has different associations according to whether we have in mind the development of an *individual*, of a *group* or *class*, or of a *whole society*. It is a part of my thesis that the culture of the individual is dependent upon the culture of a group or class, and that the culture of the group or class is dependent upon the culture of the whole society to which that group or class belongs.

We may be thinking of refinement of manners – or *urbanity* and *civility*: if so, we shall think first of a social class, and of the superior individual as representative of the best of that class. We may be thinking of *learning* and a close acquaintance with the accumulated wisdom of the past: if so, our man of culture is the scholar. We may be thinking of *philosophy* in the widest sense – an interest in, and some ability to manipulate, abstract ideas: if so, we may mean the intellectual (recognizing the fact that this term is now used very loosely, to comprehend many persons not conspicuous for strength of intellect). Or we may be thinking of *the arts*: if so, we mean the artist and the amateur or dilettante. But what we seldom have in mind is all of these things at the same time. We do not find, for instance, that an understanding of music or painting figures explicitly in Arnold's description of the cultured man: yet no one will deny that these attainments play a part in culture.

If we look at several activities of culture listed in the preceding paragraph, we must conclude that no perfection in any one of them, to the exclusion of the others, can confer culture on anybody. We know that good manners, without education, intellect, or sensibility to the arts, tends towards mere automatism; that learning without good manners or sensibility is pedantry: that intellectual ability without the more human attributes is admirable only in the same way as the brilliance of a child chess prodigy; and that the arts without intellectual context are vanity. And if we do not find culture in any one of these perfections alone, we must not expect any one person to be accomplished in all of them; we shall come to infer that the wholly cultured individual is a phantasm; and we shall look for culture, not in any individual or in any one group of individuals, but more and more widely; and we are driven in the end to find it in the pattern of the society as a whole. This seems to me a very obvious reflection: but it is frequently overlooked. People are always ready to consider themselves persons of culture, on the strength of one proficiency, when they are not only lacking in others, but blind to those they lack. An artist of any kind, even a very great artist, is not for this reason alone a man of culture: artists are not only often insensitive to other arts than those which they practise, but sometimes have very bad manners or meagre intellectual gifts. The person who contributes to culture, however important his contribution may be, is not always a 'cultured person'.

It does not follow from this that there is no meaning in speaking of the culture of an individual, or of a group or class. We only mean that the culture of the individual cannot be isolated from that of the group, and that the culture of the group cannot be abstracted from that of the whole society; and that our notion of 'perfection' must take all three senses of 'culture' into account at once. Nor does it follow that in a society, of whatever grade of culture, the groups concerned with each activity of culture will be distinct and exclusive: on the contrary, it is only by an overlapping and sharing of interests, by participation and mutual appreciation, that the cohesion necessary for culture can obtain. A religion requires not only a body of priests who know what they are doing, but a body of worshippers who know what is being done.

[From *Notes towards the Definition of Culture*, 1948]

CONDITIONS OF CULTURE

A NEW civilization is always being made: the state of affairs that we enjoy today illustrates what happens to the aspirations of each age for a better one. The most important question that we can ask, is whether there is any permanent standard, by which we can compare one civilization with another, and by which we can make some guess at the improvement or decline of our own. We have to admit, in comparing one civilization with another, and in comparing the different stages of our own, that no one society and no one age of it realizes all the values of civilization. Not all of these values may be compatible with each other: what is at least as certain is that in realizing some we lose the appreciation of others. Nevertheless, we can distinguish between advance and retrogression. We can assert with some confidence that our own period is one of decline; that the standards of culture are lower than they were fifty years ago; and that the evidences of this decline are visible in every department of human activity. I see no reason why the decay of culture should not proceed much further, and why we may not even anticipate a period, of some duration, of which it is possible to say that it will have *no* culture. Then culture will have to grow again from the soil; and when I say it must grow again from the soil, I do not mean that it will be brought into existence by any activity of political demagogues. The question is whether there are any permanent conditions, in the absence of which no higher culture can be expected.

If we succeeded even partially in answering this question, we must then put ourselves on guard against the delusion of trying to bring about these conditions *for the sake* of the improvement of our culture. For if any definite conclusions emerge from this study, one of them is surely this, that culture is the one thing that we cannot deliberately aim at. It is the product of a variety of more or less harmonious activities, each pursued for its own sake: the artist must concentrate upon his canvas, the poet upon his typewriter, the civil servant upon the just settlement of particular problems as they present themselves upon his desk, each according to the situation in which he finds himself. Even if these conditions with which I am concerned, seem to the reader to repeat desirable social aims, he must not leap to the conclusion that these aims can be fulfilled solely by deliberate organization. A class division of society planned by an absolute authority would be artificial and intolerable; a decentralization under central direction would be a contradiction; an ecclesiastical unity cannot be imposed in the hope that it will bring about unity of faith, and a religious diversity cultivated for its own sake would be absurd. The point at which we can arrive, is the recognition that these conditions of culture are 'natural' to human beings; that although we can do little to encourage them, we can combat the intellectual errors and the emotional prejudices which stand in their way. For the rest, we should look for the improvement of society, as we seek our own individual improvement, in relatively minute particulars. We cannot say: 'I shall make myself into a different person'; we can only say: 'I will give up this bad habit, and endeavour to contract this good one'. So of society we can only say: 'We shall try to improve it in this respect or the other, where excess or defect is evident; we must try at the same time to embrace so much in our view, that we may avoid, in putting one thing right, putting something else wrong'. Even this is to express an aspiration greater than we can achieve: for it is as much, or more, because of what we do piecemeal without understanding or foreseeing the consequences, that the culture of one age differs from that of its predecessor.

The causes of a total decline of culture are as complex as the evidence of it is various. Some may be found in the accounts given, by various specialists, of the causes of more readily apprehended social ailments for which we must continue to seek specific remedies. Yet we become more and more aware of the extent to which the baffling problem of 'culture' underlies the problems of the relation of every part of the world to every other. When we concern ourselves with the relation of the great nations to each other; the relation of the great to the small nations; the relation of intermixed 'communities', as in India, to each other; the relation of parent nations to those which have originated as colonies; the relation of the colonist to the native; the relation between peoples of such areas as the West Indies, where compulsion or economic inducement has brought together large numbers of different races: behind all these perplexing questions, involving decisions to be made by many men every day, there is the question of what culture is, and the question whether it is anything that we can control or deliberately influence. These questions confront us whenever we devise a theory, or frame a policy, of education. It we take culture seriously, we see that a people does not need merely enough to eat (though even that is more than we seem able to ensure) but a proper and particular *cuisine*: one symptom of the decline of culture in Britain is indifference to the art of preparing food. Culture may even be described simply as that which makes life worth living. And it is what justifies other peoples and other generations in saying, when they contemplate the remains and the influence of an extinct civilization, that it was *worth while* for that civilization to have existed.

[From *Notes towards the Definition of Culture*, 1948]

CULTURE AND THE FAMILY

THE primary channel of transmission of culture is the family: no man wholly escapes from the kind, or wholly surpasses the degree, of culture which he acquired from his early environment. It would not do to suggest that this can be the *only* channel of transmission: in a society of any complexity it is supplemented and continued by other conduits of tradition. Even in relatively primitive societies this is so. In more civilized communities of specialized activities, in which not all the sons would follow the occupation of their father, the apprentice (ideally, at least) did not merely serve his master, and did not merely learn from him as one would learn at a technical school – he became assimilated into a way of life which went with that particular trade or craft; and perhaps the lost secret of the craft is this, that not merely a skill but an entire way of life was transmitted. Culture – distinguishable from knowledge about culture – was transmitted by the older universities: young men have profited there who have been profitless students, and who have acquired no taste for learning or for Gothic architecture, or for college ritual and form. I suppose that something of the same sort is transmitted also by societies of the masonic type: for initiation is an introduction into a way of life, of however restricted viability, received from the past and to be perpetuated in the future. But by far the most important channel of transmission of culture remains the family: and when family life fails to play its part, we must expect our culture to deteriorate. Now the family is an institution of which nearly every-body speaks well: but it is advisable to remember that this is a term that may vary in extension. In the present age it means little more than the living members. Even of living members, it is a rare exception when an advertisement depicts a large family or three generations: the usual family on the hoardings consists of two parents and one or two young children. What is held up for admiration is not devotion to a family, but personal affection between the members of it: and the smaller the family, the more easily can this personal affection be sentimentalized. But when I speak of the family, I have in mind a bond which embraces a longer period of time than this: a piety towards the dead, however obscure and a solicitude for the unborn, however remote. Unless this reverence for past and future is cultivated in the home, it can never be more than a verbal convention in the community. Such an interest in the past is different from the vanities and pretensions of genealogy; such a responsibility for the future is different from that of the builder of social programmes.

[From *Notes towards the Definition of Culture*, 1948]

Other Peregrine books
are described on the following
pages

THE GREAT TRADITION

F. R. Leavis

Y20

The criticism of F. R. Leavis has always been notable for its uncompromising association of literature and morality. That association in large part explains his reasons for placing five novelists – five only – within the Great Tradition of English fiction. Those five, who 'are all distinguished by a vital capacity for experience, a kind of reverent openness before life, and a marked moral intensity', are Jane Austen, George Eliot, Henry James, Joseph Conrad, and D. H. Lawrence. Dr Leavis has devoted a separate book to *D. H. Lawrence, Novelist*, and there are special circumstances differentiating Jane Austen. Here, after an introductory essay on the Great Tradition as a whole, he deals with George Eliot, Henry James, and Conrad; and, in an appendix, with *Hard Times*, which he considers the one work of Dickens's that has the strength of 'a completely serious work of art'.

'This is critical judgement of the first order, and its force and directness come from Dr Leavis's moral directness' – Lionel Trilling

'Great criticism, some of the greatest of our time' – Gerard Hopkins in *Time and Tide*

Also available

THE COMMON PURSUIT · Y1
NEW BEARINGS IN ENGLISH POETRY · Y26

NOT FOR SALE IN THE U.S.A.

THE EIGHTEENTH-CENTURY
BACKGROUND

Basil Willey

Y21

What key-word suggests itself as a 'way in' to eighteenth-century thought – to Shaftesbury, Butler, Swift, Hume, Hartley, Holbach, and Priestley? To Professor Willey that word is 'nature', and he traces the various stages in the divinization of the idea of nature that led to the Romantic Revival. In doing so he shows the importance of this concept in religion, ethics, philosophy, science, and politics – every sphere, in fact, of the intellectual activity of the eighteenth century.

Like Professor Willey's previous seventeenth-century studies, *The Eighteenth-Century Background* is based on lectures delivered in the English faculty at Cambridge. Originally addressed to the literary student looking for extra-literary associations and explanations, it will appeal to all who are interested in the history of ideas.

'An important contribution to scholarship' – *Oxford Magazine*

Also available

THE SEVENTEENTH-CENTURY BACKGROUND · Y3